ALASKA® magazine's
ALASKA FISHING GUIDE

Including the
Alaska Highway and
Northern Canada

Another guidebook prepared by the editors of ALASKA® magazine

 **ALASKA NORTHWEST PUBLISHING COMPANY**

Anchorage, Alaska

First edition 1975
Second edition 1976
Third edition 1978
Revised and expanded edition 1979

ISBN 0-88240-126-2
ISSN 0361-3984   Key title: Alaska fishing guide
Library of Congress Catalog Card Number 75-17664

Design by Sandra Norling
CartoGraphics by Jon. Hersh

Alaska Northwest Publishing Company
Box 4-EEE, Anchorage, Alaska 99509

Printed in U.S.A.

CONTENTS

PREFACE

Before beginning to read the following pages that make up our *Alaska Fishing Guide*, we should strive to make a few things clear.

First of all, with no intent of apology, the information is of necessity sometimes vague and sometimes incomplete. There is much yet to be known of Alaska's and neighboring Canada's greatly divided geographic regions and of its vastly differing species of fish. There are surely streams and lakes yet unfished—we believe, personally, thousands—and there are likely to yet be many species of fish and variants of species discovered or recognized.

And therein lies part of the wonderful fascination of fishing in the North for the man who cherishes the thrills of exploration and discovery.

In this respect, however, we must underline the statements of biologists in pages following which would tend to warn the newcomer that there isn't quite as good "wild" fishing as one might expect in Alaska. It is true that near heavily populated areas fishing pressure has been terrific and the results to be expected. But there is really wonderful fishing in Alaska and northern Canada—"virgin" type, sometimes in the purest sense—and lots of it, scattered from Hyder on the most southern Alaska border with Canada to Attu, over 2,000 miles west in the shadow of Russian shores, and from Ketchikan to Barrow, along the Bering shores, through the immense river basins of the Great Interior, and the remote mountain valleys of a dozen great mountain ranges. But that "just-like-it's-always-been" fishing is not on the major highways or near the more populous centers.

And not "all" fishing—or even "a lot of good fishing" should be expected in a given region. Some areas are rainbow trout areas. Some have only "Dollies," some only lake trout and pike, or grayling alone, or a bit of this and that. Study this book and study it in a regional sense to better know what your fishing opportunities might be in a land which comparatively stretches a distance equal to that from Miami to San Pedro and from the Gulf of Mexico to the Great Lakes.

Study particularly the subject and regions with reference to "salmon." A great number of uninformed think of "salmon" in Alaska as more or less a single species running in a neatly bracketed area and time. Not so. There are dozens of salmon "runs" in dozens of areas (five different species), showing for a brief few weeks from early May to late October. And disregarding some growing attention to possibilities of more interest in angling for a couple of the generally "nonbiting" varieties of salmon, nearly all Alaska salmon fishing for the average sportsman revolves around runs of king salmon and silver salmon.

Know more about how and where to catch these two and from our point of view you'll understand Alaska salmon fishing better. There is some sockeye fishing in some rivers, some kings to be caught in rivers and lots of silvers (cohos), but river fish have lost their bounce and most times their color and even their flavor. Look for the salt-water areas for your salmon—and please, don't be among those snagging spawning fish that most Alaskan dogs would disdain. (Besides, it's illegal.)

Another item—don't overlook our Canadian neighbors and their often truly superb fishing for rainbows, lake trout and grayling in Northern British Columbia, Yukon Territory and Northwest Territories. We obviously do not have space to deal exhaustively with all Canadian fish in this volume, but there is some terrific fishing over there a dedicated angler will treasure.

The "best time"? This question is always asked, but the answer lies with your choice of species and areas.

And what do we personally recommend? The cutthroat—silver-sided or gold-bronze—feeding like a tiger in the salt tiderips or slashing a mosquito hatch in a landlocked lake, must be our co-favorite along with the lightning-quick, fly-taking arctic grayling. These are fish of the wild places, not hatchery bums, and the fishermen who take them are not catching these wild ones on the well-beaten trails.

In the clean surges of tidewater we pleasure at the brute rush of a bronze-backed king salmon whether he is 10

Fishing for grayling in the Chandalar River of the Brooks Range (fisherman is Jim Rearden).

pounds or 60. When you see the black gums of his strong jaws clamping at the restraining hook and leader, see the tenseness of his restrained power waiting only for release in the flashing thrust of his spotted silver and bronze tail, then you'll know and understand our respect for this truly kingly fish.

The smaller coho (silver) is another old friend—in salt water, please, or you're not getting a full measure of Mr. Coho's potential to sprain your wrist in wild leap after leap and frenzied reel-smoking rushes.

And we certainly recommend the Alaska Dolly Varden at the mouth of almost any stream in the North that gives into clean salt water. He feeds with hunger, is strong, and can be big as well as small. We think maybe we champion the Dolly a great deal because he has often been maligned—even bountied—without fair reason.

The Dolly Varden eats no more salmon eggs on the spawning beds than any other of the many fish predators. He is often beautiful and often a superior fighter. Time and again we've cooked him rolled in flour and butter, fresh from salty estuaries, and had dining friends rave about "best fish ever tasted." And he'll take flies and a variety of lures.

Best of all, "Dolly" is not only plentiful, but like my friends the cutt and the grayling, he is truly a wild creature, still in great numbers, still to be fished in hundreds of streams yet untouched, still a true member of the elsewhere diminishing family of wilderness fishes.

Perhaps that is the essence of a North Country fishing experience. There are fish and places that are yet as they must have been when Steller with Bering first expressed a naturalist's marvel at the providence of this beautiful land—clean, cold water, green unpeopled forests around—the cleansing rains and storms—tidewater beaches where you can hear the sounds of life in spurting clams, scuttling crabs, the wash of surf—a natural place where man is privileged only to temporarily pause and with respect harvest only that which he can properly use.

Read this book with our hopes that you will not only find knowledge, but pleasure, and if you are among the fortunate to partake of the North's bounty in fish, that your pleasure will be as great as ours.

You will understand that to have enjoyed the Northland's fish is only part of the story. More properly you will have come as we to love not just the fish, but a land.

Robert A. Henning

Robert A. Henning
Publisher

INTRODUCTION

Sweeping changes in ownership of Alaska's lands are making headlines as we edit this edition. President Carter, by proclamation, has established 17 new or expanded national monuments, totaling about 60 million acres. The Department of the Interior has frozen another 60 or 70 million acres to prevent state selection, mining and logging. Vast national forest areas are being established as wilderness areas where logging, mining and roads will be barred. More than 40 million acres will soon be privately owned by Alaska's Indians, Aleuts and Eskimos.

How will these changes affect sport fishing?

Generally, they will protect and preserve sport fishing, for virtually all federal lands, which will make up most of Alaska—including national monuments, national parks, wildlife refuges, national forests and unclassified Bureau of Land Management lands—will be open to sport fishing. Most of these lands will be protected from development.

The 103 million acres promised Alaska at statehood will also be open to sport fishing, although, partly as a result of the lock-up of federal lands, parts of these lands will be intensively used for all purposes, and may not offer the best sport fishing.

Thus while sport hunters have lost the privilege of hunting on a third or more of Alaska's big game ranges, sport fishermen have gained protection against loss of habitat in some of the finest fishing waters in the state, and good habitat spells fish.

Changes in land use and ownership are also coming to western Canada, an area which for the first time we include in our guide. Canada's changes have been slower in coming than those in Alaska. Virtually all of Canada's lands and waters are open to legal sport fishing.

Waters of Alaska and adjacent Canada are still mostly unpolluted, and thousands of lakes and thousands of miles of streams in this northwestern chunk of North America seldom see a fisherman. It is true that fishing near highways and urban areas is no longer tops, but the angler who is willing to hike a mile from a highway, run a boat for half an hour from a launching ramp or harbor, or charter a small plane for a brief flight, may find himself surrounded by fishing that is unsurpassed anywhere.

Availability and movements of northern fish are generally geared to the season when fishermen seek them—spring, summer and fall. It is summer and fall when millions of salmon of five species return to their fresh-water spawning streams; in the spring grayling leave the major rivers where they winter to enter clear-water tributary streams; sheefish move from coastal estuary areas inland to spawning areas, taking much of the summer for their journey; lake trout, which normally inhabit deep water, frequent surface areas at and shortly after spring breakup; the colorful, lively and variable Dolly Varden moves from lakes and streams into salt water and back again during these three seasons. Fall is steelhead time in Alaska. Halibut move into relatively shallow inshore areas in summer.

For the visitor who prefers to hire a local, knowledgeable guide while fishing, there are more and more of this unique breed making their services available in the North Country. Fishing lodges increase each year. Air taxi operators continually add to the number of fishing camps where they can fly clients, and more and more of these fly-for-pay operators stock inflatable boats to rent for float trips after fish.

There has never been a better time to fish in Alaska and adjacent Canada.

Jim Rearden
Outdoors Editor, *ALASKA*® magazine

THE NORTH COUNTRY

Upper Summit Lake on the Seward-Anchorage Highway, one of Alaska's grayling fishing lakes. (Sharon Paul, staff)

ALASKA is a vast, thinly settled state, with a climate that ranges from mild with heavy rainfall in the Southeastern Panhandle, to the extremes of the high, arid Arctic.

About 400,000 people live in the state in about 25 modern or partly modern towns of 1,500 persons or more, and in perhaps 180 villages of 25 persons or more. Most cities and villages are found on streams, large lakes or coastal bays, where fishing ranges from excellent to poor.

The largest city, Anchorage, at the head of Cook Inlet, has a population of about 200,000. The greater Fairbanks

area has 64,000 and the Juneau area (the capital city) has about 22,000.

Forests and Mountains: Alaska has vast evergreen forests, as well as extensive tundra and above timber line areas without trees. Two great mountain systems divide the state: the Brooks Range extends 600 miles across the northern part of the state, and the 1,000-mile-long Alaska-Aleutian Range arcs northwest from Canada through Southcentral Alaska and extends into the Aleutian Islands. Many of the mountains in the latter range are volcanic.

Other, shorter but nevertheless huge

and rugged mountain ranges include the Chugach Mountains, which form the rim to the central north Gulf Coast, and the Wrangell Mountains, which lie south of the Alaska Range. Both of these shorter ranges merge with the Saint Elias Mountains of Canada and extend southeast into Southeastern Alaska as the Coast Mountains.

Rivers, Lakes and the Sea: The 375 million acres of land in Alaska include tens of thousands of streams and rivers. There are 12 major river systems, of which three are tributary to the great Yukon. Four of Alaska's major rivers start in Canada. In addition, Alaska holds at least 7 million acres of lakes—while individual lakes and ponds are found in the tens of thousands.

Not all of Alaska's streams and lakes provide good angling. Some of the major rivers like the Yukon, Tanana, Susitna, Taku and Stikine are silty or muddy and are not attractive to the fisherman. Some streams that originate in glaciers are also muddy, or at least milky during months of thaw, and are not fishable, although their tributary streams are often clear and may provide top-quality fishing. Other streams are too cold or too swift to support fish life. Some lakes are shallow, and oxygen depletion during winter (when they are ice covered) prevents them from supporting fish life.

Ocean waters off Alaska are rich with plankton, which benefit from nutrients poured into the sea from the great rivers, from the minerals available from glacier action and from long hours of summer sunlight. Plankton are a link in the food chain—attracting and feeding young

salmon as they leave fresh water for the sea and providing food for a wide variety of other forms, from hordes of shrimp and crab to the huge plankton-feeding whales that move into northern seas each summer for this great wealth.

Climate: Fishermen visiting Alaska may encounter a wide range of climates. When a trip is made into Alaska's wilderness, a fisherman must be prepared to withstand extremes in wind, temperature and precipitation, whether it be rain or snow. The choice of clothing, tent, stove and sleeping bags can make the difference between life and death, or at the very least, between comfort and discomfort.

Alaska's summers are generally short, but in most areas, reasonably mild. Snow may fall during any month at high altitudes, however, and frost may occur in northerly areas during any month, even at lower elevations.

Freezeup: Alaska's rivers and lakes usually start to freeze by October, depending upon how northerly, how high and how far from the coast they are. Coastal temperatures are usually

more moderate than those of the Interior—although coastal winds commonly lower the chill factor considerably.

Freezeup in the high mountains may last well into May, with ice remaining on some lakes into July.

Communications: Telephone service is available in most towns and some villages of Alaska, and telegraph offices are found in major cities. To send telegrams from outlying towns or villages, it is necessary to reach a long-distance operator and ask for telegraph service. Mail service varies with remoteness and scheduled airline service.

YUKON TERRITORY, shaped like a triangle, is bordered on the west by Alaska and on the south by British Columbia. The northern boundary is the Beaufort Sea in the Arctic Ocean, and the eastern boundary—the long side of the triangle—angles southeast through the Mackenzie Mountains separating Yukon from Northwest Territories.

Travelers take time out to fish one of the northern British Columbia's streams along the Alaska Highway near Mile 350. (Courtesy of Canadian Government Travel Bureau)

There are 207,000 square miles in Yukon Territory. With a population of only 23,335, it is one of the least settled areas of North America. Much of Yukon is upland plateau cut by deep-gorged rivers and wide valleys and marked by mountains that are among the highest and most rugged in North America.

The Alaska Highway crosses from British Columbia into Yukon Territory about 600 miles north of Dawson Creek, BC, and continues for nearly 600 miles to the Alaska border. This highway was opened to regular traffic in 1948.

Whitehorse, the capital city, is located at Mile 916 on the Alaska Highway and is the hub of activity in Yukon Territory. This modern city provides all facilities and services and is a jumping off point for treks or flights into the vast wilderness areas of the territory. Thousands of miles of streams, large lakes and small un-named ponds offer unlimited opportunities for the fisherman.

NORTHWEST TERRITORIES is more than twice the size of Alaska, encompassing 1.3 million square miles. It extends west from Manitoba to Yukon Territory at the Mackenzie River, and extends north from Alberta and Saskatchewan through the arctic Elizabeth Islands, which sprawl north to Greenland.

Much of this land is in the Canadian Shield, a vast, U-shaped, rocky expanse surrounding Hudson Bay. The western parts of Northwest Territories include some rugged mountains and some of the wildest, loneliest wilderness lands on earth. There are few settlements.

Canada has more lakes than any other country in the world and the larger lakes and streams are home for lake trout, grayling, arctic char and whitefish. Among the largest lakes are Great Bear and Great Slave. (See "Great Bear and Great Slave Lakes," page 71 for information on where-to and how-to fish these deep icy lakes.)

Climate of Northwest Territories varies from south to north—the northern section being Arctic and subArctic, with long days in summer, and short cold days in winter. Fishing season is generally short, usually from June until September.

BRITISH COLUMBIA is Canada's most westerly province. Many call it western Canada's most beautiful province, with its geographic variety—from dry, rolling inland country to rugged coastal mountains and thousands of islands, rivers and lakes.

About 2.41 million persons live in British Columbia, 1.15 million in Greater Vancouver and the Fraser Valley. British Columbia's 366,255 square miles—up to 760 miles in length and 440 miles in width—is larger than the United Kingdom, France, the Netherlands, Belgium and Switzerland combined. The provincial capital is Victoria, on Vancouver Island.

About three-quarters of the province's rivers drain into the Pacific Ocean; largest is the Fraser, emerging at Vancouver. The Liard and Peace rivers flow to the Arctic Ocean.

British Columbia has 339 provincial parks, recreation areas and wilderness conservancies, totaling 9.4 million acres, and about 1.1 million acres in 5 national parks.

Northern British Columbia (north of the Cariboo Mountains) is a wild, relatively untouched region that offers superb fishing in many lakes and streams. Rainbow trout are abundant, as are lake trout, grayling, northern pike, Dolly Varden and cutthroat trout. It is possible to find good fishing along the road system, but, as is commonly the case in the North, best fishing can be found by hiking a short distance from the highway, or by chartering a small plane to fly a short way to relatively unfished lakes and streams.

TRANSPORTATION

The small-boat harbor at Homer, AK, provides anchorage for a wide variety of fishing craft and pleasure boats. (Sharon Paul, staff)

Alaska

ROADS: Alaska, for its size, has relatively few highways. However, most major towns and cities throughout the Gulf Coast region and Interior Alaska are connected by fairly good paved roads. These regions are also connected to Southeastern Alaska, Canada and the Lower 48 via the Alaska Highway, Canadian highways and the Haines and Klondike Highways. The vast region west and north of Cook Inlet and north of the Yukon River is largely roadless. There are no roads connecting cities in Southeastern Alaska, but small road systems radiate from each of these cities.

Open year-round, the Alaska Highway stretches approximately 1,500 miles in a northwesterly direction from Mile 0 at Dawson Creek, in northern British Columbia near the Alberta border, to Fairbanks, in the Interior of Alaska. Most of the 1,200 miles through Canada are gravel, although the first 93.3 miles are paved and sections at Fort Nelson, British Columbia, and Whitehorse, Yukon Territory, have been paved as a part of a 10-year project to pave the entire Canadian section; the Alaska portion is paved. In recent years highway construction projects have eliminated many dangerous curves and other hazards and, in doing so, have shortened the overall distance of the Alaska Highway by nearly 40

Grizzly Tackle...
made to Alaskan standards
for Alaskan size results.

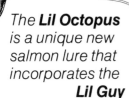

The **Lil Octopus** is a unique new salmon lure that incorporates the **Lil Guy**

and a phosphorescent skirt for the action and look of a squid.

The Lil Octopus and Lil Guy can be mooched or trolled behind an **Oregon Diver**

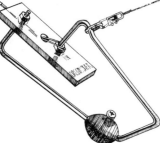

Flash Bender with flashing Vibrolite blade,

or **King Dodger** with more action and less drag at all speeds than conventional dodgers.

Jim Maxwell, President of Grizzly Inc., with a 62 lb., Chinook caught near Homer Alaska on a Lil Octopus behind an Oregon Diver.

Other Grizzly gear for Alaska includes the weighted **Spooner**

the large **Tee Lure** with smooth chrome or stepped fluted blade,

and the smaller **Trout Berry** red bead spinner for all species of trout.

grizzly
fine fishing tackle

miles. As a result, physical signs along the highway denoting miles and/or kilometers are inconsistent with the actual distances. In the summer of 1978, both the old mileposts and the newer kilometer posts were visible along the British Columbia portion of the highway. In Yukon Territory all the mileposts have been replaced with kilometer posts; the Alaska portion has only mileposts. Although this road does not compare with major highways in the Lower 48, it is no longer a wilderness road and is driven by thousands of travelers each year in all types of vehicles. Driving the Alaska Highway need not be hazardous if you exercise a little caution and common sense.

AIR: Scheduled airlines serve all of Alaska's major communities. Small communities are served by feeder lines, and mail, freight and passengers are flown once or twice a week, or less often. All large Alaskan cities and most of the major bush centers have air taxi operators.

Alaska is only a few hours by jet from any major city in the world. Fishermen traveling commercial airlines should pack their rods in crushproof cases, and especially valuable fishing rods should be insured.

Alaska has 520 airports and airstrips, 190 officially recognized seaplane landing sites and 47 heliports. There are also many remote landing strips not shown on navigation charts that are in regular use. In 1978 Alaska had 209 air taxi operations, 10 contract carriers and 20 scheduled air carriers.

Interstate: U.S. carriers providing interstate passenger service to Alaska include: Alaska Airlines, Northwest Orient Airlines (also flies Anchorage-Tokyo), Western Airlines and Wien Air Alaska.

The following are sample one-way coach fares to Alaska as of March 1979. Many airlines offer special rates. Check with the airlines or a travel agent about these special fares.

	Anchorage	Fairbanks	Juneau
New York City to	$265	$314	$326
Los Angeles to	$188	$225	$172
Chicago to	$212	$260	$212
Dallas to	$250	$280	$221

Foreign carriers, servicing Alaska through Anchorage include: Air France, British Airways, Japan Air Lines, KLM Royal Dutch Airlines, Lufthansa German Airlines, Sabena-Belgium World Airways, Scandinavian Airlines.

Intrastate (Scheduled Carriers):

From Anchorage: Alaska Airlines serves Fairbanks, Juneau, Ketchikan, Cordova, Petersburg, Wrangell, Sitka and Yakutat.

Great Northern Airlines serves Unalakleet, Talkeetna, Fairbanks, Kotzebue, Nome and Mount McKinley National Park.

Polar Airlines serves Gulkana, McGrath, Northway, Tok, Valdez and Fairbanks.

Reeve Aleutian Airways serves the Alaska Peninsula, the Aleutian Islands and the Pribilof Islands.

Sea Airmotive serves Bethel-area villages through Wien Air Alaska.

Wien Air Alaska serves Aniak, Barrow, Bethel, Dillingham, Galena, Iliamna, King Salmon, Kotzebue, McGrath, Nome, Prudhoe Bay, Saint Marys, Skwentna, Unalakleet, Homer and Kodiak.

From Fairbanks: Air North serves Fort Yukon, Chalkyitsik, Venetie, Circle City, Umiat, Rampart, Stevens

Village, Beaver, Circle Hot Springs, Eagle, Arctic Village and Birch Creek Village through Wien Air Alaska.

Alaska Airlines serves Anchorage and Southeastern Alaska cities (see list under Anchorage).

Wien Air Alaska serves Juneau, Whitehorse, YT, Barrow, Eagle, Prudhoe Bay, Kotzebue and a net work of bush villages.

Alaska Central Air serves Galena, Tanana, Minto, Manley Hot Springs and Ruby through Wien Air Alaska.

From Juneau: Southeast Skyways serves Haines and Skagway.

L.A.B. Flying Service serves Haines and Skagway and serves Excursion Bay and Hoonah through Alaska Airlines.

Channel Flying serves Angoon, Elfin Cove, Funter, Pelican and Tenakee through Alaska Airlines.

From Ketchikan: Tyee Air serves Annette Island, Craig, Klawock and Hydaburg through Alaska Airlines.

From Kodiak: Kodiak Western Alaska Airlines serves Kodiak and Afognak Islands and villages in the Bristol Bay area.

From Nome: Munz Northern Airlines serves Bethel, Stebbins, Saint Michael, Emmonak, Alakanuk, Cape Romanzof, Taylor, Kotzebue, King Island, Little Diomede Island, Candle and other villages on the Seward Peninsula.

From Petersburg: Alaska Island Air serves Kake and Saginaw Bay through Alaska Airlines.

From Sitka: Eagle Air serves Hoonah, Pelican, Elfin Cove, Tenakee, Kake, Chatham, Angoon, Saginaw Bay, Hamilton Bay, Craig, Klawock and Port Alexander through Alaska Airlines.

Channel Flying serves Angoon, Pelican, Elfin Cove and Tenakee through Alaska Airlines.

Below—*Angler unloads a hefty salmon taken during the annual fishing derby at Haines, AK. (Lael Morgan, staff)*
Right—*An air taxi takes off from Tongass Narrows near Ketchikan, AK. (Sharon Paul, staff)*

Rates and flight schedules for these communities are listed in the current edition of the *Official Airline Guide.* Contact the airlines or your travel agent for specific information.

In addition to all the scheduled air service available, there are more than 200 certificated charter and air taxi operators in Alaska.

Air taxi operators, according to State of Alaska definitions, operate from a registered base of operations and, with some exceptions, can operate throughout the state. Also with some exceptions regarding charters, air taxi operators must charge the rates published in their tariffs on file with the Alaska Transportation Commission, 338 Denali Street, Anchorage, Alaska 99501.

Short flightseeing trips cost about $30 per person with a four-person minimum, or about $115 an hour for small planes. Fly-in trips to specific destinations, such as lakes and lodges, cost from $30 to $50 an hour depending on size of aircraft. (See "Fly-in Fishing," page 18, for additional information.)

Larger charters are also available. A 19-passenger Twin Otter, for instance, can be chartered for about $400 an hour, while an 8-passenger Cessna 402 might cost about $185 an hour. Rates are about the same in Canada.

Private Aircraft: Many visitors fly their own planes to North Country destinations, generally following the Alaska Highway north.

Pilots should have the latest U.S. government flight information publication, *Alaska Supplement,* and the Canadian DND flight information publications, *VFR Supplement* and *Northern Supplement.* Also necessary are the World Aeronautical Charts for the appropriate areas. A catalog including prices, *Catalog of Aeronautical Charts and Related Publications,* is available from the NOAA offices. If there are no regional offices in your area, write the U.S. Department of Commerce, National Oceanic and Atmospheric Administration, Riverdale,

Fisherman casts into Willow Creek near the bridge on the George Parks Highway, 71 miles north of Anchorage, AK., during the salmon run in August.
(Sharon Paul, staff)

MD 20840, or to Canada Map Office, Department of Energy, Mines and Resources, 615 Booth Street, Ottawa, ON, K1A 0E9.

A free pamphlet, *Flight Tips*, containing general information on flying in the North Country, including permits, customs and immigration laws is available in Alaska from FAA Regional Office, 632 Sixth Avenue, Anchorage 99501; General Aviation District Office #1, 1515 East 13th Avenue, Anchorage 99501; Flight Standards District Office #61, 3788 University Avenue, Fairbanks 99701, or Office #62, Rural Route 5, Box 5115, Juneau 99803.

Pilots seeking information on flying within Alaska can address specific questions to the Alaska Department of Transportation and Public Facilities, Pouch 6900, Anchorage 99502.

Members of the Aircraft Owners and Pilots Association may get information on flying to Alaska by writing 7315 Wisconsin Avenue, Bethesda, MD 20014, headquarters of the association. AOPA will furnish its members a flight planned track; flight report publications on Canada, Alaska and U.S. customs, which provide information on regulations, weather, fuel, ports of entry, charts—both VFR and IFR—and other items which relate to a flight to these areas.

In Canada, *Air Tourist Information Canada* is available from Ministry of Transport, Canadian Air Transportation Administration, Aeronautical Information Services, Ottawa, ON, K1A 0N8.

RAILROAD: The Alaska Railroad, owned and operated by the federal government, stretches 470 miles from Seward through Anchorage to Fairbanks.

Daily passenger service is provided from Fairbanks to Anchorage from late May to early October; less frequently in the winter. Vehicles may be shipped via freight cars which operate twice a week, year-round. Passenger and vehicle service is available daily from Anchorage to Portage and Whittier during the summer. There is no passenger service south to Seward at any time of the year.

Fishermen and hunters commonly use the railroad as transportation to fine fishing grounds, usually in the mountain area between Anchorage and Fairbanks. Arrangements can be made with the conductor to be dropped off at any point on the route, and the train will stop to pick up anyone who signals at any point on the route.

For further information, write The Alaska Railroad, Pouch 7-2111, Anchorage 99510.

The only other rail transportation in Alaska is the White Pass & Yukon Route which provides daily service for passengers and vehicles between Skagway, AK, and Whitehorse, YT, during the summer; less frequent service in winter.

MARINE HIGHWAY SYSTEM: The Alaska Marine Highway is a ferry system that connects cities and some smaller communities in Southeastern Alaska as well as providing access to the Lower 48 with service from Seattle, WA, and Prince Rupert, BC. Alaskan communities served include Ketchikan,

Wrangell, Petersburg, Juneau, Haines, Skagway, Sitka, Metlakatla, Hollis, Kake, Hoonah, Pelican, Angoon and Tenakee.

While there is no ferry service connecting Southeastern Alaska with the Gulf Coast region, the Marine Highway system does provide service between cities in Southwestern Alaska. Communities served are Seward, Kodiak, Seldovia, Homer, Valdez and Cordova year-round. Sand Point, King Cove, Port Lions and Whittier have service during the summer only.

Many who drive to Alaska prefer to return home by a different route, thus having the opportunity to see more of

The ferry Columbia *pulls into the dock at Wrangell, AK. (Sharon Paul, staff)*

the state. The Marine Highway system, with terminals at Seattle, WA, and Prince Rupert, BC, on the southern end and Haines and Skagway on the northern end, offers a pleasant and relatively inexpensive way to travel between Alaska and the Lower 48. It is also an inexpensive way to reach the unique fishing areas of Southeastern Alaska. It is 490 miles from Prince Rupert to Skagway, direct; via Sitka it is 697 miles.

It is also possible to ride the ferry as a foot passenger, without a car. During spring, summer and fall months especially, reservations are necessary for cars and for staterooms. Coast Guard regulations prohibit passengers from visiting the car deck while ferries

AVERAGE RUNNING TIME

Seattle to Ketchikan	40 hours
Prince Rupert to Ketchikan	6 hours
Ketchikan to Wrangell	6 hours
Wrangell to Petersburg	3 hours
Petersburg to Juneau	7½ hours
Petersburg to Sitka	9 hours
Juneau to Haines	6 hours
Juneau to Sitka	8 hours
Haines to Skagway	1 hour

Tariffs: Rates in the tables below and on page 10, were announced for 1979 and are subject to change; regard them as a guide only. Reservations are needed well in advance for summer travel on the Marine Highway. For further information consult *The MILEPOST®* (please see page 21 for details), for complete summer schedules and tariffs or write the Division of Marine Highway Systems, Pouch R, Juneau 99811. Note: The Division of Marine Transportation will not accept out-of-state personal checks.

Winter rates, in effect between October 1 and April 30, are different.

1979 PASSENGER AND VEHICLE TARIFFS
EFFECTIVE MAY 1, 1979 THROUGH SEPTEMBER 30, 1979

BETWEEN AND	PIER 48 SEATTLE	PRINCE RUPERT	KETCHI-KAN	WRANG-ELL	PETERS-BURG
Passengers 12 years and older (meals and berths not included)					
Ketchikan	73.00	15.00			
Wrangell	80.00	29.00	14.00		
Petersburg	85.00	37.00	22.00	8.00	
Sitka	95.00	54.00	39.00	25.00	17.00
Juneau	95.00	54.00	39.00	25.00	17.00
Haines	105.00	65.00	50.00	36.00	28.00
Skagway	109.00	71.00	56.00	42.00	34.00

Tariffs for children 6-11 are approximately half the adult fare; Children under 6 are transported free.

	PIER 48 SEATTLE	PRINCE RUPERT	KETCHI-KAN	WRANG-ELL	PETERS-BURG
Vehicles to and including 19 feet					
Ketchikan	257.00	46.00			
Wrangell	287.00	82.00	45.00		
Petersburg	299.00	99.00	62.00	26.00	
Sitka	337.00	149.00	112.00	74.00	57.00
Juneau	337.00	149.00	112.00	74.00	57.00
Haines	369.00	182.00	139.00	101.00	86.00
Skagway	374.00	187.00	144.00	106.00	91.00

Tariffs are progressively higher with increased size of vehicle.

SURCHARGES: Unaccompanied vehicles except motorcycles and scooters are assessed a surcharge as follows: To or from Seattle $20. To or from Prince Rupert $10. Surcharges also apply to all vehicles more than 8 feet in width, and all single-unit vehicles more than 46 feet in length. Apply to any Marine Highway office for rates involving surcharges.

M.V. MALASPINA - M.V. COLUMBIA
CABINS SOLD AS A UNIT

FOUR BERTH CABIN/SITTING ROOM — COMPLETE FACILITIES

BETWEEN AND	Pier 48 Seattle	Prince Rupert	Ketchikan	Wrangell	Petersburg	Haines	Sitka	Juneau
Ketchikan	97.00	36.00						
Wrangell	107.00	50.00	36.00					
Petersburg	110.00	55.00	41.00	36.00				
Sitka	119.00	66.00	52.00	45.00	38.00			
Juneau	119.00	66.00	52.00	45.00	38.00	38.00		
Haines	129.00	74.00	59.00	52.00	46.00	46.00	36.00	
Skagway	132.00	77.00	62.00	55.00	49.00	49.00	38.00	36.00

FOUR BERTH CABIN — COMPLETE FACILITIES

BETWEEN AND	Pier 48 Seattle	Prince Rupert	Ketchikan	Wrangell	Petersburg	Haines	Sitka	Juneau
Ketchikan	87.00	31.00						
Wrangell	96.00	44.00	31.00					
Petersburg	100.00	49.00	36.00	30.00				
Sitka	110.00	59.00	46.00	40.00	33.00			
Juneau	110.00	59.00	46.00	40.00	33.00	33.00		
Haines	119.00	66.00	52.00	47.00	41.00	41.00	31.00	
Skagway	122.00	69.00	55.00	50.00	44.00	44.00	33.00	30.00

TWO BERTH CABIN/SETTEE — COMPLETE FACILITIES

BETWEEN AND	Pier 48 Seattle	Prince Rupert	Ketchikan	Wrangell	Petersburg	Haines	Sitka	Juneau
Ketchikan	60.00	23.00						
Wrangell	67.00	32.00	23.00					
Petersburg	70.00	36.00	27.00	22.00				
Sitka	77.00	43.00	34.00	29.00	25.00			
Juneau	77.00	43.00	34.00	29.00	25.00	25.00		
Haines	82.00	48.00	39.00	34.00	30.00	30.00	22.00	
Skagway	85.00	51.00	42.00	36.00	32.00	32.00	24.00	22.00

TWO BERTH CABIN — COMPLETE FACILITIES

BETWEEN AND	Pier 48 Seattle	Prince Rupert	Ketchikan	Wrangell	Petersburg	Haines	Sitka	Juneau
Ketchikan	55.00	21.00						
Wrangell	61.00	29.00	21.00					
Petersburg	64.00	32.00	24.00	19.00				
Sitka	70.00	38.00	30.00	26.00	23.00			
Juneau	70.00	38.00	30.00	26.00	23.00	23.00		
Haines	75.00	43.00	34.00	30.00	27.00	27.00	20.00	
Skagway	77.00	45.00	36.00	32.00	29.00	29.00	22.00	19.00

DORMITORY ROOM - RATE PER BERTH

BETWEEN AND	Pier 48 Seattle	Prince Rupert	Ketchikan	Wrangell	Petersburg	Haines	Sitka	Juneau
Ketchikan	28.00	12.00						
Wrangell	31.00	15.00	12.00					
Petersburg	32.00	16.00	12.00	12.00				
Sitka	35.00	19.00	15.00	13.00	12.00			
Juneau	35.00	19.00	15.00	13.00	12.00	12.00		
Haines	38.00	22.00	17.00	15.00	14.00	14.00	12.00	
Skagway	39.00	23.00	18.00	16.00	15.00	15.00	12.00	12.00

Dormitory rooms may be assigned as needed and sold on a per berth basis, however, the occupants must be willing to share the cabin.

NOTE: M.V. *Matanuska* has comparable rates, but accommodations also include five-berth and three-berth cabins. Rates on other vessels vary according to size and accommodations.

Fishermen in one of the many creeks along the Sterling Highway in Alaska. (Sharon Paul, staff)

are under way; sleeping on the car deck is not permitted. However, many people ride the ferries overnight without stateroom accommodations by making themselves as comfortable as possible on one of the reclining lounge chairs and waiting patiently each morning for access to the public washrooms. Some unroll sleeping bags in empty corners or on deck.

The 1979 schedule has ferries departing Seattle twice weekly between May 1 and September 30, and once a week in winter. Sailings from Prince Rupert are scheduled four times a week from June 1. During the summer, vessels depart Prince Rupert northbound at 8 A.M., while departures from Skagway are scheduled at varying times.

Yukon Territory

ROADS: Yukon Territory is accessible via the Alaska Highway from Dawson Creek, BC, and connects with Alaska's highway system, offering access to major cities and the Alaska Marine Highway system via Haines. The Alaska Marine Highway system is also accessible from Yukon Territory

Nisutlin Bay Bridge spans a wide arm of Teslin Lake at Mile 803 on the Alaska Highway. These waters offer excellent fishing including an occasional lake trout up to 40 pounds.
(Patrick Hawkes, staff)

For information on operating private aircraft in the North see page 7.

RAILROAD: The White Pass & Yukon Route provides daily service for passengers and vehicles between Whitehorse, YT, and Skagway, AK, during the summer; less frequent service in the winter.

Northwest Territories

ROADS: Access to Northwest Territories by highway is relatively new. The highway extends north from Edmonton, AB, to Yellowknife, NWT, on the northern shore of the Great Slave Lake, east to Fort Smith and northwest through Fort Simpson along the Mackenzie River as far as Wrigley. The Mackenzie Route officially begins at Grimshaw, AB.

The 448-mile Dempster Highway from Dawson City, YT, to Inuvik, NWT, was completed in 1978. There

via the Klondike Highway between Whitehorse, YT, and Skagway, AK.

The Cassiar Highway in northern British Columbia also connects with Yukon Territory's road system and is reached from Yellowhead Highway 16 midway between Prince George and Prince Rupert, BC. The Yellowhead Highway can be reached by several access roads from northwestern United States as well as from Trans-Canada Highway 1.

Prince Rupert is also accessible via ferry from Vancouver Island in southern British Columbia and via the Alaska Marine Highway system (see page 8).

AIR: Daily jet service to Whitehorse and Watson Lake, YT, from Vancouver, BC, and Calgary and Edmonton, AB, is provided via Pacific Western Airlines or Canadian Pacific Airlines, with connecting flights to most cities in the Lower 48 and eastern Canada. Direct flights are also available from Juneau and Fairbanks, AK, via Wien Air Alaska. Regular scheduled flights are available from Winnipeg, MB, via Yellowknife, NWT. Several other communities in Yukon Territory have scheduled air service and all fishing areas can be reached via charter flights from major air terminals.

was no ferry service across the Peel River near Fort McPherson at press time, but the government does plan to provide ferry service at this crossing. *CAUTION:* The Dempster Highway is open only during the summer. Because of limited facilities (the only services are at Mile 231) inclement weather, possible lack of ferry service and highway maintenance problems, driving the Dempster Highway can be extremely hazardous. *DO NOT* start out under any conditions without first checking with the RCMP in Dawson City.

AIR: Daily flights from Edmonton, AB, to Yellowknife, NWT, connect with extensive scheduled air service to most small communities throughout the territory. Charter flights are available to several wilderness resorts and fishing camps at lakes and streams as well as into the Arctic Coast regions.

For information on operating private aircraft in the North see page 7.

Northern British Columbia

ROADS: Northern British Columbia can be reached easily from the Lower 48 by driving from Washington State or Montana via several access routes, or by ferry from Seattle, WA, via Prince Rupert, BC. An alternative route is to take the ferry to Haines or Skagway, AK, drive the roads north, then south through Yukon Territory and northern British Columbia and return via one of the access routes.

Transcontinental highways from eastern Canada also connect with the highway system leading to northern British Columbia.

AIR: Daily jet service from Vancouver, BC, and Calgary and Edmonton, AB, via Canadian Pacific Airlines or Pacific Western Airlines to Dawson Creek, BC, Whitehorse and Watson Lake, YT, provides access to feeder lines serving communities in northern British Columbia. Connecting jet service is available from most cities in the Lower 48 and in eastern Canada.

Charter service into British Columbia fishing country is provided from air terminals in Yukon Territory and British Columbia.

For information on operating private aircraft in the North see page 7.

PLANNING YOUR NORTH COUNTRY FISHING TRIP

Upper Russian Lake on the Kenai Peninsula offers good rainbow fishing. (Jim Rearden)

☐ If you plan to fish salt water from a boat that you run yourself, or if you plan to venture into a remote stream or lake, tell someone as specifically as possible where you are going and who you will be with. If you don't return as planned, that person can notify authorities and a search will be made for you.

☐ If you venture away from the road on a fishing trip, be sure to be warmly dressed, with good rain and foot gear. Use top-quality tents and sleeping bags, and have with you extra food when you camp. If you fish where there are bears, brown/grizzlies or black, have with you a firearm capable of stopping a charge. Bears haunt coastal streams especially during salmon spawning season.

☐ Be sure to carry a well-equipped first-aid kit.

☐ Study the sport fishing seasons and bag limits for the area you plan to fish, and check with local wildlife authorities for any regulation changes: in Alaska, especially, summer field announcements are often made to close some streams to salmon fishing, if salmon runs don't measure up.

☐ Clean up your camp. Don't litter streams, lakes or salt water when fishing. Keep the Northland clean.

The following chapter provides information that should help you plan and prepare for your fishing trip in the North. The subject material is arranged alphabetically. For names and addresses of where to write for additional information on these and other subjects see "Information Sources" on pages 20-22.

Accommodations and Services

Facilities providing lodging, meals and automotive services are present in most communities and along all the major through highways in the Northland. Facilities are fewer along the less-traveled roads leading to a single destination. Some communities, accessible only by air, also have complete facilities, but most bush villages do not. Fishing lodges in remote areas vary from luxury accommodations to primitive wilderness necessitites. (See "Resorts, Lodges and Fishing Camps" for more information.)

Baggage

Baggage allowance refers to the weight and number of pieces allowed per person without additional charge when traveling on scheduled air carriers.

Most major airlines allow two items up to 70 pounds each, plus a carry-on (under seat size, 20 by 16 by 9 inches). Scheduled carriers in the Northland generally operate with smaller aircraft and baggage allowances are limited to weight rather than the number of pieces. For example, Wien Air Alaska has a limit of 40 pounds; Reeve Aleutian Airways, 66 pounds; Pacific Western Airlines, 44 pounds; with no limit on the number of pieces.

Fishing rods are considered as a piece of baggage. It is recommended that rods be packed in a sturdy container. Often several rods can be packed in a single container such as a shotgun carrying case which would be considered one piece of luggage.

When traveling by smaller aircraft, especially the type used for fly-in trips, it is best to have gear packed in duffel bags or other pliable containers as many of these aircraft have smaller baggage compartments with narrow doorways.

Aerosol pressure cans should not be put into suitcases that are to be checked as baggage: high-altitude flights frequently cause them to burst. Many travelers have found clothing and other items ruined because they included a pressurized can of mosquito repellent in their suitcase.

Bears

Alaska and western Canada have more bears, and more of a variety of bears, than any other land. Coastal streams used by spawning salmon attract bears—both the black and the big brown, or brown/grizzly.

Bears like to travel along streams and lake shores anywhere, and fishermen are likely to encounter them in any part of Alaska or Canada. They are most active during early morning and evening, although when salmon are running, they may actively catch fish and feed at midday.

Any bear is potentially dangerous, including the black bear. Fishermen who expect to angle coastal waters when salmon are spawning should carry a heavy rifle (.30 caliber or larger) for protection.

Bears occasionally attack without provocation, and it is for such incidents that fishermen should be alert. Normally bears avoid encounters with humans. Occasionally, when a bear is surprised, its reaction is to attack. Therefore it pays to make plenty of noise when you travel in bear country—especially if you are along a brushy stream.

Garbage and such things as fish entrails attract bears. Careful campers burn or bury garbage. Food left in the open is more of an attraction than that which is covered. Don't leave food in your tent. Store foods in plastic bags away from camp, preferably suspended out of reach.

Boats

Salt-water Charters: All the larger communities of Southeastern Alaska offer a wide variety of charter boats. They range from large luxury craft capable of accommodating large groups for several days and nights, to boats less than 30 feet, designed for day-cruises.

Valdez, Cordova, Whittier, Seward, Homer and Kodiak in the Gulf of Alaska, have numerous day-cruise charters and a few overnight charters are available. In other communities, commercial fishing boats are sometimes available for charter.

Charter boats generally provide tackle, lures and bait.

Rentals: Skiff rentals for salt-water fishing are not common—the waters are generally too rough and dangerous for the usual small boat-outboard type of rental operation. There are exceptions, of course, but generally speaking, Alaska's salt-water fishing areas have not developed the skiff-rental facilities found in coastal Oregon, Washington and British Columbia.

Boat rentals for fresh-water fishing are available at some resorts and towns. However, during the peak season, many of these rentals may be reserved for guests at the resorts.

Using Your Own Boat: The Northland's great variety of fishing waters calls for many different types of boats. In Alaska, the 33,904 miles of coastline includes some of the wildest, stormiest waters in the world. It also includes fine, sheltered, scenic waters, as in Southeastern Alaska, where the angler can travel on boats in the 18- to 20-foot class, provided they are seaworthy.

Inland waters also vary greatly. Many large lakes can be extremely hazardous during sudden storms.

Salt-water Boats: Most boats used by sport fishermen in Alaska's coastal waters are vee- or round-bottomed cabin cruisers, with outboard or in-

Sport fishing in Resurrection Bay near Seward. (Sharon Paul, staff)

board drive. Most are at least 18 feet in length, and most are fast, safe and seaworthy. Open skiffs may be used in sheltered bays and in some inside coastal waters.

Unpredictable winds, strong tidal currents, tiderips and other hazards confront anyone taking to Alaska's coastal waters. Boats should be in top condition, and their operators should have marine charts and should learn of local hazards from fishermen experienced in the area before venturing any distance.

Car-top Skiffs: These are handy boats for small ponds and lakes, slow, meandering streams and a few salt-water lagoons and sheltered bays in Alaska and Canada. Boats of this type are generally too small for the large lakes and bays. Violent weather is too frequent and calm waters turn rough too quickly to take a chance with a boat that is not big enough for complete safety.

Rubber Rafts, Inflatable Boats and Kayaks: These are popular for fly- in or pack-in fishing trips. An effective method of fishing the pack-in country is to charter a plane and have it drop you and a dependable inflatable boat, with camp gear, upstream on a fine fishing stream—one that is safe for a float trip. The pilot can pick you up a day or a week later downstream at a predetermined point.

Modern, tough, inflatable boats are superior to the life rafts military surplus stores often sell. The cheap life rafts often puncture easily, and the bottom wears out if dragged over gravel.

Many air taxi operators have inflatable boats they rent for fly-in float trips.

Kayaks are a special type of boat, good for fast water when handled by an expert. They have little room in them for camp gear, and they are not as safe or practical for a fishing float-trip as a good-sized inflatable boat.

Canoes: Many lakes and streams in Alaska and Canada are suitable for canoes. Square-stern metal models are popular because they are tough enough to withstand striking bottom in shallow, swift streams—a frequent occurrence. A number of fine one-day to several-day canoe trail trips have been mapped by the U.S. Fish & Wildlife Service for the Kenai National Moose Range, and by the Bureau of Land Management in several areas of the state. Fishing is good to excellent on these planned trips.

Write for *Alaska Canoe Trails,* U.S. Bureau of Land Management, 555 Cordova, Anchorage, Alaska 99501; for canoe trails on the National Moose Range write to the Refuge Manager, Kenai National Wildlife Refuge, Box 500, Kenai, Alaska 99611.

Some rivers are too dangerous for canoeing. Never launch a canoe into an unknown river. Make local inquiries

before trying any canoe trip. Big lakes can turn from flat calm into dangerous white-waved death traps within minutes, so if you travel in a large lake, stay close to shore where you can land when it gets rough.

Riverboats: Alaska and northern Canada have thousands of miles of glacial rivers, winding streams that may or may not be shallow, streams that are often too hazardous for the small sport-type boats usually carried as car-toppers. Such rivers are the Stikine, Taku and Unuk in South-eastern Alaska. In central Alaska, the Copper River is especially hazardous. The Kenai River and the Susitna are silty, often shallow, and hazardous to navigation. Most boats used on these rivers are specially designed, flat-bottomed, shallow-draft riverboats. Many of Canada's rivers can also be classified as hazardous.

The vast Interior rivers north of the Alaska Range, the Yukon River and its many tributaries—(the Tanana, the Koyukuk, the Porcupine)—are also generally traveled with flat-bottomed riverboats, powered with outboards. Such riverboats range from 15 to 30 feet in length and use outboards to 75 or more horsepower. Jet units are often attached to riverboat outboards.

Large loads—many passengers, much camp gear, plenty of fuel—can be carried in these riverboats, which are designed to ease over riffles only inches deep. The "john boat" of the Midwest and South is a near relative to these northern riverboats.

Camping

Alaska: State campgrounds and waysides require an annual $10 permit. No permit is necessary to enter Alaska's national forests, however most USFS campgrounds charge a $2 overnight fee. The Bureau of Land Management maintains about 25 camping areas in the state. There is no charge with the exception of Delta Campground. Mount McKinley National Park has 7 campgrounds with fees from $1 to $3 per night depending upon the facilities.

USFS cabins in Alaska are available for a fee of $5 per night. These cabins are very popular and must be reserved well in advance. The Bureau of Land Management has 3 public use cabins in

the Fairbanks District. Reservations necessary; user fee is $2 per night.

Yukon Territory: Territorial campground fee is $10 per season or $2.50 per night.

Northwest Territories: Territorial campground fee is $5 per season.

British Columbia: Provincial park campgrounds are serviced from early spring to early fall and are gated from 11 P.M. to 7 A.M. Fee is generally $3 per night.

Canada's national park campgrounds generally have a per night fee—$3 for a site not equipped with water, sewer and electrical hookups; $5 for a site with electricity; $6 for a full-service site.

City and Commercial Campgrounds: Many community and commercial campgrounds are also maintained throughout the Northland. In addition there are many areas suitable for camping by self-contained recreational vehicles along the roads, lakes and streams.

Camping Equipment: If you plan to use your own tent be sure it is capable of keeping you dry and warm. In Southeastern Alaska, in Prince William Sound or on the Alaska Peninsula—all damp coastal areas with frequent heavy and continuous rains, and on the peninsula, commonly high winds, you'll want a tent with a fly (an extra, outside cover) that will turn rain. You'll also want some type of heat in the tent even during summer months. A wood stove with an old-fashioned wall tent makes a safe and comfortable camp. Modern tents are

often so tight that it is dangerous to use gasoline-burning stoves inside them without ventilation.

When camping near your car, such as in sites along the Alaska Highway, in the Interior or on the Kenai Peninsula, you don't need as watertight a tent, or necessarily one with heat during summer months. If you are in a campground with your car near, you can always pack up and leave if you get wet and cold.

If, however, you drift down the Yukon or one of the other large river systems or have an air taxi operator drop you off at a lake or a river so that you are entirely dependent upon a tent for shelter, be sure you have a good one, and be sure it is plenty roomy for the size of your party. Manufacturer's specifications for tents are on the optimistic side, and seem meant for a casual, one-night camping trip. A four-person tent is crowded for four on a week-long trip, and in actuality is about right for two.

If you plan to sleep on the ground in your tent, remember that the ground almost everywhere in Alaska and northern Canada is wet. If you use cots, you can use a tent without a floor. For sleeping directly on the ground, use a tent with a waterproof floor and a foam sleeping pad under you to insulate from the cold ground and provide a cushion. An air mattress

allows the cold to come through, but is all right if you have sufficient bedding under you for warmth. The insulating pad, of course, provides both comfort and warmth.

It is best when camping, to have both a saw and an ax. A bow saw is superior to an ax for cutting firewood. An ax is handy for splitting kindling, driving stakes and a hundred and one other chores around camp.

During late May, June, July and early August, daylight hours in northern Canada and Alaska exceed dark, and the farther north you go the more pronounced this is. Above the Arctic Circle from mid-May until mid-July, it is essentially daylight all the time, eliminating need for a lantern or flashlight.

Sleeping Bags: If you plan a fly-in fishing trip or a long river float and will be isolated from civilization and are entirely dependent upon your camping equipment, you should have a top-quality bag. If, however, you plan to camp in campgrounds and will be near your car, you can get by with a bag of lesser quality.

Spring, summer and fall temperatures in the North, when most sport fishing is popular, are seldom extreme. Freezing weather is gone south of the Arctic Circle (unless you are in the mountains) by early May and doesn't appear again until early August.

Care of Fresh-caught Fish

Fish should be killed as soon as caught. The sooner they are cleaned after they are dead, the better. Salmon and trout especially ferment rapidly if not properly cared for. Gills should be removed, for they are a fine medium for bacteria that cause spoilage. Kidney tissue—the dark, soft structures along the backbone—should be removed.

Do not wash fish until just before cooking or freezing. Water hastens spoilage; dry fish keep longer.

A workable method of preserving fish in the field is, after cleaning, to place it in the hot sun for about 10 minutes to allow it to glaze. The glaze seals the flesh, so it will not dry, and it prevents bacterial development on moist surfaces.

Do not keep fish in plastic bags.

Smoking fish lightly over a low fire of alder or poplar (not spruce, fir, pine or any of the resinous conifers) will extend the time that the fish will keep.

Fish can be split along one side of the backbone and hung to dry or smoke. Tons of salmon are preserved in this manner by Eskimos in the North.

For information on smoking fish see page 69. Also see "Want That Fish Mounted?" on page 95.

Clothing

Dress for Alaska and northern Canada is generally informal. Small villages, towns, lodges, ferry travel, traveling along the highway and fly-in trips all call for comfortable, durable clothing, with a minimum of light dress-up clothes. Anchorage, Fairbanks, Juneau, Whitehorse and other cities are modern, with fine restaurants and hotels. However, even here summertime dress especially is fairly informal.

For actual fishing, clothing needs depend on whether you are after salmon in often-rainy Southeastern or hiking into a grayling stream in the Interior, or boating on a lake in the subarctic of Northwest Territories. In any case, normal needs are for durable, com-

fortable, loose-cut clothing. Wool shirts and jackets are necessary for evening and morning wear. Light rain gear—the kind you can roll up and put in your pockets—will keep you dry in most areas.

Footgear, again, depends on whether you are planning to hike a lot or whether you will be wading or riding in a chartered or other type boat. The ground in Alaska and northern Canada is often damp or wet and calls for rubber footgear. Rubber-bottomed, leather-topped shoepacks are perhaps the most popular of all types of footgear. Most stream fishermen use lightweight sport hip boots—the kind that are comfortable to walk in. Some use waist-high waders.

Because of the wet ground, woolen socks in rubber-bottomed shoes are needed to keep your feet warm. Bring plenty for frequent changes. Avoid sponge-rubber shoe soles that soak up water—some draw water right through and wet your feet when walking on the tundra or damp ground.

Modern flotation jackets are popular in the North, whether used for stream wading or worn aboard a boat. If you fall overboard, they keep you afloat. They are light, comfortable and warm.

A visit to the Bering Sea coast or the Arctic coast, even in summer, calls for somewhat warmer clothing. A light- or medium-weight down parka, a pair or two of light underwear (Duofold is popular), along with the other woolen clothes needed elsewhere, will usually suffice.

A pair of inexpensive cotton gloves comes in handy. Hands can get cold on foggy days on a boat, or during early morning or evening as the temperature drops.

Customs Requirements

Identification: Citizens or permanent residents of the United States can cross the United States-Canada border either way without difficulty or delay. They do not need passports or visas. However, they should carry some identifying paper that shows their citizenship. Permanent residents who are not citizens are advised to have their Alien Registration Receipt Card (U.S. Form 1-151). Visitors to the United States who have a single entry visa should check with the office of the U.S. Immigration and Naturalization Service to make sure that they have the proper papers to get back into the United States.

Motorists should have car registration. If you do not have legal title to the car you are driving, you should have a document from the legal owner of the car, giving the owner's permission for you to drive it out of the United States.

Financial Responsibility: Border officers of Canada Customs generally ask how long you plan to stay in Canada and may ask for evidence that you have enough money to pay expenses during your stay including extra funds to cover emergencies.

If traveling from the Lower 48 to Alaska the average basic cost from Great Falls, MT, or Seattle, WA, to Fairbanks, or Anchorage, AK, allowing eight days, with two adults and three meals a day is about $700 ($200 for meals, $300 for lodging and $200 for gas and oil). Those who sleep in tents, campers or trailers or make the trip in less than eight days spend less.

Recreational Equipment: Visitors may bring in sporting outfits and other equipment by declaring them at entry. These can include fishing tackle, portable boats, outboard motors, ice boats, camera (with a reasonable amount of film) and other sports equipment. It will facilitate entry to have a list of all items with a description and serial numbers when possible.

Firearms: Revolvers, pistols, fully automatic firearms and "any firearm that is less than 26 inches in length or that is designed or adapted to be fired when reduced to a length of less than 26 inches by folding, telescoping or otherwise," are PROHIBITED. Federal customs regulations permit the entry into Canada of rifles and shotguns (other than fully automatic) without permit. A description of such equipment and serial numbers of the guns must be provided so they may be readily cleared upon return.

Insurance: Automobile insurance is mandatory in all Canadian provinces and territories. Proof of financial responsibility and liability insurance may vary, but Yukon Territory generally demands proof upon entry.

Restrictions apply to the transporting of animals, plants, the amount of alcohol, tobacco or food allowed. For complete information obtain the free brochures available from Canada and U.S. customs offices.

Driving Tips

Many Northland roads are gravel and can be dangerous. Skids are hard to control, and flying gravel from fast-

moving vehicles endangers other traffic on the road. Dust also hinders visibility. When wet these gravel roads become extremely slippery. Hard surfaced roads are subject to frost-heaves and holes which also make driving hazardous. The best advice for safe driving on these roads is to slow down.

Best travel time is from about mid-May until early October. Deep cold may be encountered from November through March, although winter roads are usually smooth. Breakup may cause soft spots in April and early May. During the winter some facilities along the highways are closed. Be sure to check ahead before starting out, have plenty of fuel and carry extra food and water. If you travel in winter have down-insulated sleeping bags and heavy winter clothing that will protect you to at least -50°F. Cars used on the highway from mid-October through March should be winterized, including antifreeze in the radiator and winter-weight oil or grease for crankcase, transmission and differential. A moisture remover should be added to the gas tank with every third fill-up, and tank should be kept filled to prevent condensation. Electric engine heaters are helpful—most lodges have electrical outlets for the cars of guests.

Turn lights on under dusty conditions, keep gas tank topped and don't travel with an overloaded vehicle. Special screens to protect cars against bugs and gravel can be attached to the front of a car, and plastic headlight covers are available. Some drivers cover the bottom of their gas tanks with rubber to protect them from flying gravel.

Fly-in Fishing Trips

The best fishing, other than some salt water areas, is by fly-in trips to remote areas. Many air taxi operators offer package trips for flying in to lakes, streams or beaches. Often air taxi companies have cabins available at remote spots, or they have tents and other camping gear they will loan or rent. Also, many of the USFS cabins can be reached only by flying in. (See "Resorts, Lodges and Fishing Camps" for information on their package trips.)

Air taxi operators offer various

Protective screens over windows and in front of radiator, such as on this camper, help eliminate the hazards of driving graveled roads. (W. H. Truesdell)

types of planes for charter, and fishermen can arrange to be flown to any area of their choice. Some current approximate sample air taxi charter rates for Alaska (Canadian rates are comparable) are:

Fairbanks and Bettles Field

Cessna 185 (floats), 1,200-pound useful load, 4 passengers, $148/hr.

DeHavilland Beaver (piston engine, floats), 1,200-pound useful load, 6 passengers, $148/hr.

Cessna 207 (wheels), $140/hr.

Cessna 185 (wheels), $138/hr.

Nome

Cessna 172 (wheels), $90/hr.

Cessna 185 (wheels/skis), $119/hr.

Cessna 207 (wheels), $125/hr.

Piper Aztec (wheels), $190/hr.

Beechcraft D-18 (wheels), $255/hr.

Anchorage

Flat seat rates are offered by various air taxi companies to well-known fishing holes. Family and party rates are also available.

Cessna 185 (floats), $130/hr.

Cessna 206 (floats), $140/hr.

DeHavilland Beaver (piston engine, floats), $170/hr.

Juneau

Cessna 180 (floats), $105/hr.

DeHavilland Beaver (piston engine, floats), $145/hr.

Grumman Goose (twin engine, amphibian), $240/hr.

DeHavilland Otter (piston, single engine, floats) $220/hr.

Homer

DeHavilland Beaver (piston engine, floats), $140/hr.

DeHavilland Otter (piston, single engine, floats), 2,200-pound useful load, 9 passengers, and will also carry a kayak or small canoe, $250/hr.

Piper Super Cub (floats), 700-pound useful load, 1 passenger, $75/hr.

Cessna 207 (wheels), $110/hr. Standard fares to some local fishing areas. Family rates available.

Cessna 172 (wheels), $65/hr.

Standby rates vary. Various air taxi operators charge standby rates according to charter rate. Most also charge a minimum of 4 hours charter for each day of standby time, but this may be lower for extended standby time, or during slow months.

Consult with individual operators for standby rates for your particular needs.

Air Taxi Operators: Air taxi operators work from a registered base of operations with aircraft of 12,500 pounds gross takeoff weight, or less. Unless otherwise restricted, air taxi operators may operate aircraft in all areas of the state.

Tips on Fly-in Trips: In chartering a plane, cost normally includes the time required to fly to the fishing area *and return to the origin of charter.* Because of this the "package" prices that most air taxi operators offer for fishermen are usually more economical than a charter. Further, sometimes weather will prolong a charter, increasing the estimated time involved in flying. A package price is not changed, regardless of weather or other delays.

All small-plane flights depend on weather. High winds, low clouds, fog and darkness keep small planes on the ground. These conditions may occur anywhere in the North, and during any month.

Weight and bulk are both problems in flying. If you plan to charter for a fly-in camping-fishing trip, plan your outfit carefully so that you can get it and yourself to your destination and back in the least possible amount of flying time—and in the smallest plane practical for the trip. The smaller planes are normally less expensive.

Take extra food along if you plan to be dropped off and left. Weather can turn bad and delay the pilot in retrieving you. In wilderness areas—the objective of most fly-in trips—take a good first aid kit and be especially careful with an ax or other tools and

when walking in rough terrain. You will have to wait until your pilot comes for you to get medical care for a serious injury.

Always go with another person. In an emergency at least one person should be capable of providing shelter, getting food or signaling for help.

In an emergency, unless you *know* where other people are and are sure you can get there in a short time, it is best to stay where your pilot left you. Signal for help to passing planes. A white cloth waved in the air will usually stop an observant pilot. Three fires, three smokes or a flashlight flashed in series of three is the universal call for help.

Letters scuffed in the sand or spelled out with pieces of wood will attract attention. Toilet paper can be used to spell out words.

Best foods to take on a fly-in trip are the freeze-dried items available at most grocery stores and at sporting goods stores. Their extra cost may save on plane charter, if weight is a factor. Talk to your pilot first.

Don't try to take huge boxes, bundles or packages in a small plane. Many small items pack better and are more easily lifted in and out.

With a large party it is usually cheaper to charter a large plane that will haul everyone at once. When a small plane is used for repeated ferry trips, especially if you are going any distance—say more than an hour's flight—weather could trap some of the party at one end or the other for days at a time.

Hunting

Hunting regulations can be obtained from license vendors or by writing to: Alaska Department of Fish & Game, Subport Building, Juneau, AK 99801; Director of Game, Box 2703, Whitehorse, YT, Y1A 2C6; Fish & Wildlife Service, Department of Natural and Cultural Affairs, Government of the Northwest Territories, Yellowknife, NWT, X1A 2L9; British

Columbia Government, Fish & Wildlife Branch, Parliament Buildings, Victoria, BC V8V 1X4.

For a full insight into hunting possibilities order *ALASKA®* *magazine's Alaska Hunting Guide*, (includes Northwestern Canada), from Alaska Northwest Publishing Company (see page 21 for details).

Information Sources

Alaska: Fish and game regulations and brochures on when and where to fish. Ask for: "'Alaska Sport Fishing Seasons and Limits," "Alaska Sport Fishing Predictions," and "Alaska Sport Fishing Guide" ($1.00), Alaska Department of Fish & Game, Subport Building, Juneau, AK 99801.

List of registered Alaska guides: Alaska Department of Commerce, Pouch D, Juneau, AK 99811.

Information about Alaska's many federal wildlife refuges: The U.S. Fish & Wildlife Service, 1011 East Tudor Road, Anchorage, AK 99502.

General information on Alaska's wildlife, and public lands managed by the Bureau of Land Management: The Bureau of Land Management, 555 Cordova, Anchorage, AK 99501.

Information about Southeastern Alaska's Tongass National Forest (including USFS cabin rentals): U.S. Forest Service, P.O. Box 1628, Juneau, AK 99802.

Information about Alaska's Chugach National Forest (north Gulf of Alaska coastal region and Afognak Island)—also includes USFS cabin rental information: U.S. Forest Service, Pouch 6606, Anchorage, AK 99502.

Maps and information on maps of Alaska: U.S. Geological Survey, Map Sales Office, 508 West Second Avenue, Anchorage, AK 99501.

Travel and visitor information: Alaska State Division of Tourism, Pouch E-907, Juneau, AK 99811. Ask for "Discover . . . The Worlds of Alaska."

Publications on Alaska:

The following are published by Alaska Northwest Publishing Company. For complete information on these and other publications about the Northland write to: Alaska Northwest Publishing Company, Box 4-EEE, Anchorage, AK 99509.

The MILEPOST®, All-the-North Travel Guide®, includes information on traveling throughout western Canada and Alaska with mile-by-mile logs of all major highways. $5.95.

ALASKA® magazine, $15 per year.

The ALASKA JOURNAL®, history and arts of the North, quarterly, $8 per year.

ALASKA GEOGRAPHIC®, quarterly publication of The Alaska Geographic Society, $20 per year.

Illustrated Keys to the Fresh-Water Fishes of Alaska, by James E. Morrow, $2.95.

Selected Alaska Hunting & Fishing Tales, Volumes 2-3, $3.95 each; Vol. 4, $4.95.

ALASKA® magazine's *Alaska Hunting Guide*, $5.95.

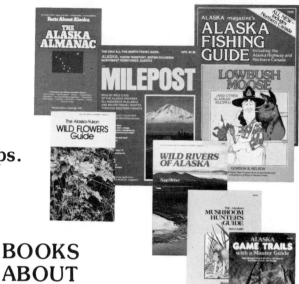

Yukon Territory: Fish and game regulations, information on fishing: Federal Fisheries Service, 122 Industrial Road, Whitehorse, YT.

Travel and visitor information: Department of Tourism & Information, Box 2703, Whitehorse, YT Y1A 2C6. Ask for "Hospitality Yukon."

Northwest Territories: Fish and game regulations, information on fishing: Fish & Wildlife Service, Department of Natural and Cultural Affairs, Government of the Northwest Territories, Yellowknife, NWT X1A 2L9.

Travel and visitor information: TravelArctic, Yellowknife, NWT X1A 2L9. Ask for "Explorer's Guide."

The government of the Northwest Territories publishes an annual *Publications Catalogue*, a complete guide to the pamphlets, books and other printed materials available from the Northwest Territories government; free from Chief of Publications and Production, Department of Information, Box 1320, Yellowknife, NWT, X1A 2L9.

British Columbia: Fish and game regulations, information on fishing: British Columbia Government, Fish and Wildlife Branch, Parliament Buildings, Victoria, BC V8V 1X4.

Travel and visitor information: Tourism British Columbia, 1117 Wharf Street, Victoria, BC V8W 2Z2. Ask for "Directory of British Columbia Tourist Accommodations."

Insects

In some places at certain times insects in the North can make it impossible for humans to relax and carry on normal activities. Low-lying wet tundra areas in the Interior and Arctic and along major river systems are the worst. Here, during June and July and even into early August, any outdoor activity requires the liberal use of good insect repellent.

In camp, a smudge of damp wood helps to keep pesky insects away. Buhack, a brand of powdered pyrethrum commonly marketed in bush areas, burned inside a tent or a cabin will kill any insects that the punkylike smoke touches.

Several brands of modern insect repellent have been found effective. They can be found at shopping centers in every town and in every village general store.

In some areas—and in some seasons—even insect repellent is not sufficient, and one must resort to head net and gloves. Bed nets are necessary in these areas during insect months.

Mosquitoes are found everywhere in Alaska and northern Canada. They are mostly absent from major cities, at higher altitudes where there is a constant breeze, or where it is dry. Generally good repellents can make life possible where there are mosquitoes, but there are exceptions.

No-see-ums, or tiny almost-below-vision-level biting flies, are found throughout Interior Alaska and Canada in June, July and early August. These tiny creatures bite a chunk of flesh from exposed areas, and their bite feels like the end of a red-hot match.

Blackflies, or their relatives, are also found in parts of Alaska and Canada. Insect repellent works for these pesky biters when they aren't too numerous—but there are times, especially in June, when head nets are required.

Parks, Monuments and Forests

Alaska: Mount McKinley National Park is open from about June 1 to September 10. There are seven campgrounds available on a first-come, first-served basis. There is a hotel within the park (reservations are necessary). Commercial lodges and campgrounds are located nearby. No fishing license is required. Glacier Bay National Monument is open May through mid-September and offers wilderness camping, boating and fishing. Accommodations are available at private lodges and aboard charter craft. Alaska fishing license is required. Katmai National Monument is open June to September, has a free tent campground with 10 sites and a private lodge. Alaska fishing license is required.

A presidential proclamation in December 1978 established 14 new national monuments and enlarged the 2 existing monuments and park in Alaska. No facilities have been established in these areas as yet and an Alaska fishing license is required on all waters.

Alaska's State Parks are newly formed. They are simply large areas that are designated as parks, and are protected as such. Hunting and fishing are allowed in these parks, which include the Chugach State Park and Denali State Park near Anchorage and the Kachemak Bay State Park and Kachemak Bay State Wilderness Park near Homer on the lower Kenai Peninsula.

Alaska's Two National Forests: The 4,726,000-acre Chugach and the 16-million-acre Tongass are the two largest of all U.S. national forests. Both offer a wide variety of fishing, camping, hiking, hunting and other recreation. State fishing regulations apply.

There are more than 130 USFS maintained public cabins in the Tongass National Forest of Southeastern Alaska, and 35 in the Chugach Forest of Southcentral Alaska. Reservations are necessary to use the cabins, with a fee of $5 a day and varying time limits, depending upon cabin and time of year.

Some cabins can be reached by chartered plane, others by boat, still others by hiking. Some are on lakes, streams or coastline where fishing can be found. Many of those that are located on lakes also have a skiff available for public use.

Cabins are equipped with bunks, stoves (wood or oil) and pit toilets but not with electricity.

Bedding, a lantern, food, cooking and eating utensils are about all that is needed to move into and be comfortable at one of these well-built cabins. Most will accommodate four to eight persons.

For information on locations of various cabins and what fishing opportunities are available at each, write to the Office of Information, U.S. Forest Service, P.O. Box 1628, Juneau 99802, and request the free brochure on the cabins available in the Tongass National Forest.

For information on cabins in the Chugach National Forest, write to U.S. Forest Service, Pouch 6606, Anchorage 99502 and ask for the free Chugach National Forest brochure that lists cabins.

The brochures include a map showing cabin location and a table indicating what fish species can be found at each, plus method of access. Instructions are given on procedure in making reservations, which must be made as much as six months in advance.

Yukon Territory has only one national park. Kluane National Park is located in the extreme southwest corner of the territory about 130 miles from Whitehorse. There is only one campground in the park at Kathleen Lake just off the Haines Highway, 17 miles south of Haines Junction. There are 44 sites, each with a picnic table and firepit. Firewood, garbage cans, water and flush toilets are provided. Several public and private campgrounds as well as motels and lodges are located along the Alaska and Haines Highways near the park. A special fishing license, supplementary to the regular Yukon angling license is required when fishing in the park.

Information and brochures are available at the park headquarters at Mile 1019, Alaska Highway or by writing: Superintendent, Kluane National Park, Haines Junction, YT, Y0B 1L0.

Northwest Territories has three national parks.

Auyuittuq National Park is representative of a portion of the vast arctic regions that constitute more than one-third of the Canadian landscape. It is located on Cumberland Peninsula of Baffin Island, 8,290 square miles along the 66th parallel. It has spectacular fjords and deeply carved mountains and is dominated by a massive icecap.

A commercial airline operates a daily jet service to Frobisher Bay, 180 miles from the park, and there is also regular service to Pangnirtung, 20 miles from the southern boundary and to Broughton Island at the eastern terminus of the park.

Park information may be obtained by writing to the Superintendent, Auyuittuq National Park, Pangnirtung, NWT, X0A 0R0.

Nahanni National Park is located in the southwest corner of the Northwest Territories. This 1,840-square-mile wilderness area contains the South Nahanni River, one of North America's finest wild rivers. Upper reaches flow through tundra-capped mountains inhabited by mountain goat, Dall sheep and caribou.

The major cataract of the South Nahanni is Virginia Falls where the river plunges 316 feet, with four acres of water face shrouded with mist. A short distance downstream treacherous rapids mark the river's journey

Pat Martin steps out of the USFS cabin to do some coho fishing in the Situk River near Yakutat, AK. (Dianne Hofbeck)

through Hell's Gate. Another six miles downstream the Nahanni is joined by the Flat River.

Steep canyons, with walls that rise 3,500 feet are found, with many caves in steep limestone formations. Sulphur hot springs are also found here.

Nahanni National Park lies 90 miles west of Fort Simpson, NWT, and 650 miles northwest of Edmonton, AB. There are no roads to Nahanni, and access is by air or riverboat, with Fort Simpson and Watson Lake, YT, as major jumping-off points. Both are served by regular air service and all-weather highways via Edmonton. Charter aircraft are also available at both locations. Nahanni Butte at the mouth of the South Nahanni River has a dirt airstrip, but no fuel.

Wood Buffalo National Park, 17,300 square miles of Alberta and the Northwest Territories, represents Canada's boreal plains. It was established to protect Canada's only remaining herd of wood bison. Since then, plains bison

were introduced to the park, and the two species have interbred, and there are now about 7,000 buffalo there.

There are camp and picnic sites, summer and winter trails, and canoe routes. The park road system is usually open to the public from May 1 to November 1. Park headquarters are at Fort Smith, NWT, 500 miles by air from Edmonton. Fort Smith has regular air service and an all-weather road from Edmonton. Write to: Superintendent, Wood Buffalo National Park, Fort Smith, NWT, X0E 0P0.

Northern British Columbia has six provincial parks. Atlin Provincial Park, 50 miles due north of Juneau, AK, on the Alaska-Canada border, accessible via boat from Atlin, BC; Mount Edziza Provincial Park, which lies south and east of Telegraph Creek and Tahltan, BC; Spatsizi Plateau Wilderness Provincial Park at the headwaters of the Stikine River; Kwadacha Wilderness Provincial Park, about 60 miles west of the Alaska

Highway at Prophet River; Muncho Lake Provincial Park straddles the Alaska Highway about 50 miles south of the Yukon border, and Stone Mountain Provincial Park at Summit Lake on the Alaska Highway. The last two are the only ones accessible by road.

There are no national parks in northern British Columbia.

Rentals of Cars and Recreational Vehicles

NOTE: One-way rental of vehicles is not available in many parts of the North. Where it is available the drop-off charges are extremely high.

Alaska: In Anchorage car rentals are available from Airways, American International, Avis, Hertz, National and Stepp Bros. Lincoln, Mercury Rent-A-Car. Many other cities in Alaska have car rentals through one or more of the major companies. Rental agencies for recreational vehicles in Anchorage are: Alaska RV Tours, Alaska Land Cruises, Great Land Campers, Number One Motorhome Rentals of Alaska and Sourdough Camper Village. Some agencies in other cities have pickups and pickups with campers for rent.

Yukon Territory: Avis, Hertz and Tilden have car rental agencies in Whitehorse. Avis has agencies in Watson Lake and Faro. Tilden has agencies in Faro and Dawson City.

Northwest Territories: Car rentals available in Yellowknife.

Northern British Columbia: Car rentals in Prince George and Fort Nelson are available from Avis and Hertz; in Dawson Creek from Avis.

Resorts, Lodges and Camps

Fishing lodges, resorts and camps of varying qualities of comfort and service are found scattered throughout Alaska and Canada. Some are primitive camps with tents, others have plush hotel- or motel-like quarters. Some provide boats, guides and/or small planes to take guests to fishing grounds. Others simply provide lodging and meals and leave the guests to fish on their own.

A few lodges are found along the road system, however most are located in remote areas accessible only by air or boat. (See "Fly-in Fishing.)

Many fishing resorts are located in the Bristol Bay region of Alaska. Southeastern Alaska also has several fine fishing resorts. Great Bear and Great Slave lakes in Northwest Territories have many fine lodges. Lodges are located in various parts of Yukon Territory and British Columbia.

The Guide Post® in *ALASKA®* magazine ($15 a year, Box 4-EEE, Anchorage, AK 99509) gives current listings for various fishing lodges and fishing guide services throughout the North.

SEASONS, LIMITS AND FEES

Pike taken at Minto Lakes near Fairbanks, Alaska. (Jim Rearden)

The following seasons, limits, fees and other regulations are provided as a guide only, and were effective as of Spring 1979. All are subject to change by government regulatory agencies. Fishermen should obtain current official regulations from appropriate agencies before fishing. See "Information Sources," page 20.

Alaska

Condensed from the *Alaska Department of Fish & Game Sport Fishing Seasons and Bag Limits*

Sport Fishing License: Any person 16 years of age or older, with the exception noted below, must have a valid sport fishing license in his actual possession while taking or attempting to take any fresh-water, salt-water or anadromous fish for personal use and while sport-digging razor clams or dip-netting for smelt (hooligan). Licenses must be shown upon request to any authorized representative of the Alaska Department of Fish & Game or the Alaska Department of Public Safety.

Alaska residents who are 60 or older and have had 30 or more years of continuous residency within the state do not need a sport fishing license. A special identification card is available from the Alaska Department of Fish & Game, Subport Building, Juneau, AK 99801. Application forms for this card are available from designated license agents or Fish & Game offices.

Licenses are available from designated issuing agents or by mail from Department of Revenue, Fish & Game License Division, 240 South Franklin, Juneau, AK 99801.

Sport Fishing Seasons and Bag Limits: Each December the Alaska Board of Fisheries reviews and usually makes many changes in the state's sport fishing regulations.

During the year the Department of Fish & Game has authority to alter

Jim and Bill Knott from Pennsylvania hold up a coho salmon taken in the Situk River near Yakutat, Alaska. (Dianne Hofbeck)

regulations by field announcement or emergency regulation. Anglers should check with local Department of Fish & Game offices if there are questions about season or regulation changes.

Regulations are designed to be effective from January 1 through December 31 of each year. However, delays in implementing new regulations frequently occur, and sometimes new

regulations do not go into effect until as late as March.

For current local seasons, bag limits and gear restrictions, consult the printed summary of current *Alaska Sport Fishing Seasons and Bag Limits*, available free from license vendors and all Alaska Department of Fish & Game offices, or write to the Alaska Department of Fish & Game, Subport Building, Juneau, AK 99801.

For additional information consult the local Department of Fish & Game representative or Department of Public Safety Fish & Wildlife Protection Officer in:

Anchorage	Kodiak
Bettles	Kotzebue
Cordova	McGrath
Delta Junction	Nome
Dillingham	Palmer
Eagle River	Petersburg
Fairbanks	Seward
Glennallen	Sitka
Haines	Soldotna
Homer	Tok
Juneau	Valdez
Ketchikan	Wrangell
King Salmon	Yakutat

License Fees (As of Spring 1979)

Resident sport fishing license	$10.00
Resident (blind) sport fishing license	.25
Resident hunting and sport fishing license	22.00
Resident hunting, trapping and sport fishing license	25.00
Visitor's special sport fishing license	
Valid for 1 day	5.00
Valid for 10 days	15.00
Nonresident sport fishing license	30.00
Nonresident hunting and sport fishing license	90.00

The license period is from January 1 through December 31, inclusive, of the current calendar year.

Fresh-water and salt-water fishermen who fish for salmon and steelhead in Cook Inlet waters must have a special punch card in their possession.

Fishermen dip for hooligan (smelt) at the mouth of Twentymile River in Turnagain Arm south of Anchorage, Alaska. (Staff photo)

SUMMARY OF ILLEGAL ACTS

It is unlawful . . .

☐ in fresh water to snag any fish. Fish hooked elsewhere than in the mouth must be released.

☐ to take razor clams without a valid sport fishing license or by any means other than a manually operated clam gun, shovel, fork or by hand.

☐ to sport fish with more than one line having attached to it more than one plug, spoon, set of spinners, two flies or two hooks or as indicated in "Sport Fishing Methods and Means" or for a specific regulatory area.

☐ to sport fish in fresh water with live fish for bait.

☐ to use explosives or toxicants to take fish.

☐ to take grayling by any means other than by hook and line.

☐ to sport fish within 300 feet of an artificial barrier, weir, dam, fish ladder or other obstruction, unless the obstruction is a total barrier to fish passage.

☐ to knowingly disturb, damage or destroy a notice, poster or marker, or any other property of the department used in the administration or enforcement of these regulations.

☐ to sport fish in stocked or planted waters when so designated or posted by closure signs placed by the Alaska Department of Fish & Game.

☐ to cast, drift or place by any means a hook, bait, lure or fly into closed waters.

☐ to possess, transport and release any live fish or live fish eggs (marine fishes exempted), or mark any live fish except in accordance with the terms of a permit issued by the Commissioner of Fish & Game.

☐ to molest or impede spawning or the natural movement of fish contrary to the methods and means of sport fishing.

☐ to intentionally waste or destroy any species of sport-caught fish which have bag limits provided for in these regulations.

☐ for anyone to possess unpreserved fish or part thereof not legally taken by himself unless he furnishes on request of an officer authorized to enforce these regulations a statement signed by the person who took the fish stating the type of fish, number of fish and location and date taken. This statement is unnecessary if the person possessing the fish is accompanied by the person or persons who took the fish.

☐ to buy, sell or barter sport-caught fish.

SPORT FISHING METHODS AND MEANS

Sport fishing may be done only with a single line held in the hand or attached to a hand-held or closely attended rod. The line may not have more than one plug, spoon, spinner or series of spinners or two flies or two hooks attached to it, except as indicated for a specific regulatory area. Two rods, each with one hook or one artificial lure, may be used while fishing through the ice.

Fresh-water sport fishing may not be done by means of:

☐ Fixed or weighted hook(s) or lure(s), except those of standard manufacture, or multiple hooks or lures to which a weight is attached in such a manner that the weight follows the hook when retrieved by the angler.

☐ Multiple hook with gap between points and shank larger than ¼ inch unless attached to a plug, spoon, spinner or artificial lure.

☐ Plug, spoon, spinner or artificial lure having multiple hook(s) with gap between points and shank larger than ½ inch except as permitted in Area 8.

☐ Spear (except as provided for in Areas 2 and 8). Note: grayling may only be taken by hook and line.

☐ Arrow.

Underwater sport fishing may be done by underwater spear in salt water and in accordance with applicable seasons and bag limits, by persons completely submerged.

Burbot (fresh-water ling) may be taken year-round without limit and with more than one line and hook (see Area 2 summer exception in complete, official Alaska Department of Fish & Game regulations) provided that:

☐ The total aggregate of hooks does not exceed 15 in number.

☐ The hooks are single hooks with gap between point and shank larger than ¾ inch.

☐ Each hook is set on the bottom of the lake or stream.

☐ Each line is identified with the angler's name, address and sport fishing license number.

☐ Each line is physically inspected at least once during each 24-hour period.

Smelt and herring may be taken year-round in salt water using up to 15 unbaited single or multiple hooks.

Yukon Territory

Condensed from the Fish and Wildlife Branch of Yukon Territory official regulations

Yukon Territory angling licenses are available from lodges along the Alaska Highway, all Fish and Wildlife Branch offices, various sporting goods, hardware and general stores throughout the Yukon, and Fisheries Service office in Whitehorse. All licenses other than short-term licenses expire March 31 of the year following issuance. An angler must have his license in his possession and display it upon official request.

Fishing regulations and Yukon angling license apply to all tidal and nontidal waters of Yukon Territory. An additional license is necessary when fishing in Kluane National Park. Various regulatory changes may be made starting in late 1979. For further information write Fish and Wildlife Branch, P.O. Box 2703, Whitehorse, YT, Y1A 2C6.

License Fees (as of Spring 1979)

Resident . . . . $ 3.00
Nonresident (alien) full term 10.00
Nonresident (alien) 5-day short term. 3.50
Children under 16 . . . . No license required
Supplementary license for Kluane National Park 4.00

Season, Catch and Possession Limits.
There is no closed season for sport fishing.

Species	Daily Limit	Possession Limit
Arctic grayling.	7	2 days
Lake trout.	5	catch limit,
Dolly Varden	5	all species
Kokanee	5	
Rainbow trout	5	
Cutthroat trout	5	
Northern pike	10	
Arctic char	2	
Inconnu	5	
Whitefish	5	
* Salmon	2 (over 18 inches in length, of which one may be a chinook)	
Salmon	5 (under 18 inches in length)	

* Fishing prohibited in area around dam at Whitehorse during salmon run.

No person shall continue to angle for game fish after taking his or her daily limit. To determine catch and possession limits two whole fillets shall be deemed to be one fish.

Wellesley Lake, at 62°20′, and 139°59′, is a trophy lake. No person shall angle in or on a trophy lake with barbed hooks. Daily catch limit for lake trout is 2, of which only 1 may be 20 pounds or over. Possession of lake trout is 4, of which only 1 may be over 20 pounds. Daily catch limit for pike is 5, of which only 2 may be over 20 pounds. Possession of pike 10, of which only 2 may be over 20 pounds.

GENERAL SPORT FISHING REGULATIONS

No person shall:
☐ while angling use more than one line, except in trolling where two lines may be used.
☐ except when fly fishing, use on a line any gear that is designed to catch more than one fish at a time.
☐ abandon game fish or portions of game fish suitable for human consumption.
☐ stone, club, shoot with any firearms, or in any manner molest, injure or kill fish in any stream or lake.
☐ use torches, artificial lights, spears, arrows, jigs or snares in fishing for game fish.
☐ use explosives of any kind in water frequented by fish without prior written approval of the Regional Director or a fishery officer.
☐ introduce live fish or fish eggs into Yukon Territory or transfer live fish or fish eggs from one body of water to another within Yukon Territory.
☐ sell, barter or attempt to sell or barter fish caught by angling.
☐ use a lure having a single hook with a distance between the point and the shank greater than ¾″, or a lure with a treble hook with a distance between the points and the shank greater than ½″ in the following waters during its specified time: Klukshu River, Takhanne River, Blanchard River, Village Creek, Tatshenshini River, June 1-August 30. Tatchun Creek, Klondike River, July 15-September 15. Takhini River, August 1-September 15.
☐ when sport fishing use a landing gaff, or landing net with openings larger than 2 feet in diameter or handles longer than 4 feet in the waters referred to above.

Special Conditions: Any person holding a valid angling license may: (a) jig to capture cisco; (b) spear fish as carried out by a skin-diver under the same regulations that apply to angling; (c) use hand nets and gaffs to land fish caught by angling, other than in the size and waters referred to above.

Minimum Size Limit: No person shall fish for, catch or kill by angling, grayling or trout of any kind under 8 inches in length, and when such fish are caught they shall be immediately returned to the water unharmed.

Northwest Territories

The following information is condensed from the *Northwest Territories Fisheries Regulations*

Fishing licenses are available in most communities from local hardware and sporting goods stores, from fishing lodges, and the 60th Parallel Visitor Information Centre at the Alberta-Northwest Territories border on Highway 1.

An angler must carry his or her license and produce it at the request of a federal fisheries officer, a Fish and Wildlife officer of the Northwest Territories or the RCMP.

Authorities recommend that fishermen use barbless hooks so that fish can easily and safely be released after catching. Keep only your limit, or what you can eat.

GENERAL SPORT FISHING REGULATIONS

These regulations apply in all waters of the Northwest Territories and in the tidal waters of the provinces of Manitoba and Ontario.
No person shall:
- ☐ take, be in possession of or use live fish for bait when sport fishing.
- ☐ use a gaff while sport fishing.
- ☐ engage in sport fishing while he is acting as a hired guide for an angling or fishing party.
- ☐ angle in open water with more than a single line or rod and line.
- ☐ angle in ice-covered water with more than two lines, or two rods and lines, or have more than two hooks attached to one line. He must remain within 45.7 meters (50 yards) of his line or lines.
- ☐ fish by snagging.
- ☐ catch, kill, molest or injure fish by using spears, arrows, gaffs, lights, sticks, stones, clubs, snares or hand nets (however hand nets may be used to land fish caught by angling).
- ☐ kill by angling in the Tree River any arctic char in any year after 700 arctic char have been taken.

Current regulations should be consulted for more complete information. For information write: District Manager, Fisheries and Marine Service, Box 2310, Yellowknife, NWT.

License Fees (as of Spring 1979)

Resident sport fishing license . . . . $ 3.00
Nonresident sport fishing license 10.00
Children under the age of 16 . . . . No license required
Fishermen over 65 years of age . . . . No license required

Catch and Possession Limits

Type of Fish	Daily Maximum Limit	Maximum Possession Limit
Lake trout	3	5
* Grayling	5	10
Walleye	5	10
Northern pike	5	10
Humpback and broad whitefish	10	20
Dolly Varden	4	7
Brook trout	3	5
Inconnu	5	10
Goldeye	5	10
All Ciscos	no limit	no limit
** Arctic char	4	7
Rainbow trout	3	5

* Grayling caught in the portion of the Mackenzie River and the tributary streams lying west of a line drawn from Pointe de Roche to Slave Point and east of the inlet of Mills Lake, must have a fork length of not less than 14 inches.
** Except in waters of Tree River entering Coronation Gulf, 137 kilometers (85 miles) east of Coppermine, where maximum limits are daily maximum limit, 2; and maximum possession limit, 2.

North Arm of Great Slave Lake in Northwest Territories. (Daniel Montroty)

There is good fishing for grayling and Dolly Varden along the Cottonwood River, Mile 307, Cassiar Highway in northern British Columbia. (Patrick Hawkes, staff)

British Columbia

The following information
is condensed from the
*British Columbia Sports Fishing
Regulations Synopsis*

Fishing licenses are available from most Fish and Wildlife Branch offices and sporting goods stores. It may be difficult to obtain licenses in remote areas of British Columbia. Purchase all necessary licenses before traveling to remote areas.

Fishermen must have their licenses in their possession and display it upon request by any authorized official.

None of these licenses are valid in any national park.

Nonresident short term angling licenses are valid for 3 consecutive days only. More than one may be purchased.

Steelhead licenses are valid only if the holder also carries a basic annual angling license. Only one steelhead license may be purchased by an angler in one year (April 1 to March 31). Any licensed steelhead angler who takes and keeps a steelhead trout must immediately punch out the appropriate perforation of the steelhead license and

License fees (as of Spring 1979)

Residents of Canada	$ 5.00
Residents of Canada over age 65	1.00
Residents of Canada under age 16	No fee
Nonresidents of Canada, age 16 and over	15.00
Nonresidents of Canada, short term (3 days)	6.00
Supplementary:	
Steelhead, residents and nonresidents	10.00
Steelhead, residents of Canada over age 65	3.00
Special rivers, nonresidents	25.00
Special lakes, nonresidents	15.00

<table>
<tr><td colspan="3">Province-wide Catch Limits: Catch and possession limits, common to all regions, for angling, spear fishing and bow fishing. Consult with the full British Columbia Sport Fishing Regulations Synopsis currently in effect.</td></tr>
<tr><td></td><td>Daily Limit</td><td>Possession Limit</td></tr>
<tr><td>Salmon over 50 cm, fork length</td><td>2</td><td>6</td></tr>
<tr><td>Aggregate salmon</td><td>8</td><td>24</td></tr>
<tr><td>Aggregate bass</td><td>8</td><td>24</td></tr>
<tr><td>Aggregate Northern pike & walleye</td><td>8</td><td>16</td></tr>
<tr><td>Aggregate whitefish (one exception in Region 3)</td><td>25</td><td>75</td></tr>
<tr><td>Grayling</td><td>8</td><td>16</td></tr>
<tr><td>Burbot, regions 4 & 6</td><td>10</td><td>20</td></tr>
<tr><td>Burbot, other British Columbia waters</td><td>no limit</td><td>no limit</td></tr>
</table>

write on that license the date upon which the steelhead was caught and the name of the stream or water from which the steelhead was taken.

Some of the waters of British Columbia supporting angling of exceptional quality have been designated as Special Lakes or Special Rivers. Nonresidents of Canada wishing to angle in these waters require a Special License in addition to their basic annual nonresident angling license.

No person under age 16 requires a license to angle. However, an angler under 16 who is not a resident of British Columbia must be accompanied by a person who is in possession of the appropriate angling license(s). Any fish caught and kept by the unlicensed angler under 16 shall become part of the daily catch and possession limit of the accompanying license holder. Persons under 16 may purchase an angling license if desired.

Note: Trout, char, kokanee and sturgeon limits appear under "Regional Regulations" in the *British Columbia Sport Fishing Regulations Synopsis*, however they have become complicated and some anglers find them difficult to interpret. They may best be explained by example:

Take a river where daily trout and char limits are: steelhead, 1; aggregate trout and char over 50 cm, 2; aggregate trout and char (all sizes), 8. This may be restated as follows to clarify intent —"The daily limit for trout and char (all species and all sizes combined) is 8 fish of which no more than 2 may be over 50 cm fork length, and no more than 1 of the latter may be a steelhead.

Steelhead: Only for steelhead are

there annual catch limits. Those limits, for the period April 1 to March 31 of the year next following are: 10 fish from all non-tidal waters by a person not a resident of British Columbia; 20 fish from all non-tidal waters by a person who is a resident of British Columbia, except no more than 10 of those fish can be taken from any single river or stream. Single refers to separately named waters (i.e. though the Thompson and Fraser rivers are part of the same system, a British Columbia resident may take 10 steelhead from each). One exception is the Vedder-Chilliwack rivers which are considered a single river.

GENERAL RESTRICTIONS AND PROHIBITIONS

It is unlawful to:
☐ take, kill or have in possession any fish that are smaller than the minimum size limit or larger than the maximum size limit. Any undersized or oversized fish that may be taken must be returned immediately to the water, unharmed.
☐ continue to angle for a species of game fish, burbot, sturgeon or whitefish, after taking the daily catch limit for that species; for chinook or coho salmon after taking the daily catch limit for either of those species.
☐ fish for, catch or kill sockeye, pink or chum salmon in the non-tidal waters, and any of these species accidentally taken must be immediately released.
☐ use more than one line while angling, except that a person may

use two lines when alone in a boat on any lake but the West Arm of Kootenay Lake.
☐ use any gear on a line when angling that is designed to catch more than one fish at a time, except fly fishing where the use of two artificial flies is permitted.
☐ use a spear, spear-gun or bow and arrow to take salmon in any non-tidal waters; game fish or burbot in Region 4 waters; game fish, whitefish or sturgeon in streams of Regions 1, 2, 3, 5, 6 and 7.
☐ use snares, lights or firearms for fishing.
☐ use any set line except by special permit.
☐ catch or attempt to catch a fish by impaling it on a hook through some part of its body (commonly known as jigging or snagging) instead of luring it to take the hook in its mouth as in angling.
☐ use a bare or unbaited hook to take fish, other than a gaff hook used as an aid in landing a fish.
☐ use any explosive for any purpose in water frequented by fish.
☐ fish in any manner within 25 metres downstream from any obstacle or leap or the lower entrance to any canal or fishway.
☐ stone, club, shoot or molest fish in any way.
☐ fish for or molest kokanee in streams.
☐ trap or pen fish in rivers or streams or on their spawning-grounds.
☐ use or possess for bait any fish or fish product other than crustacea or roe, except in Regions 1, 2, 6 or 7 where trout, Pacific herring and smelt may be so used or possessed.
☐ deposit any fish eggs, corn, meat, bones or other material to attract fish for the purpose of catching fish.
☐ introduce any fish or fish eggs alive into British Columbia waters or transport fish or fish eggs alive within British Columbia, except by permission of the Minister of Fisheries (Canada).
☐ remove from British Columbia waters or transport within British Columbia any live aquatic invertebrate organisms other than insect larvae or crayfish.
☐ export game fish from the province without a permit, unless the fish are being transported by the person who caught them. Periodic checks are made at border crossings,

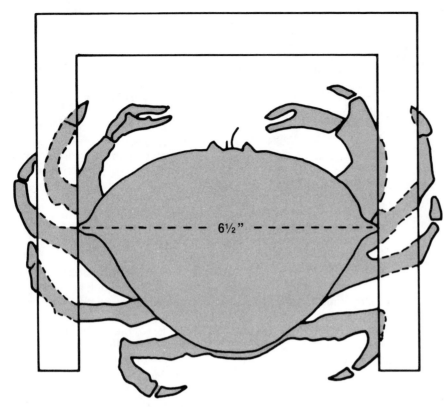

Calipers for measuring legal size of crab (illustrated above) can be cut from plywood, heavy cardboard, plastic, sheet metal or masonite. When crabbing, be sure to check on size restriction for the area. (Illustration courtesy of British Columbia Department of Fisheries and Environment.)

anglers should retain their angling license.
- [ ] sell, trade or barter any fish taken in non-tidal waters of the province, except fish taken under authority of a Commerical (Class A), or a Coarse-fish (Class C) or a Commercial Fish Farm License.
- [ ] can or bottle trout or char in British Columbia other than at the residence of the angler, as shown on his angling license.
- [ ] engage in breeding or rearing of fish (except aquarium fish) without a license.
- [ ] fish for, molest or remove fish from any fish-holding facilities or fish-collection structure owned or operated by the Fish and Wildlife Branch.
- [ ] leave fish offal or other deleterious material on the ice when fishing through the ice.

Salt-water Sport Fishing Regulations, for tidal water fishing only.

Licensing: No licenses are required for Canadian residents. Vessels owned by nonresidents of Canada which fish or which transport or tow auxiliary fishing vessels must be licensed. Individual nonresident fishermen do not require a personal fishing license.

Gear Restrictions
No person shall:
- [ ] use more than one line in angling except while trolling, strip casting or "mooching."
- [ ] use gear designed to catch more than one fish at one time in angling except when fly fishing, or herring fishing, or when fishing in Fraser River tidal waters where gear designed to catch not more than two fish may be used.
- [ ] use artificial power to operate a gurdy or other device in handling sport fishing gear.
- [ ] use more than one gill-net or set net, maximum length 25 feet, in fishing for smelts or sardines.
- [ ] use gear other than a hook attached to a handline or rod to catch halibut.
- [ ] use gear except dip nets or open ring nets to catch crab in Pender Harbour or Fulford Harbour at any time or in Naden Harbour from May 1 to September 30.

- [ ] fish with a downrigger to which a line with a lure is attached otherwise than by means of an automatic release clip.

General Prohibitions
It is illegal to:
- [ ] use rockets, explosives, shells, stones, clubs or firearms or in any other such manner, hunt, kill, molest or injure fish.
- [ ] use torches, artificial lights, spears, jigs or snares in fishing for salmon, trout or steelhead.
- [ ] trap or pen fish in their spawning ground or in rivers or streams leading thereto.
- [ ] use jigs, gaffs, spears, rakes or any sharp-pointed instrument to take crab; or suction devices, spears or any sharp-pointed instrument to take abalone.
- [ ] use bare unbaited hooks or grapnets for taking sturgeon.
- [ ] fish for game fish or salmon for personal use except by angling.
- [ ] purchase or possess fish caught under special permit conditions (i.e. Indian Food Permit).
- [ ] buy, sell, barter or expose for sale or barter any fish or game fish caught in sport fishing.
- [ ] possess sport-caught halibut aboard a vessel when other fish or shellfish aboard the vessel are destined for commercial use.
- [ ] bring ashore any grilse with the head or tail removed or any crab with the shell or carapace removed.
- [ ] use a commercial troller while sport fishing unless the lines are removed from the power gurdies.
- [ ] transport or export from the province salmon or game fish in excess of the possession limit.

New and Revised Regulations: The 1979 regulations on size limits, daily bag limits, possession limits, season and area closures, and spear fishing were not available at press time.

Further Information: Local time and area closures for sport fishing may be made. Regulations are also subject to change. For current information, contact any Fishery officer, or the Regional Director, Fisheries Management, Pacific Region, Department of Fisheries and Environment, 1090 West Pender Street, Vancouver, BC, V6E 2P1. ☐

TROPHY FISH CONTEST RULES

REPRINTED FROM ALASKA® MAGAZINE

A 10-pound, 4-ounce arctic char, taken by angler Frank Beeler of the Alaska Peninsula.
(John Walatka, courtesy of Jim Rearden)

STATE OF ALASKA
TROPHY FISH AWARD PROGRAM

Trophy fish awards are issued by the Alaska Department of Fish & Game to give special recognition to anglers taking fish that meet minimum weight qualifications for each species. Trophy fish rules and affidavits are available at all Department of Fish & Game offices. Affidavits must be signed by at least one witness (preferably two) and be accompanied by a picture of the fish indicating size (color picture, if possible). Incomplete forms may disqualify the applicant. Entries must meet the following minimum weight qualifications:

Arctic char/Dolly Varden	10 pounds
Arctic grayling	3 pounds
Brook trout, Eastern	3 pounds
Burbot	8 pounds
Cutthroat trout (all varieties)	3 pounds
Halibut	100 pounds
Kokanee	1 pound
Lake trout	20 pounds
Northern pike	15 pounds
Rainbow/Steelhead trout	12 pounds
Salmon, chinook (king)	60 pounds
Salmon, chum (dog)	12 pounds
Salmon, coho (silver)	18 pounds
Salmon, pink (humpback)	8 pounds
Salmon, sockeye (red)	10 pounds
Sheefish	30 pounds
Whitefish	4 pounds

Attractive 8x10-inch parchment certificates suitable for framing will be presented to all contestants winning an award under the Trophy Fish Award Program. Three types of certificates are awarded:

Trophy Certificate of Record: This will be presented to each individual submitting an entry complying with the minimum weights established above. Only one certificate is allowed each angler per year per species.

Annual Certificate of Record: This will be presented to the individual submitting the largest (weight) entry for each species during each calendar year.

Champion Certificate of Record: This will be presented to any individual submitting an entry that establishes a new record as the largest (weight) fish of any species in Alaska.

For additional rules and regulations contact any Department of Fish & Game office.

ALASKA DEPARTMENT OF FISH & GAME
TROPHY FISH CONTEST RULES

Fish weight will be the criteria for determining the class winners. Fish must be weighed on a currently certified scale, in the presence of witnesses. Certification date of the scale must be entered on the affidavit.

Length and girth measurements will be made with a metallic tape. Length measurement must be straight line measurement, not along the curve of the fish. Failure to complete the affidavit form in full will disqualify the applicant.

1. Fish must be played on conventional rod, reel and line, hand held, and must be hooked and played by only one person. Assistance is permissible in landing or boating a fish.

2. Fish must be legally caught in compliance with all current Alaska Department of Fish & Game regulations. A fish caught from waters not open to the general public is not eligible.

3. The affidavit form, or an exact copy, must be completed in full for each entry. Incomplete forms will disqualify entrants.

4. Affidavits must be received at Alaska Department of Fish & Game, Subport Building, Juneau, AK 99801, no later than December 31 of the current calendar year.

5. A contestant's largest entry for the calendar year shall be the only entry of that species for which he may receive an award. In the event of two or more entries, identical in weight, identical awards will be given to each contestant.

6. A clear photograph, preferably in color, showing a closeup side view of the fish must accompany each contest entry form. Fish will be hand held, or if photographed alone, must have a size reference object included in the picture. All photographs must be identified with the angler's name, date, type of fish and fish weight on the back, or attached paper. Writing on photograph back must be done with soft marking pencil, to avoid defacing impressions. The photograph will not be returned, and may be used by the Department.

7. A 3-foot sample of the line used in catching the fish must accompany each contest entry form, if the contestant wishes to make the entry eligible for possible later subdivision of classes. For fly casting, the leader tippit should be submitted. Samples will be accurately tested for breaking strength. Rough or abraded portions of samples will not be used in testing.

8. The Alaska Department of Fish & Game reserves the right to check on fish identification or to refuse any questionable affidavits. Decision of the judges will be final.

9. Certificates will be issued only once each year, normally during January or February of the following year. Please keep us advised of any address changes to be sure of prompt delivery of your certificate. Address all correspondence to Sport Fish Division, Department of Fish & Game, Subport Building, Juneau, AK 99801.

ALASKA DEPARTMENT OF FISH & GAME
TROPHY FISH AFFIDAVIT

Trophy Fish Board, I hereby swear that the following statements are true, that in taking this fish I complied with all the rules of this contest, and that the witnesses hereto actually witnessed the weighing and measuring of this fish.

Kind of fish _____

_____lbs._____ozs. Round/dressed weight.

Length_____inches to nearest 1/8 inch.

Girth_____inches to nearest 1/8 inch.

How caught: Casting, Spinning, Trolling, Fly, Bait, Lure, Marine

    or Freshwater.   Date caught _____

Where caught, in detail _____

Type of reel_____Line test _____

Lure, bait or fly used _____

Sport Fishing License No. _____

Contestant's name (please print) _____

Street _____

City_____State_____Zip _____

Local newspaper_____

Street _____

City_____State_____Zip _____

We, the undersigned, witnessed the weighing, measuring and opening of the fish described above, and verify the weight and measurements recorded.

1. (Signature) _____

   (Address)_____

2. (Signature) _____

   (Address)_____

Contestant's signature _____

Certified by me this_____day of_____19 _____

Official's signature _____

Official's address_____

Scale Certification Date_____

(SEE RULES. TAPE DOWN HERE 3 feet of the line used or sample of the leader tip used as specified)
(ATTACH photo of fish)

The following information should be inserted in the appropriate spaces:

Fish species: e.g., silver salmon, grayling, etc.

Weight: To be in pounds and ounces, indicate round or dressed weight.

Length: Give to the nearest 1/8 inch.

Girth: Measurements are to be taken just in front of the dorsal fin as a complete circumference to the nearest 1/8 inch.

How caught: Circle appropriate words to indicate by what means the fish was caught, e.g., the words "bait," "marine," "trolling" would be circled to indicate this type of fishing.

Where caught: Name of lake, drainage area, etc. necessary to positively identify the waters or area where the fish was caught.

Reel: Indicate casting, spinning, trolling or fly reel.

Line type: Actual line test in pounds. If this figure is unknown, insert the word "unknown."

Lure, bait or fly used: If lure or fly has a commonly accepted name, this should be listed. In lieu of this, such descriptive names as "a wobbling spoon," "hook with spinner," etc., is sufficient.

Sport fishing license number: Copy from current sport fishing license.

Contestant's name: The full name *printed* legibly.

Address: Mailing address in full.

Local newspaper: This information is not mandatory. Names and addresses of the contestant's local newspapers should be given if known and if the contestant so desires.

The affidavit: If possible, the signature and addresses of two independent witnesses should be given in addition to the official. *At least one signature as a witness is mandatory.*

The contestant must sign the affidavit in the presence of the official.

The official is to include his address and his affiliation, such as "Totem Sport Shop," Anchorage, after his signature.

The scale certification date, as copied from the certification seal, is to be placed in the space provided.

Fill out in triplicate, *Official to retain* first carbon. *Entrant to submit* original with photograph of the fish and may retain remaining copy for personal file. Submit entries to Alaska Department of Fish & Game, Subport Building, Juneau, Alaska 99801.

Danette English with her father's 16-pound, 8-ounce annual record chum salmon, taken near Bell Island in Alaska. (W. Daniel English)

1978 RECORD FISH OF ALASKA

Three new state champions were recorded in the 1978 trophy fish programs, for halibut, Northern pike and whitefish.

Annual awards for the largest fish registered for 1978 (except for record fish, which are listed at the left), were given for:

Arctic grayling—two fish tied at 4 pounds, 0 ounces. One caught from Ugashik River by Richard A. Cook of Concordia, KS. The second from Ugashik outlet by Carroll C. Dick, of Kelso, WA.

Burbot—one fish of 13 pounds, 7 ounces, jointly claimed caught from the Tanana River by Jim Klepek and Alan Townsend, Fairbanks, AK.

Chum salmon—16 pounds, 8 ounces, caught in Behm Canal at Bell Island by W. Daniel English of Salt Lake City, UT.

Coho salmon—18 pounds, 2 ounces, caught in Karluk Lagoon, Kodiak Island, by R. M. Neville, Santa Rosa, CA.

Cutthroat trout—3 pounds, 9 ounces, caught in Mosquito Lake, Mile 27, Haines Highway, by Ken E. Bryant, Ketchikan, AK.

King salmon—82 pounds, caught in the Kenai River near the Soldotna Bridge, by Gerald Thompson, Anchorage, AK.

Lake trout—27 pounds, 1 ounce, caught in the Brooks Range by Jim Coulter, Birmingham, MI.

Pink salmon—9 pounds, 8 ounces, caught in the Swiftwater area of the Kenai River by J. C. Burton, of Whittier, CA.

Red salmon—14 pounds, 8 ounces, caught at the confluence of the Stuyahok and Mulchatna rivers by Leif Jerlstrom, Degerfors, Sweden.

Sheefish—37 pounds, 4 ounces, caught in the Kobuk River at Ambler, by Raimund Illek, of Tulln, Austria.

Steelhead—16 pounds, 12 ounces, caught 1 mile up Sitkoh Creek, Sitkoh Bay, by Linda G. Seymour. □

RECORD FISH OF ALASKA

These are official records as recorded by the Alaska Department of Fish & Game since the establishment of the Trophy Fish Award program of 1964. It is recognized that larger fish may have been taken in Alaska, but they were taken before the program was initiated, or were not entered into the competition.

Species	Lbs.	Oz.	Where taken	Year	Length (inches)	Angler
Arctic char/ Dolly Varden	17	8	Wulik River	1968	36	Peter Winslow
Arctic grayling	4	11	Ugashik Lake	1975	21-1/2	Duane Weaver
Burbot	24	12	Lake Louise	1976	43	George R. Howard
Chum salmon	27	3	Behm Canal	1977	39-3/8	Robert Jahnke
Cutthroat trout	8	6	Wilson Lake	1977	26-1/4	Robert Denison
Halibut	440		Point Adolphus	1978	97-1/2	Joar Savland
King salmon	91		Kelp Bay	1977	50	Howard Rider
Lake trout	47		Clarence Lake	1970	44-1/4	Daniel Thorsness
Northern pike	38		Fish Creek, 15 mi. east of Tanana	1978	48	Rhoda Edwards
Pink salmon	12	9	Moose River	1974	30	Stephen Lee
Rainbow/steelhead	42	2	Bell Island	1970	43	David White
Red salmon	16		Kenai River	1974	31	Chuck Leach
Sheefish	52	8	Kobuk River	1968	48	Jim Keeline
Silver salmon	26		Icy Straits	1976	35	Andrew Robbin
Whitefish	7	2	Tolovana River	1978	25-1/2	Glen W. Cornwall
Kokanee	2		Lake Lucile	1977	21-1/4	James E. Gum, Jr.

GAME FISH
OF THE
NORTH

*Dianne Hofbeck lands a 13-pound coho with unsolicited help from husband, Joe,
from the Situk River near Yakutat, AK. (Pat Martin)*

PRIMITIVE METHODS OF FISHING

Long before whites arrived, the Natives of Alaska and Canada depended heavily upon various species of fish for food. Salmon especially was important. Others commonly taken by primitive means included halibut and cod, whitefish, burbot, pike and shellfish of all types.

Salmon were caught in streams by various traps and weirs. Halibut were caught with bone lures, or even wooden lures, with rock weights. When available, pieces of sharpened metal were attached to the lures as hooks.

The Aleuts of Alaska used skin boats and angled for halibut and cod—and were found doing this when they were first discovered by the earliest Russians.

Fish spears were used by every group of Natives in Alaska. Many were several-pronged with barbed points. Others were simple fire-hardened and pointed poles.

Smelt were caught with fine-mesh nets, dip nets, or traps.

Eskimos and Interior Indians fished through the ice for sheefish, grayling and burbot. Eskimos also fished for tomcod in salt water. Walrus ivory lures were used, and commonly an ivory lure was worked just under the water's surface to attract fish, where they were speared when they came within range.

Split green spruce traps are still used to catch fish in some areas of the Yukon Basin, as they were before the arrival of whites.

Straight-grained green spruce trees, without knots, are selected and repeatedly split with wedges into quarter-inch-diameter pieces that are about 12 feet long.

The tough green wood does not break when made into a cylinder, using spruce roots or the under bark of willow for tying the spiral outer form-holding strips in place. A funnel entrance is constructed, and the other end of the trap is closed.

Although these traps are brittle and break easily when dry, they are tough when wet, and they will hold many pounds of fish. Fish remain alive in them as long as they are submerged.

GAME FISH VARIETY

Between 40 and 50 species of fish are found in lakes and streams of Alaska and Canada. Some are primarily salt-water forms, like the flounders that have wandered temporarily out of their natural home. Many are anadromous—that is, like the five species of Pacific salmon found in Alaska and western Canada, they spawn in fresh water and mature in the sea. Of these about 15 are important to anglers.

Far more species and subspecies of fish inhabit the thousands of miles of salt-water coastline—several hundred, probably—but few of these, perhaps a dozen, are commonly sought by sport fishermen.

By far the most important group of sport fish in Alaska and western Canada are the members of the salmon family—the salmon and the trout. Cool, clean waters, multitudes of summer insects and nearness to the rich North Pacific Ocean and Bering Sea have created an ideal environment for these finicky fish.

THE PACIFIC SALMON

Five species of Pacific salmon spawn in about 2,000 different rivers in Alaska and hundreds of rivers in British Columbia and Yukon Territory. All five are important to commercial fishermen, and two—the coho and the king—have long been regarded as among the top game fish of the world. A third species, the pink salmon, is of moderate interest to sportsmen. In recent years the sockeye salmon has become increasingly popular with Alaska's sportsmen as they have learned techniques of catching it on lures. (See pages 89-90.)

Salmon was one of the most important foods of many of the North Country's Indians and Eskimos before the arrival of Caucasians. The abundance, ease of preserving through smoking and drying, high food value, and ease of capture as they returned to their home streams to spawn made possible an easy life for these early residents. This was especially true in South-

An old canoe paddle modified into a fish spear by an Alaskan Athabascan Indian (not the holder). Points are nails bound to the spear with rawhide. (Jim Rearden)

eastern Alaska and British Columbia, where a complex civilization and social structure evolved amongst these peoples—primarily because food gathering took such little time.

All of the Pacific salmon (there are six species—one of which, the masu salmon, rarely occurs in Alaska but is found in Japan and northern Korea) are anadromous, breeding in fresh water and maturing in the sea. All display homing instinct and attempt to return to the stream of their origin to spawn, with the king salmon and sockeye probably having the most pronounced homing instinct. All species deposit their eggs in fresh water or, occasionally, with pink salmon and chum salmon, in the intertidal zone at stream mouths. The female does all of the nest digging, and the male fertilizes the eggs with his milt at the time the eggs are deposited.

Eggs are covered with gravel, the depth and coarseness varying with area and species. Eggs must respire and may be suffocated if a deposit of mud or silt occurs on them. They hatch in two to six or more months, depending upon water temperature.

Length of fresh-water life varies both with species and within species, with the exception of the pink and chum salmon, which descend to the sea shortly after they hatch. The length of time spent in the ocean varies from a few months to several years, depending upon species and individual, with the exception of the pink salmon, which invariably returns to its home stream to spawn at the end of the second year of its life or two years after being deposited as an egg.

All five species are silvery when at sea and have spotted or speckled back and fins. When they enter fresh water—or as they mature sexually as they near their fresh-water spawning streams—these fish develop a hooked snout, and the silvery sides change color variously from brick to crimson red or to brown or blackish, depending upon the species.

All Pacific salmon die after spawning.

Identifying Young Salmon in Fresh Water

Young salmon in fresh water are never black-spotted; most trout are black-spotted in fresh water. Salmon have 13-19 rays in the anal fin; trout have 9-12, rarely 13.

The parr marks—the large, dark, round, irregular or oval-shaped marks on the sides—of young salmon are useful in identifying the species in fresh water.

King salmon young in fresh water: parr marks are vertical bars, occasionally long ovals, almost bisected by the lateral line. The parr marks are usually wider than interspaces.

Silver salmon young in fresh water: vertical parr marks are usually narrower than interspaces. The first two or three rays of the anal fin are elongate, forming a "flag." The lower fins are sometimes orange or white-tipped.

Red salmon young in fresh water: parr marks are short, elliptical or oval, extending little if any below the lateral line. Parr marks are usually quite distinct.

Chum salmon young in fresh water are two to three inches long at most, and slim. Parr marks are short elliptical or oval, extending little if any below the lateral line. Parr marks are usually indistinct, and are more irregular in position than parr marks on young red salmon.

Pink salmon young in fresh water have no parr marks. Fish are a deep blue to greenish on the back and maximum size in fresh water is about two inches.

King Salmon

Breeding male king salmon

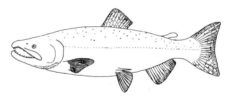

Mature female king salmon

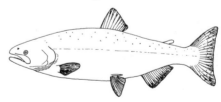

REPRINTED FROM ILLUSTRATED KEYS TO THE FRESH-WATER FISHES OF ALASKA

Oncorhynchus tschawytscha: Also called the chinook, tyee or spring salmon; the largest and longest-lived of the Pacific salmon, with occasional weights of over 100 pounds. The average weight of commercially caught kings is about 20 pounds, with fish up to 80 pounds not being unusual. The current record in Alaska taken in salt water on sports tackle is a 91-pound fish taken at Kelp Bay in 1977 by Howard Rider.

A young fisherman holds up a king salmon taken from the Anchor River on the Kenai Peninsula in Alaska in early June. (Phyllis Leiren, staff)

In Alaska and British Columbia, king salmon arrive at the mouths of their home streams usually in the spring, although they continue to arrive throughout summer and fall. Feeder kings may be caught at any time of the year along the Alaska and British Columbia coastline.

The longest stream migration of Alaska's salmon is that of the kings that enter the Yukon River in June, bound for headwater spawning streams in Yukon Territory and in British Columbia, almost due east of Juneau—a fresh-water migration of more than 2,000 miles. These are the richest of all, for the fat stored by these fish provides the energy necessary for their long journey. Pacific salmon do not feed after they enter fresh water on a spawning migration.

Young king fry may go to sea soon after hatching, or they may remain in a lake or river for one to two years before traveling downstream to salt water. While in this stage, young kings feed mostly on aquatic insects and may accidentally be taken by sport fishermen on flies or spinners. They can be identified as salmon by their parr marks (see key).

Kings commonly range along the Pacific coastline from California through the Bering Sea, feeding as they mature. Age at time of spawning varies considerably, and fully mature fish may be from 3 to 7 years old.

Jack kings—male fish that have matured sexually after a year at sea—may return at 3 or 4 pounds. They are capable of breeding. Jacks may be more numerous in some years and in some river systems.

For spawning, kings normally choose wide, deep rivers. At spawning time their color turns from bright silver to a dark brown or dull reddish, sometimes even approaching black.

Most king salmon have red flesh, but some are white fleshed. Commercial operators pay less for white kings, although nutritive value is the same for both.

Fishing for kings: King salmon are taken in both salt and fresh water in Alaska and Canada, with various techniques, baits and lures—fished from the beach and from boats.

King salmon fishing is prohibited in all drainages from Dixon Entrance to Cape Fairweather (this includes all of Southeastern Alaska)—thus restricting fishing for king salmon to salt water in Alaska's Panhandle.

Best fresh-water fishing for kings in Alaska is probably in June in the Bristol Bay region. (See fishing maps.) In Yukon Territory the best area for kings is the Klukshu, Tatshenshini, Takhanne and Blanchard rivers which are accessible from the Haines Highway. These rivers have excellent runs of salmon early in July. The fish run big here, averaging 20 pounds with specimens up to 60 pounds having been taken. Also due to their short migration run these kings are in fine condition. Stout spinning rods and 25- to 40-

pound test line are prerequisites on these rivers. Pixie or Kit-a-mat spoons are favorites as their weight brings them down close to the bottom of the turbulent streams.

Fresh-water fishing methods for king salmon include drifting gobs of salmon eggs into holes on the bottom where the fish may lie, use of various fairly large spinners and spoons, and fluorescent tee spoons or Okie Drifters. Some experts also effectively use fluorescent (and, in clear water, nonfluorescent) wet flies, and get good results by drifting them on the bottom into deep holes. Fish deep and slow for kings.

Heavy spinning rods and reels, with at least 200 yards of 20- or 30-pound test line, are most popular, although some fishermen use salt-water star-drag reels with heavy 8- to 10-foot poles, or even heavy fly rods with big, single-action reels.

Salt-water fishing methods vary greatly. Best results come from boat fishing and trolling with a motor or rowing. Some anglers "mooch" by drifting and casting, using natural baits and light sinkers. The bait (usually herring or a strip of herring) is rigged to spin slowly as tidal action works it or as it is retrieved after a cast.

Others mooch by anchoring boats in a tiderip area or near a deep drop-off where the tide is running, where they may allow the tide to pull their baits out or down to the depth of feeding kings (or cohos).

Salt-water king fishermen who troll or mooch commonly use rods that are 7½ to 10 feet long, with a sturdy butt and a fairly springy tip. The limber tip acts as a shock absorber and gives good sport when playing smaller fish.

Fishermen who fish unusually deep or use wire line or planers usually use a shorter, stiffer rod.

Many fishermen use heavy-duty salt-water spinning reels, although others prefer star-drag multiplying reels. The adjustable drag on both star-drag reels and spinning reels must be carefully set to avoid line breakage—and to avoid the fish being able to take the line out too freely.

Salt-water-caught kings are at their peak of strength, and when they have plenty of room to run, they can and will take out great amounts of line. Most fishermen use up to 1,500 feet of 20-pound-test line, or 1,100 or 1,200 feet of 30-pound-test. Monofilament nylon is most popular.

The key to catching kings is lure action. Most lures are designed to resemble a crippled or erratically swimming herring, a species king salmon depend upon heavily for food. A feeding king will slash through a school of herring, leaving in his wake stunned or crippled fish, which he will return for. If a fishing lure is presented to a king in such a way as to appear like a crippled herring, chances are he'll hit it.

This means that metal lures should be polished and bright. Kings usually feed deep, except at dawn or dusk or on cloudy days. A dull lure won't show up well in the dim light of the depths.

Sharp hooks are important. King salmon have tough mouths, and a dull hook will slide off. Hooks must be

needle sharp to start the penetration as the fish hits. When you are sure you have a fish holding your lure or bait, set the hook by yanking your rod—hard.

King salmon travel close to shore. Feeding fish may be in 60 to 90 feet of water, except that at dawn or dusk or on dark days, they may be much shallower or actually at the surface. Kings like places along the shoreline where shallow water drops abruptly into deep. Points that water flows around and eddies and tiderips, where feed fish collect, also attract kings.

Kings seem to prefer a slowly trolled bait or lure, rather than one that is moving fast. A lure that spins lazily, wobbles about, falters and drops, and then picks up again, seems to attract a king salmon more quickly than any other.

For this reason, lures that don't have good action at slow speeds are not good king salmon lures. Whole herring, cut plugs and strips of herring can

be made to work well at slow speed. Flatfish and some wobblers also work well.

Kings often lightly mouth a bait before turning to make off with it. Experienced fishermen may drop their rod tip and let the line run free for 5 to 10 feet at the first gentle nudge. When the fish pulls strongly, the hook is set, *hard.*

Best salt-water fishing for kings is in the vast network of bays, channels, islands and tidal estuaries of Southeastern Alaska and northern British Columbia, not to take away anything from coastal waters farther south. Kings feed here year-round and are found in greater numbers during their spawning migrations.

While kings may be found almost anywhere, fishermen have found concentration areas where fishing is best. The listing in the fishing map section is general, and more detailed information on where to find kings can often be obtained locally.

HOW TO USE HERRING AS BAIT

Cut spinner: Select large herring for cutting strips of spinners. A spinner may be cut from each side. Bevel at head of spinner determines roll of spin. Generally fast-turning spinners are best for cohos, while kings prefer a slow roll.

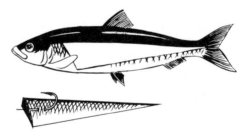

Whole herring: Two hooks may be effectively used with whole herring. Small herring are usually preferred.

Plug cut: By slicing head from herring at an angle, bait is activated by the slightest rod or tidal action.

REPRINTED FROM ALASKA SPORTSMAN®'S 1970-71 ALASKA FISHING ANNUAL

Silver Salmon

Breeding male silver salmon

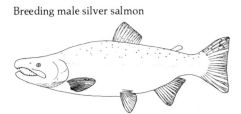

Mature female silver salmon

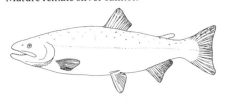

REPRINTED FROM ILLUSTRATED KEYS TO THE
FRESH-WATER FISHES OF ALASKA

Oncorhynchus kisutch: Also called coho or silversides; the most popular game fish of the Pacific salmon. Average weight of an adult is about 9 pounds, but fish weighing more than 30 pounds have been taken. The current record coho in Alaska is a 26-pound, 35-inch fish caught by Andrew A. Robbin in Icy Strait in 1976.

The coho or silver is a fall-run fish, returning to its home stream as an adult starting in late July, appearing more abundantly in August and tapering off in September and October, although some Alaskan streams have the peak of the silver run in September. In much of Southeastern Alaska coho fishing drops off swiftly after Labor Day. In some areas, migrating adult spawners enter streams until at least December.

Found along the British Columbia and Alaskan coastline as far north as Kotzebue Sound, silver salmon commonly spawn in smaller streams than do king salmon, and the females dig their redds (nests) in finer gravel. Unlike king salmon, which may remain in fresh water for several months before spawning, silver salmon usually spawn within a couple of weeks after entering fresh water.

Young silver salmon may descend to sea shortly after hatching, or they may remain in fresh water for a year before descending to the sea. They may return to spawn at the end of their third year of life, or, occasionally, at the end of their fourth year.

Like king salmon, male silver salmon occasionally mature sexually after a year at sea and return to spawn as 2 to 3 pound "jacks."

Silver salmon turn a dark brick red or even brownish when they mature sexually.

When maturing at sea or on feeding runs in coastal areas, silver salmon are voracious feeders, slamming into herring, pilchard, sand lances and other prey species with wild abandon.

Fishing for silver salmon: Silver salmon are taken in both salt and fresh water, where they take a wide variety of lures and baits.

Fresh-water fishing methods for silver salmon include drifting gobs of salmon eggs into holes on the bottom where fish may lie; use of various medium-sized spoons and spinners, and various flies. Silvers frequently take polar bear wet flies, even in salt water.

When in rivers, silvers like slow and deep runs and holes. They frequently roll or leap out of the water, revealing themselves to the alert fisherman. Fish the quietest, deepest holes, where there are overhanging banks, rocks or overhanging brush. Use fluorescent lures in muddy, silty or even murky water. Good lures include golf tee spinners, wobblers, spoons; even bucktail flies are sometimes effective silver lures in streams.

Most popular are medium to heavy spinning rods, 7 to 9 feet long, with spinning reels and 8- to 10-pound-test

with this battling fish. Most of the lakes planted with rainbow trout also contain coho. Most of the 12- to 18-inch fish are caught through the ice in winter, however, excellent summer fishing can be had by using dry or wet flies and by trolling small diving plugs. Corn and natural baits are also very productive.

Good fresh-water stream fishing for silver salmon in Alaska (better in lower river reaches nearest to the sea) can be had almost anywhere in Southeastern, in the Yakutat area, in Prince William Sound, Cook Inlet, Kodiak-Afognak Islands and the Bristol Bay-Alaska Peninsula area; in British Columbia streams nearest the sea; in Yukon Territory in the Klukshu-Tatshenshini River system.

Salt-water fishing methods for silver salmon generally resemble those used for king salmon. Frequently, when fishing for silver salmon, anglers hang a king salmon, and therefore often use tackle suitable for either. Star-drag reels holding 1,000 feet of 20-pound-test monofilament line are often used, as are heavy-duty salt-water spinning reels. Some fishermen prefer lighter line for silvers when they know they aren't likely to hang a king salmon, and line down to 12-pound-test or less can be successfully used.

The silver, like the king, feeds voraciously on herring, sand lances and other small schooling species. Erratic action of a lure that makes it resemble a crippled small fish is usually

A silver salmon (coho). (Courtesy of Alaska Department of Fish & Game)

monofilament line. Fly rod enthusiasts use fairly heavy rods with long monofilament leaders and large, single-action reels with a couple of hundred feet of backing.

Landlocked coho are found in a large number of small lakes in southern Yukon Territory. The Federal Fisheries Service has stocked numerous lakes

successful in enticing a silver salmon to strike. Both artificial lures and herring, mooched or trolled, are successful in taking silvers. Sharp hooks are a must.

Size of the lure depends somewhat upon what type food silvers may be taking. If they are feeding on shrimp, squid and small herring, a small lure such as a small spoon or bucktail flies (which are usually more effective in taking silver salmon than in taking kings) or small spinners are most successful. Smaller spoons (generally under 5 inches) are more effective for silver salmon than for kings.

Silver salmon prefer a lure with more action to it than king salmon do. Shorter leaders often cause a lure to behave more erratically; therefore, shorter leaders are usually best for silver salmon fishing.

Silver salmon normally travel at shallower depths than do kings—usually 30 feet or less. Silver salmon are more commonly found on the surface than are king salmon. Another peculiarity: silver salmon seem to like a lure that is trolled or retrieved rapidly—far more rapidly than lures used for king salmon.

Like the king salmon, silvers are often at the surface and feeding heavily at daylight. They like tiderips and currents, and areas where bait fish concentrate naturally. Eddies on a point and where tiderips—a line where current on one side is moving differently on the other side—are attractive to salmon of all species.

Mooching is as effective for silver salmon as it is for kings. However, kings prefer a slowly spinning bait, while silvers are more attracted by bait that spins rapidly.

Silvers are less fussy about time of feeding and may feed actively through the day, although peak feeding periods occur at dawn, dusk and tide changes.

Silvers often show themselves in salt water by frequent jumping. They feed and cruise near the surface commonly, and at such times streamer flies trolled or cast on the surface are extremely effective. When trolled, no lead is needed. Use a 10- to 15-pound-test monofilament line and trail from 25 to 50 feet behind the boat. Trolling should be fast—so fast that a clear "v" wake is left by the moving fly. It helps to zigzag, with frequent changes in speed.

Fishermen often lose silvers that strike flies trolled in this manner because they try to set the hook too quickly. It is best to wait until the fish turns and is swimming off with the fly in his mouth. Silver salmon strikes are explosive, and usually a fisherman's reaction time is about right to set the hook, but fish are occasionally lost because fishermen react too quickly.

Top salt-water fishing areas for silver salmon are found throughout

TERMINAL GEAR FOR SPORT SALMON ANGLING

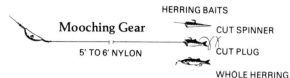

Mooching Gear: This type of equipment is a favorite of fishermen looking for maximum sport. Sinkers of 1 to 6 ounces are used. Herring is activated by trolling, wind or tide action, or by reeling or stripping line in.

Coho Fly: These colorful flies are killers for coho when trolled fast near the surface with little or no lead. Polar bear hair is usually used for hackle. Coho flies fished deep behind dodgers or flashers will take kings.

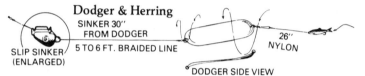

Dodger and Herring: The bright, erratic flash of the dodger attracts both kings and silvers, while the herring offers good food appeal. Spoons or coho flies are often successfully substituted for herring.

Standard Large Spoon or Plug Gear: Maturing kings found at river mouths are attracted to this gear. Advantages are that fish other than salmon are not so likely to hit, and that plugs and spoons are working all the time.

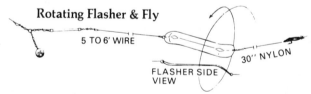

Rotating Flasher and Fly: This rig is designed to do the same job as the dodger, but is often fished with heavier weight. Because of the rotating action, the drag is heavy, and stiffer rods are in order. Herring or spoons are sometimes used with flashers.

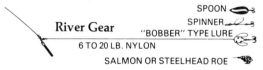

River Gear: Bright salmon sometimes hold in lower reaches of a river, and at such times these lures and bait are effective. Lures are either cast and permitted to swing with the current, or are anchored by the sinker near the bottom where the current activates them.

WASHINGTON STATE DEPT. OF FISHERIES

British Columbia and Southeastern Alaska (see fishing maps). Other good Alaskan areas include Prince William Sound, Lower Cook Inlet (south of the silt line, which is roughly at Ninilchik), and the Kodiak-Afognak area.

Red Salmon

Breeding male red salmon

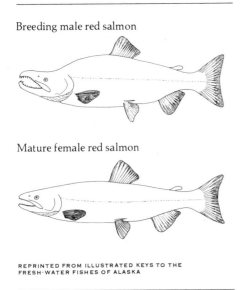

Mature female red salmon

REPRINTED FROM ILLUSTRATED KEYS TO THE FRESH-WATER FISHES OF ALASKA

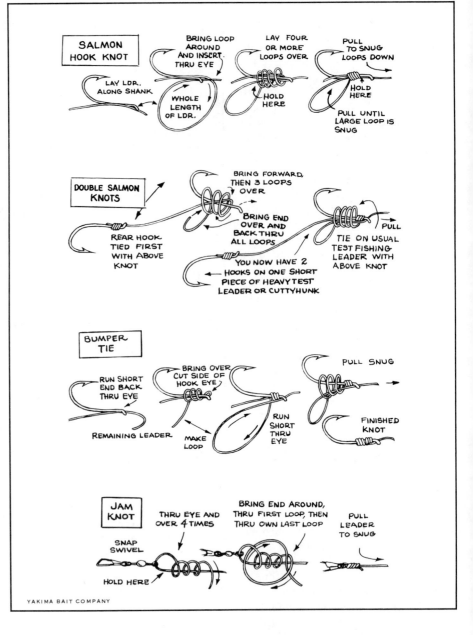

Oncorhynchus nerka: Also called sockeye and blueback; of great commercial value because of their rich, oily, ruby-red flesh. They are found in streams and lakes along the Alaskan coast as far north as the Seward Peninsula. Anglers are prohibited from taking red salmon in fresh water in British Columbia.

Weighing from 6 to 12 pounds as adults, when at sea red salmon are blue-tinged silver. Both sexes turn to varying shades of red when they reach their spawning grounds—frequently even a spectacular, brilliant crimson, with their heads remaining dark green. The males also develop a humped back and sharply hooked nose. Females retain their sea-going shape.

Sockeye spawn in streams that have lakes in their watersheds; when they hatch, young red salmon spend from 1 to 3 years in lakes before migrating to sea.

Red salmon are primarily plankton feeders, but as they grow they start taking smaller food fish.

The mass migration of sockeye fingerlings from lake to sea takes place shortly after the ice goes out. They move into estuaries and then into the Gulf of Alaska and the North Pacific.

Age at maturity, when they return to spawn, ranges from 3 to 6, occasionally 7 years. Adults returning to spawn weigh from 6 to 12 pounds. Current Alaska sport record for red salmon is 16 pounds, held by Chuck Leach of Anchorage, with a fish he took in the Kenai River in 1974.

Sockeye that become landlocked are commonly found in lakes from Oregon into Alaska. Called "kokanee," or "little redfish," they follow the same life cycle as their sea-going relatives, except that they grow to maturity in lakes, and they mature at a much smaller size—rarely exceeding 15 to 16 inches in length in Alaska.

Current Alaska sport fish record for kokanee is 2 pounds, held by James E.

Gum, Jr. Fish was caught in Lucile Lake in 1977.

Fishing for red salmon is spotty, for the species is moody and characteristics for hitting lures vary from river to river.

For many years sportsmen believed that red salmon would not hit a lure, and few attempts were made to fish for them. Then fishermen at Brooks Lake in the Katmai Monument started to catch red salmon on wet flies.

Next, sports fishermen in the Russian River, tributary to the Kenai River on the Kenai Peninsula, discovered that properly fished wet flies of the right pattern would consistently take the red salmon in that system. Red salmon fresh from the sea are powerful, swift fighters, equal pound-for-pound to any other Pacific salmon.

Despite this, fishermen report that the techniques that catch red salmon in one system often fail in others.

Fresh-water fishing for red salmon, using flies, boils down to one simple rule: fish on the bottom. Red salmon hug the bottom. Cast upstream if swift and deep water keeps a fly cast otherwise from reaching the bottom. In shallow water, cast across and/or slightly downstream.

There are many methods for getting a fly on the bottom and keeping it there. A sinking fly line may do it. Sometimes the fly has to be lightly weighted, even with a sinking fly line.

Spin fishing is where the problem comes in getting a fly on the bottom. It is necessary to keep a tight line so that strikes can be felt (and red salmon sometimes just tap the lure, and it merely pauses momentarily). If you miss the strike, fish usually spit the lure out. A rod with a light sensitive tip is a must in this type of fishing. Otherwise strikes cannot be sensed.

A red salmon sockeye). (Courtesy of Alaska Department of Fish & Game)

The steelhead-type rig is popular for getting flies to the bottom, but others work as well. See diagrams for fly hook-ups for red salmon on pages 90-91.

Most red salmon fishermen work their flies too much. Best results are obtained with the natural drift. Flies that work on reds can be purchased in Alaskan tackle shops, or if you tie your own, sparsely tied yarn flies on a No. 4 or No. 6 hook are effective. Just ordinary red yarn will do. Red hackle flies are also good. When water is murky, fluorescent colors of pink, yellow or orange are also helpful. In clear conditions, the old favorite, the Muddler Minnow, is often effective in taking red salmon—provided it is fished right on the bottom.

Good Alaskan fresh-water streams for red salmon include the Russian River on the Kenai Peninsula (see fishing maps). Two runs of red salmon, sometimes totaling 50,000 or more fish, enter this river each year. The first run normally starts between June 5 and 10 and tapers off by early July. This run averages perhaps 20,000 fish.

The second run begins between July 15 and 20 and lasts for 2 to 3 weeks.

Brooks River, in the Naknek River

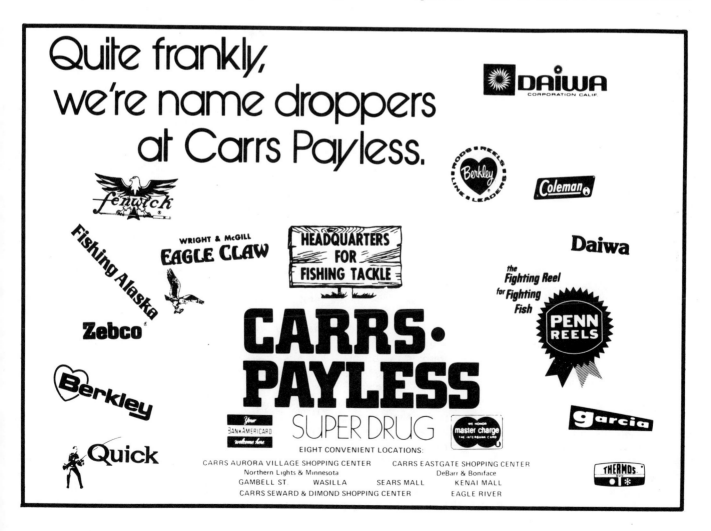

system, offers fly fishing for reds in late June and early July. Wien Air Alaska has a fish camp there, and charter services from King Salmon are available to take anglers into the area on their own.

Undoubtedly good red salmon fishing will develop in other streams in Alaska as fishermen learn which lures work for this finicky fish, and how to fish them.

In Yukon Territory the only accessible area for sockeye is the Klukshu-Tatshenshini system. These rivers have excellent runs of 6- to 12-pound fish early in July and then again in late August. The early run coincides with the run of kings so the same tackle is recommended. Sockeye will also hit weighted streamer flies retrieved slowly along the stream bottom. Kokanee are caught occasionally in Kathleen Lake.

Salt-water fishing for red salmon has not developed in Alaska. Commercial salmon trollers south of Alaska reportedly have taken large numbers of red salmon in some years. In time sportsmen will likely find places in bays and estuaries where they can consistently catch red salmon.

Pink Salmon

Breeding male pink salmon

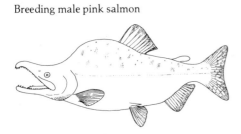

Mature female pink salmon

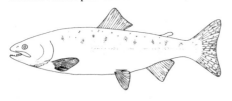

REPRINTED FROM ILLUSTRATED KEYS TO THE FRESH-WATER FISHES OF ALASKA

Oncorhynchus gorbuscha: Smallest of the Pacific salmon, this species averages about 4 pounds at maturity, although weights to about 10 pounds are commonly reported. Current state record for a sports-caught pink is 12

pounds, 9 ounces for a 30-inch fish taken at the confluence of the Moose and Kenai rivers by Stephen A. Lee of Los Alamitos, California in 1974.

It is also the most abundant of the Pacific salmon in some years. It is generally the least valuable per pound of the five Alaskan salmon, for its flesh is often softer than that of the others.

Pinks are often turning color from a bright ocean silver to a pale gray and eventually to black, with white undersides, when they arrive at the mouths of their spawning streams. As sexual maturity progresses, males develop an almost grotesque hump on the back—hence the name "humpback" salmon.

This is the two-year salmon. Adults arrive at spawning streams from July

A pink salmon (humpback). (Courtesy of Alaska Department of Fish & Game)

through September, sometimes a bit later in some areas, and usually spawn in small streams a short distance from the sea, although pink salmon do ascend several hundred miles up some large streams.

Young fry, an inch to two inches long, descend streams almost as soon as they are hatched and enter the sea in March, April or even May. They spend about 15 months in salt water and invariably return at the end of their second year of life to spawn.

Various areas in the pink salmon's range have "even year" and "odd year" runs. That is, few areas have a heavy run of pink salmon each year. Once the pattern is established, it seems to remain even or odd for decades, although there are records of runs reversing from odd to even, and vice versa, in some areas.

Fishing for pink salmon can be exciting and productive when they are present, fresh from the sea, and in clear water. Alaskan anglers take them in both fresh water and salt although British Columbia prohibits anglers

from taking pink salmon in fresh water. Artificial lures are most commonly used, with spoons, spinners and other bright, glittery lures being most successful. The Pixie spoon is a current favorite. Humpback salmon use the Yukon River system to reach Yukon waters as far inland as Nisutlin and Teslin lakes. Because of the lengthy migration they are not greatly sought after in these waters.

Fresh-water fishing methods are basically the same as in salt water. Fishermen most commonly use light spinning tackle, with 4- to 6-pound-test lines, and small spoons, spinners, wobblers or other metallic lures that can be easily cast and retrieved.

Pink salmon change rapidly when they arrive in fresh water, and within a week of their arrival are slab-sided, thin and the males hump-backed with projecting teeth—a not-very-attractive food fish. Anglers frequently catch and release such fish in attempting to catch bright, fresh-from-the-sea pinks.

Pinks that are bright and fresh from the sea are fairly scrappy, although not in the same class as silver salmon or red salmon, even of the same size.

Slow runs, deep holes, eddies behind rocks and other resting places are the best spots to fish. A retrieve of varying speed (slow, then fast, then slow) often entices these fish into striking.

Good fresh-water fishing for pink salmon is found throughout Southeastern Alaska, in the Yakutat area, in Prince William Sound, in Cook Inlet from the lower Kenai Peninsula into the Susitna drainage, in the Kodiak-Afognak area and throughout the Bristol Bay area.

Salt-water fishing methods for pink salmon call for light tackle, spoons, spinners, wobblers and other glittery lures. Spinning equipment is most popular. Pinks are often taken when trolling for silvers and kings during the fall months.

In areas where pink salmon migrate into streams, fishermen are often successful in fishing clean, steep-sloping gravel or sandy beaches, casting offshore beyond the fish (which migrate close to the shore) and retrieving through traveling schools. Pinks frequently jump and fishermen can often spot a traveling school as it follows along a beach and be prepared to cast into it.

Pinks often concentrate in huge balls or schools at the mouths of spawning streams, or in salt-water lagoons near spawning streams. They remain in such schools, sometimes of many thousands of fish, for several days at a time. Most fish in such a school ignore a lure, but there always seems to be a few aggressive ones that will strike.

Chum Salmon

Breeding male chum salmon

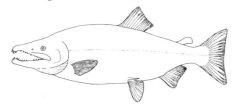

Mature female chum salmon

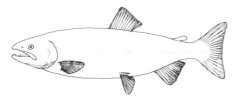

Oncorhynchus keta: Also called dog salmon and occasionally calico salmon for the varied-color pattern that develops on its sides as it approaches sexual maturity.

This is a summer and fall—occasionally late fall—running fish that spawns in lower tributaries along the coast, usually less than 100 miles from the ocean, with the Kuskokwim and Yukon runs of chums being exceptions. The species ranges from Oregon to Arctic Alaska, farther north in Alaska than any other Pacific salmon. It is

common to Kotzebue Sound and is found sparsely on around to the Mackenzie River in arctic Canada.

Average weight is about 9 pounds but varies from 7 or 8 to 18 pounds, with extreme weights reported to nearly 40 pounds. The current state record is a 27-pound, 3-ounce, 39-3/8-inch-long fish taken in Behm Canal in 1977 by Robert Jahnke.

Chum salmon have a lower oil content than other salmon and are especially good for smoking.

Chum fry, which are long, slim and silvery, go directly to sea from their natal streams nearly as soon as they are hatched. They reach maturity in 3 or 4

A chum salmon (dog salmon). (Courtesy of Alaska Department of Fish & Game)

years, when they return to their home streams to spawn.

Males develop a sharply hooked nose, and their large doglike teeth become totally exposed. Both sexes develop barred coloration along the sides—coloration that includes distinct dark vertical bars, with colors that range through blacks and grays to a reddish hue in advanced stages of spawning.

In common with the red and pink

salmon, the chum is heavily dependent upon planktonic forms of food, especially when the salmon is small. Adult chums feed on small fish, however, and larger planktonic forms. Normally it is difficult to get a chum salmon to strike a lure either in salt or in fresh water, and this species is of least interest to sport fishermen of the five Pacific salmon in Alaska. When rarely hooked, however, the "green" (bright silver) dog in salt water puts up a terrific scrap. It's a shame this fish does not readily strike a lure.

Fishing for chum salmon is usually an exercise in futility, for they seldom strike lures. When they do, it appears to be in annoyance. Bright, shiny spoons, spinners and wobblers seem to be lures that cause chums to react more than anything else.

Freshly arrived chums appear in some areas in July and enter streams in late July and in August. Southeastern Alaska has a late run of chums that may appear in August and September. Chum salmon are protected from fishermen in the fresh waters of British Columbia.

TROUT

Included in this general category are the rainbow, cutthroat and lake trout, the chars (Dolly Varden, arctic char and eastern brook trout); all more or less related.

These fish prefer cool, clear waters and may live in the sea, lakes, rivers or small streams. The rainbow, cutthroat, Dolly Varden and arctic char commonly descend to and live in salt water for varying amounts of time.

All have spots—some black, some red, others brown or even white—on bodies and fins. All can be slam-bang feeders, and they accept artificial lures of all kinds.

Rainbow Trout

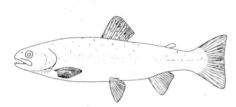

Salmo gairdneri, the sea-run of which is known as the steelhead, is a black-spotted trout native to western North America. In Alaska it is found naturally as far north as Stony River, a tributary of the Kuskokwim. The greatest development in size and numbers is reached in the great arc of clear-water lakes and streams that pour into Bristol Bay. Northern British Columbia has hundreds of fine lakes and streams holding heavy stocks of both rainbow and steelhead.

Rainbow trout are native to only one or two areas in the western part of Yukon Territory. The Federal Fisheries Service however, has introduced rainbow to several small lakes in the south Yukon. In addition there are several unmarked and virtually unknown lakes that were stocked by a commercial company years ago. The location of these lakes is a closely guarded secret among Yukon anglers but should a visitor stumble upon one of these lakes he will discover rainbow fishing most anglers only dream about.

Some rainbows are found on the north side of the Alaska Peninsula north of the Aleutians. They are found on Kodiak Island, in the great drainage of the Susitna at the head of Cook Inlet, on the Kenai Peninsula, in Prince William Sound, in the Yakutat area and throughout Southeastern Alaska.

They have also been transplanted to Interior Alaska, mostly in the vicinity of Fairbanks.

This chunky trout in fresh water has a liberal sprinkling of black spots on a dark background above, light to almost white below, and a rosy stripe from gill cover to tail on the middle of each side. A steelhead returns from the sea large and silvery, blue-gray above and white below. It turns color when it spends any time in fresh water, gaining spots and the rosy band along the sides grows in size and its faint pink trace gradually darkens to a real red.

Steelhead may spawn, return to the sea to spend a year or more, and again migrate into fresh water to spawn perhaps two or even three times.

The rainbow thrives in a wide range of habitats, from large lakes to tiny creeks or large rivers. It has been known to survive water temperatures to 83°F, but much prefers cooler temperatures. Low oxygen in its home water can be a limiting factor, with the lower limit close to about four parts per million.

The rainbow has been widely transplanted in Alaska. Spawning season varies for the species, but normally it is a spring spawner. Some steelhead, as those on the lower Kenai Peninsula, enter streams in August, September and October, and may spend the winter in fresh water, returning to sea thin and spawned out in the late spring.

Fishing for rainbows varies with the type of fishing gear an individual prefers. Fly fishing, with dry or wet flies, can be superb. The spin caster, with light- or medium-weight gear, can use bait or lures. Generally rainbows are less active when water temperatures are below about 40°F. Since most Alaskan streams are above this temperature during late spring, summer and fall, these are the months when rainbow fishing is best. Steelhead fishermen often fish in winter and spring when the fish are moving into fresh water from the sea. Water temperatures may be hovering close to the 40° mark at such times.

Nonmigratory rainbow in Alaska, especially the smaller fish, are generally easier to catch than are steelhead. They are used to taking a wide range of food, including flies or insects of various kinds, smaller fish and occasionally even unwary mice or shrews.

Best baits for rainbow in Yukon lakes are floating plugs such as the flatfish or Lazy Ike trolled very slowly. Dry flies in the blue dun and mosquito patterns work well while shrimp flies and nymphs are the wet patterns that produce. Natural baits such as grasshoppers, nymphs and worms are deadly and marshmallows, cheese and corn have been used with some success.

An inspection of the stomach con-

The rainbow trout of Walker Lake, 3 years after planting, weighed between 3 and 4 pounds. (Edward H. Bielejec)

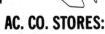

tents of a fish will often give the angler a clue to the most effective bait.

The steelhead, on the other hand, is wary, and baits and a lure must be presented in a form that will not frighten it. It must be drifted to pass close to the fish, for steelhead usually will not pursue a lure in fresh water. The old standby, a cluster of fresh salmon eggs drifted on the bottom and into a hole where steelhead may lie, is

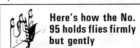

perhaps the most effective way of catching these fish.

A variety of artificials are effective on steelhead. They will occasionally take an ordinary spoon or spinner, but this is not the most effective method of taking steelhead. Fluorescent wet flies floated on the bottom are sometimes effective steelhead lures, or semi-floating lures that resemble a cluster of eggs.

Productive stream areas are those located either just above or below rough rapids. Slick areas upstream or downstream of long shallow areas are good—they give the steelhead a hiding place. Sometimes steelhead wait until darkness to pass through these shallow areas where they can easily be seen, and a number of fish will pile up in a hole.

Upstream casts are effective for steelhead; they put the bait or lure on the bottom where the fish are. Since Northern streams are often full of logs, rocks and other natural debris, a lot of tackle is lost in steelhead fishing.

Experienced steelhead fishermen find a favorite lure or bait and usually stick with that, for they know how to get it to the fish consistently.

Because steelhead are powerful and often large, most experienced fishermen use 10-pound-test leaders, with monofilament line of about the same test if they are spin fishermen, or fly lines if they use fly rods. The current state record rainbow/steelhead weighed 42 pounds, 2 ounces and measured 43 inches long. It was taken by David White at Bell Island in 1970.

A rod of 7- to 9-foot length gives the steelhead fisherman a tool with which he can present his lure easily, and it also allows him to handle a big and scrappy fish. A shorter rod, which is generally stiffer, may result in more fish breaking off—and in catching few fish, for accuracy in casting can suffer if you can't reach around bushes or hold the tip of the rod out over a stream during a retrieve.

When water is low and clear, the wise steelheader *crawls* to the hole he plans to fish to prevent fish from seeing him and spooking.

Big fresh-water rainbows are somewhat similar to steelhead in that they hug the bottom. They are used to feeding in fresh water (steelhead are not) and will take small fish, fish eggs and items other than insects. Small rainbows are the insect feeders. Big

rainbows need more sustenance than is generally obtainable from insects.

One of the most effective fishing techniques for big rainbows (in the 10-pound and above class) includes bottom-bouncing whatever lure you choose to use. It works with spoons, spinners or egg-cluster imitations. You'll lose lures by hanging up—but there's no choice. Either fish down where the fish are, or be satisfied with the smaller surface-feeding rainbows.

Best steelhead waters in Alaska for April and May (best in late April, early May) are the Naha and the Karta in the Ketchikan area; Eagle Creek, Kah Sheets, Anan and Thomas creeks in the Petersburg-Wrangell area; Alex's Creek on Kuiu Island; and Sitkoh, Eva and Port Banks creeks in the Sitka area.

Good fall steelhead streams in Alaska include the Naha and Karta in the Ketchikan area and the Situk near Yakutat.

Top fresh-water streams in Alaska for big rainbows are Lower Talarik Creek on Lake Iliamna, Newhalen River, Copper River, Gibraltar Lake and Iliamna River, also on Lake Iliamna, in the Bristol Bay area. The Naknek system is also tops for fresh-water rainbows, as is the Wood River system north of Dillingham.

Lakes near Whitehorse in Yukon Territory that have been planted with rainbow include Judas, Marcella, Scout and MacLean. These lakes offer excellent fishing for trout in the 3- to 6-pound category. Some of these lakes hold a few lunkers of 12 and even 18 pounds so hold onto your rod.

Cutthroat Trout

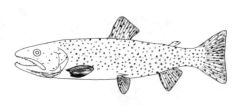

REPRINTED FROM ILLUSTRATED KEYS TO THE FRESH-WATER FISHES OF ALASKA

Salmo clarki is another black-spotted trout, found throughout British Columbia and Southeastern Alaska, north to Montague Island in Prince William Sound.

This is the common native trout of

A black-spotted cutthroat trout. (Neil French)

Southeastern Alaska and coastal British Columbia. It is also found in coastal streams of Washington, Oregon and northern California. Its body color varies with its environment. In fresh water its body is generally dark bluish-green on the back, fading to a pinkish-purple stripe on the sides with a lighter colored belly. Body and fins are heavily spotted, and its name comes from the two red streaks (sometimes absent) that are found under its chin.

In salt water, which it frequents, the cutthroat has a silvery body with no spots or only a few spots, and the red slashes under the jaw are frequently absent. After time in fresh water the sea-run cutthroat reverts to the darker coloration and black-spotted pattern.

Cutthroats which have spent 3 years or so in salt water may weigh as much as 4 pounds, with an occasional 6-pounder. Cutthroats that live year-round in streams seldom reach this size. The current state record cutthroat weighed 8 pounds, 6 ounces and was 26¼ inches long when presented for weighing by Robert Denison. He caught it in Wilson Lake near Ketchikan in 1977.

The sea-run fish start to enter creeks in the fall on their spawning migration which may continue until December. Spawning takes place in April and May, after which surviving sea-run cuts return to salt water—an estimated one-third of those that have made the spawning run. Like steelhead that spend the winter in fresh water, they are snaky and thin when they return to the sea.

Young may hatch from May to June, as water warms, and they spend from 1 to 3 years in fresh water before they enter salt water, if they do. Evidence indicates that sea-run cutthroats seldom stray far from the mouth of the home stream when they go to salt water.

The cutthroats, like their cousin trout and char, often follow salmon upstream and feed on drifting salmon eggs for the duration of the salmon run. At such times they are often gorged and not easily enticed into striking a lure.

Best fresh-water fishing for cutthroats in Southeastern Alaska and British Columbia is generally in steep-sided, deep lakes where the fish are found in shallower bays, and near stream mouths where aquatic food

organisms abound. Cold, deep areas of lakes are poor producers of fish.

In streams, cutthroats are most often found at heads of pools, where they feed on drifting aquatic organisms.

Famous cutthroat waters in Alaska include Chilkat Lake near Haines, Hasselborg and Thayer lakes near Juneau, the Stikine River and Virginia Lake in the Petersburg-Wrangell areas, the outlet of Redoubt Lake near Sitka and the Naha River near Ketchikan.

Sea-run cutthroat fishing is good in inlets and estuaries along the coast. Top fishing occurs often at stream mouths, which are highly productive of food such as shrimp, small salt-water and fresh-water fish and sticklebacks.

Fishing methods for cutthroats depend upon the angler, for cutthroat trout will strike wet and dry flies, and any variety of spoon and spinners.

Top-quality fishing often occurs at high tide, near large stream mouths, at evening or early morning, when the water is calm. Dry flies will take sea-run cuts, or they will strike a bucktail fly with great vigor.

Eastern Brook Trout

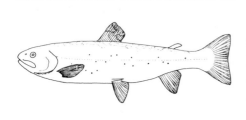

Salvelinus fontinalis is an eastern species that was introduced to Southeastern Alaska.

This cold-water fish is native to brooks, small streams and clear waters of the eastern United States. It is a fall spawner, preferring to spawn in gravel of spring-fed streams.

This is a dark gray or olive fish, marked with small round gray, whitish or red spots, paler than the main color, and the spots are often surrounded with still paler borders. The dorsal fin and, to a degree, the back are mottled with green wavy marks.

A 5-pound brook trout is a large one in its native range. In Alaska most brook trout are small—12 to 15 inches

being about maximum. Its nearest relative in Alaska is the Dolly Varden.

Eastern brook trout can be caught in Ward Lake and Grace Lake near Ketchikan; in Green Lake, Heart Lake and Thimbleberry Lake in the Sitka area; and also are found in Salmon Creek reservoir near Juneau. See fishing maps.

Fishing techniques for eastern brook trout are those for taking any of the trout. Wet and dry flies are popular, as are various forms of hardware. Smaller sizes of spoons and spinners should be favored for the brookies found in Alaska. This trout, like other trouts, will also take bait—worms, salmon eggs in clusters or single egg hooks.

Dolly Varden Trout

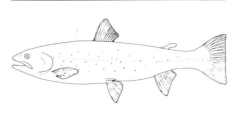

Salvelinus malma has the widest distribution of any trout (or char) in Alaska and western Canada. It is a highly variable fish in coloration and size. Some Interior and Kenai Peninsula Dollies are locally called "golden-finned trout" or "golden trout" because of their high color. In short and steep mountain streams of Southeastern Alaska fjords country, a dwarf version of Dollies lives in the streams apparently the year-round. They also are red or "golden-finned" and their brown sides and white to red spots remind one of eastern brookies.

The Dolly may reach 20 pounds, tail is well forked, becoming squarish in large individuals.

After dropping down into salt water from wintering over in chosen lakes, the Dolly takes on a bright silver sheen for the next few months until he begins to ascend the streams. Gradually, faint white spots show through the silver and the silver fades. Soon the Dolly's spots become faintly pink, then progressively stronger almost-red pinks, and silver sides become a gray only lightly brushed with silver. By fall, when spawning time arrives, the Dolly

Varden's sides have become dark gray to brown, with great livid red spots, a rosy belly in sharp contrast to the gray-brown above. Ventral fins turn bright orange with white trim, as do the pectoral and anal fins to a lesser degree. Gill covers blacken and when open reveal an alternate white and black barring. Bellies become redder and at the peak of his spawning period, Dolly is a truly colorful creature. Soon after spawning, he loses weight swiftly and his bright raiments dull. He will not turn silver again until midwinter and not bright silver until he returns to the sea in the spring.

The Dolly is abundant along the Pacific coast from British Columbia through Southeastern Alaska, the Alaska Peninsula and Aleutians through Bristol Bay and around the coastline to Canada. Scattered populations are found in Interior Alaska, Yukon Territory and Northwest Territories.

This is primarily a salt-water trout in Alaska but strictly fresh-water forms are known.

Spawning takes place in streams from September to November, although it is reported that at the tip of the Alaska Peninsula and perhaps in the Aleutians, Dollies spawn much later.

The female deposits the eggs in depressions or nests. After eggs are deposited and fertilized by the male, the female covers them with a layer of gravel.

Eggs incubate for about 3 months before hatching. Upon hatching the young move deeper into the gravel, where they remain for 2 to 4 months before working to the surface and launching themselves into life in the stream.

Usually in about their fourth year of life, in spring, Dollies in coastal areas make their first seaward migration. They actively feed on small crustaceans and fish and grow rapidly. After 2 or 3 months at sea, they migrate back into the streams they left, still feeding, now often on loose salmon eggs if salmon are spawning in the stream. If the stream they ascend does not have a lake in which they can winter-over, the Dollies will return to sea and search out another stream, seeking one with a connected lake. Eventually the Dollies spend the winter in a lake. They usually lose weight during winters in fresh water.

Come spring, the Dollies return to sea, feeding voraciously and gaining weight, to follow the same pattern—entering fresh-water streams in fall in order to winter-over in a lake.

At one time the salmon-oriented Territory of Alaska paid a bounty for the tails of Dolly Varden—2½ cents at the time the practice was stopped—on the theory that Dolly Varden ate large numbers of salmon. The bounty was cut off when it was discovered that bounties were being paid for tails of young salmon, rainbow trout and other species, as well as for Dolly Varden.

It is true that Dolly Varden seem to follow salmon spawning runs and that they feed on salmon fingerlings and salmon eggs. Many other species do the same thing, though, and the Dolly is not unusual.

The abundance of Dolly Varden sometimes is nearly incredible. During fall spawning runs they often blacken the bottom of streams.

Dolly Varden are often found around active salmon canneries, feeding on the offal dumped into the water. Such fish may be huge—8 to 15 pounds or so—but they can seldom be tempted with a lure, or even with bait, gorged as they are—a frustrating experience for an eager angler.

Fishing for Dolly Varden calls for knowledge of their habits. They can be caught in the spring as they migrate from lakes to sea. However, they are thin at this time of year—April to June.

Salt-water fishing is best from May through July, when the fish are cruising about, often in small or even large schools, feeding along the shoreline. Sandy beaches with a steep drop seem to attract them, as do beaches with fine gravel and many streams mouths.

Virtually all coastal streams from Southeastern Alaska throughout their range are good fishing for Dollies in August and September. Good fishing can be had near spawning salmon, in deep holes and at the creek mouth on incoming tides.

Dollies are often at the lower end of deep holes in rivers and streams, where the water is slack.

Lake fishing for sea-run Dolly Varden is good from late August through November, as the fish return to lakes to winter-over.

Best sport with Dollies is in salt water in late May and June, when they have fed for a time in salt water and

Three Dollies taken at the end of Mud Bay Road near Haines, AK. (Courtesy of Department of Economic Development)

gained weight and strength. It is also during this period when the Dolly is at its finest in the frying pan—one of the best tasting fish that swims, many say. Poorest fishing in terms of sport is when they are thin, and on their seaward migration after wintering-over.

Best lures for Dolly Varden depend upon the angler, for the Dolly will usually readily strike almost anything, except when gorged with salmon eggs on the spawning grounds. It is rare, then, to get good fishing with anything other than fresh salmon eggs. During spring try small spinning lures in the lake outlet streams and where streams enter salt water. In spring and summer streamer flies that resemble small fish are effective.

Coastal streams in August and September can produce excellent fishing for spinning lures, or even for a single salmon egg bounced along the bottom. Occasionally flies, both wet and dry, are good in both streams and lakes. A sea-run Dolly Varden caught on light tackle gives a vigorous fight. It may leap like a rainbow or dive and use bull strength and head-shaking tactics.

A few hot spots for Dolly Varden include Unuk River, 50 miles north of Ketchikan (see fishing maps), and Karta and Hana rivers, also near Ketchikan. The Stikine River (in the Wrangell area) is good, as is Salmon Bay Lake, 40 miles west of Wrangell. Hasselborg Lake on Admiralty Island at times provides excellent Dolly fishing. The Situk River in the Yakutat River system is especially good for Dollies in August. The Buskin River on Kodiak Island offers good Dolly fishing in the fall. Virtually all Bristol Bay watersheds offer fine Dolly fishing at different times. The Sinuk River on the Nome-Teller Highway is exceptional. One of the best Dolly streams in Alaska is the Wulik River near Kivalina, north of Kotzebue Sound. Almost any stream in coastal Alaska that enters tidewater is likely to produce Dollies.

Dolly Varden are not particularly abundant in Yukon Territory with the exception of the Rancheria River and some streams and lakes along the Dempster and Haines Highways. Dollies, or bull trout, as they are sometimes called, can reach 20 pounds in weight although the average for Yukon waters is under 2 pounds.

Arctic Char

An arctic char (similar to Dolly Varden). (Clifford Myers)

Salvelinus alpinus, a close relative of the Dolly Varden, is found from Kodiak Island, the Alaska Peninsula and the Aleutian Islands along the coast of Alaska north and east to the Mackenzie River. It is also found in scattered locations in Interior Alaska, including Wonder Lake in Mount McKinley National Park. It is common in some areas of the Brooks Range. Yukon Territory has excellent runs of char along its arctic coast, especially in the Firth River. Most of these areas are accessible only by air. Chapman Lake and the Blackstone River on the Dempster Highway contain some small char running between ½ and 1½ pounds.

Arctic char and Dolly Varden are awfully close to being the same fish—a southern Dolly Varden and a northern Dolly Varden. They are so close to being the same fish, only taxonomists should be really bothered by the differences. For example, it would appear most southern Dollies have 15-19 gill raker counts on the first arch, northern Dollies 21-23. There are slight differences in count of the *pyloric caeca,* little protuberances on the large intestine of the stomach, and the vertebrae of the southern is 56-67, while the northern counts 63-71—but most fishermen are unlikely to be counting tummy stuff or vertebrae, let alone gill rakers on the first arch.

And to confuse things still further, the ichthyologists also find intermingling of both species in the same waters. So many arctic char pictures are taken in the short Arctic summer where in mid-August spawning coloration has already begun, one would have a tendency to think of all northern area Dollies as highly colored and therefore arctic char, but that is not necessarily true. And it does not also follow that most southerly Dollies are usually silver or gray-silver with pink spots in stream areas near salt water, or often brownish or pale gray in land-locked specimens, just because most anglers fishing southern Dollies in the summer miss the fall (usually September) strong spawning colors of the Dolly, which in most cases are just as brilliant as those of their northern cousins in the Arctic a few weeks earlier. So where are you most likely to catch an arctic char or a Dolly Varden (northern Dolly and southern Dolly)? From our personal experience, and not counting gill rakers, etc., we'd say that the northern Dolly begins to show in the Bristol Bay region as a minority, then gradually becomes more prevalent in the Seward Peninsula streams and at some point between Nome and Barrow, a majority. And thence clear around the Arctic Slope to some point on the Atlantic side where perhaps, and we believe undoubtedly, an Atlantic "southern char" takes over.

The arctic char, is usually a lake-spawning fish. It is especially abundant in the Wulik River near Kivalina, Alaska, where the current arctic char/Dolly Varden state record of 17 pounds, 8 ounces is held; the fish was taken in 1968 by the late Peter Winslow of Fairbanks. Arctic char are also abundant in the Noatak and Kobuk drainages (Alaska). It grows to huge size in the lower Mackenzie River and its tributaries of Yukon Territory and Northwest Territories. Little is known about this fish. It is heavily utilized by Eskimos for food, and it is a highly colored fish, particularly at spawning time, when males especially are virtually crimson red. Like the Dolly, it spends much time in salt water, although forms that never leave fresh water are known.

Donald Rearden of Portland, Oregon, playing a large arctic char in a stream at Ugashik Lake on the Alaska Peninsula. (Jim Rearden, staff)

Lake Trout

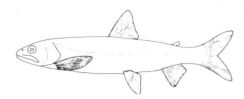

REPRINTED FROM ILLUSTRATED KEYS TO THE
FRESH-WATER FISHES OF ALASKA

Lake trout, from Chenik Lake on the west side of Cook Inlet, are heavily spotted. These average about 14 inches long. (Jim Rearden, staff)

Salvelinus namaycush is found in most suitable lakes from the Alaska Peninsula northward. It is found in the Copper River drainage (near Cordova), but not in Southeastern Alaska. It is found in British Columbia and throughout Northwest Territories where it reaches its greatest size, probably in Great Bear and Great Slave lakes. In Yukon Territory lake trout are numerous in almost all of the large clear lakes.

It is variously called Great Lakes trout, mackinaw, and togue in different parts of its range. This is a large trout with a strongly forked tail, profusely pale spotted body and dorsal and tail fins spotted or reticulate. Basic color varies from very dark to pale gray or even greenish on the side. In parts of its range it reaches perhaps 100 pounds. Alaska's current record is a 47-pounder that measured 44¼ inches long, taken in 1970 in Clarence Lake by Daniel Thorsness.

This is a deep-water fish, often found at depths of more than 100 feet. During summer months fishermen often troll deeply for lake trout in the larger lakes. But in Alaska, lakes are often smaller and shallower than elsewhere in this trout's range, and casting from shore with heavy light-reflecting gold or silver lures will often bring results. Lakers are often found where stream currents carry forage fish and insects into the lake.

Lake trout spawn in the fall, in rocky shoals from 6 to 15 feet deep. They are less migratory than other trout, remaining in their home lakes normally during their lifetime.

Lake trout are large-mouthed and feed heavily on other fishes. Whitefish, lake herring, smelt, grayling, arctic char, stickleback all are utilized. For this reason baits that resemble wounded fish are often effective in taking lake trout when others do not attract it.

Eating qualities of lake trout are superb; they are rated by many as among the best of the trout or chars. Their flesh is orangish or yellowish colored. The flavor is delicate.

Best fishing for lake trout is immediately after the ice leaves a lake, at which time lakers big and small are commonly found near the surface, feeding on anything that moves.

Flat-wing flies of many types, streamers and bucktails of various designs are effective during this brief period. Spin fishermen using spoons, wobblers, spinners or other glittery lures likewise catch many lake trout when they are feeding near the surface at ice-out time.

During summer and fall, lake trout fishing is good at stream inlets, where they pour into a lake. Trolling seems to take the largest and most trout during summer months, when the fish are normally deep.

In Yukon Territory, the best lake trout fishing is to be had just after ice-out until early July and then again in September and October. Some of the top waters for lakers from 5 to 40 pounds are Teslin, Tagish, Atlin,

Kusawa, Dezadeash, Kluane, Kathleen, Ethel, Aishihik and Frances. Many of the smaller lakes dotting the territory contain good populations of fish in the 2- to 6-pound category. Fish the mouths of creeks flowing into lakes in early summer and troll around rocky points and islands later in the season.

Lures and baits vary from lake to lake with the all-around favorites being the Kit-a-mat and Pixie spoons. The Pixie, a heavy, hammered metal spoon with a colored plastic insert, has to be the most widely used Yukon line. Many stores often run out of these early in the season so pick up several in varying sizes as soon as possible. Other spoons and large streamer flies will also produce good catches, especially early in the year. In midsummer many anglers switch to lead core line in some lakes as the fish tend to head for deeper, cooler waters during the height of the summer.

Best lake trout fishing in Alaska is probably in the Bristol Bay region, at the outlet of the Tikchik Lakes (see fishing maps); in inlet streams in Lake Clark (choose clear-water streams here); in Battle River or Nonvianuk Lake. Naknek Lake is good. Abundance of lake trout, not size, is the attraction in the Bristol Bay region. For size try Crosswind Lake, Clarence Lake or Lake Louise, off of the Glenn Highway. Good lake trout fishing is also available in lakes along the Denali Highway.

OTHER SPECIES

Arctic Grayling

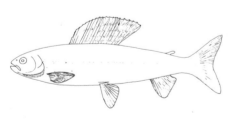

Thymallus arcticus is the major game fish in many parts of central and

An arctic grayling shows its colors. Grayling have delicate coloring that is visible as long as they are live and in the water. They fade to a dull gray when removed from the water. (Jim Rearden)

northern Alaska. It is found from the north side of the Chugach Mountains to the Arctic Ocean. It is also found in the Susitna drainage and throughout the Copper River drainage. Large grayling have been reported from Saint Lawrence Island in the Bering Sea. It is found in northern British Columbia, throughout Yukon Territory and in most systems of northern Northwest Territories.

The arctic grayling is a slender, graceful, active and troutlike fish of cold streams. It has a small, tender mouth and a long, high dorsal fin marked with bright spots and sometimes bands. The male's dorsal fin is larger than that of the female—and both have the largest dorsal fin of any American species. (When depressed, the dorsal fin of a 12-inch male commonly reaches to or beyond the adipose fin.) The blue and red spots on the dorsal fin are highly colored as long as the fish is in the water. In death, they quickly fade.

Sparse black spots are commonly found along the sides of the arctic grayling. Fish vary in color, depending upon water they are found in, from dark, almost black, to a bright pearl color.

Most grayling caught by anglers are from 10 to 15 inches long. Any grayling that approaches 20 inches is very large. The current Alaska record is a 4-pound, 11-ounce, 21½-inch-long grayling that was taken in Ugashik Narrows by Duane Weaver of Marshall, Minnesota, in 1975.

Grayling are equally at home in streams and lakes, preferring clear waters. However, they do occur in some silty lakes and streams.

As ice melts in lake tributaries in the spring adult grayling leave lakes and enter streams to spawn. They also leave the major rivers—the Yukon, the Tanana (Alaska)—and enter tributary streams. Throughout summer these fish are found in spawning areas. By fall many of them have moved back into the lakes; and by winter, many more return to the big rivers, like the Yukon and Tanana, where they apparently spend the winter.

They spawn in spring or summer as water temperatures approach 40°F. Eggs hatch in about 20 days.

Grayling feed mostly on aquatic insects, although their diet at times includes smaller fish, such as stickleback, young salmon or young trout.

Because of its varied food preferences, the grayling is a good sport fish; it will strike at a wide variety of lures.

Best sport fishing for grayling is with dry flies, which they often take readily. Small, dark flies such as the black gnat or gray flies such as the mosquito are often used successfully. A grayling in gin-clear water can often be seen several feet away as it rises to take a fly, and anglers are often tempted to set the hook before the fly is struck.

Grayling are sometimes fussy and refuse to hit dry flies. When this happens anglers use nymphs (flies tied to imitate the aquatic stage of various stream insects) with some success.

Grayling also hit small spoons, spinners, wobblers and even small plugs, thus making the grayling a good fish for the spinning-rod fisherman.

Largest grayling in Alaska come from the Ugashik Lakes on the Alaska Peninsula. Good grayling fishing is available in most clear-water Interior streams. Top grayling fishing can be had in many of the Bristol Bay waters, including the Wood River system, the Igushik River system, the Tikchik Lakes, the Nushagak River, the Alagnak (Branch) River system and the Naknek River drainage (see fishing maps). Exceptionally large grayling have been reported from Saint Lawrence Island, but few anglers have had the opportunity of fishing for them there.

Grayling can be found almost anywhere in Yukon Territory with the largest coming from Quiet Lake, the Yukon River and the Teslin River and Teslin Lake. They average 2 pounds with some large lake fish running to 4 pounds. Best times are from ice-out to early June and then again in late August in the streams and rivers and all year in the lakes.

When lake fishing watch for the grayling's distinctive swirling rise along rocky shorelines and points of land. These fish travel in large schools so once a feeding school is located cast #1 or #0 Mepps spinners or flies into the midst of the fish. Stream fishermen should try drifting black gnat or nymph flies into riffles and pools. Grayling have very tender mouths so avoid setting the hook too hard.

Sheefish

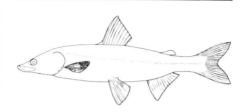

REPRINTED FROM ILLUSTRATED KEYS TO THE
FRESH-WATER FISHES OF ALASKA

Stenodus leucichthys is a little-known sport fish outside of Alaska and northern Canada. Variously called the inconnu, or unknown fish, the shee, cony, and shovelnose whitefish, it is known as the white salmon in Russia. A member of the whitefish family, it is slender with a long, tapering head. Teeth are tiny, but numerous. Body color is silvery on the underside, darkening to dark silver on the back. Freshly caught fish may have a purplish sheen. It has no spots, and the scales are large—they have often given rise to the nickname "tarpon of the Arctic."

It is found in the Kuskokwim, Yukon, Selawik and Kobuk drainages of Alaska, as well as many of the tributaries of the Yukon. A slightly different species is found in the Mackenzie River of Canada, ranging into Yukon Territory and Northwest Territories.

Alaskan sheefish probably reach 60 pounds, although any sheefish over 25 pounds is a very large one. Present state record for sheefish is 52½ pounds, for a 48-inch-long fish taken in the Kobuk River in 1968 by Jim Keeline.

Most sheefish spend part of the year in brackish water, at the mouths of large rivers that empty into the ocean, or in shallow, brackish lakes such as Hotham Inlet or Selawik Lake in Alaska. Other populations probably live year-round in fresh water.

During winter the fish seem to congregate in schools as they feed on schools of ciscos. When ice goes out, in late May or early June, sheefish run up the Kobuk, Selawik and Tuklomarak rivers of Alaska. Most of these fish are on spawning migrations, although some are nonspawners. Migration is slow, for spawning doesn't take place until September, when water temperatures drop to about 36°F. Sheefish, like salmon, don't feed during the latter stages of spawning migrations, but they will strike artificial lures. Best fights come from fish taken near the sea. The long trip upstream, the last distances without food, takes much of their energy.

Spawning takes place on the surface of the water and the tiny eggs, which average 2.5mm in diameter, sink to the bottom and lodge between rocks and in gravel. One female may lay from 100,000 to 350,000 eggs, but egg mortality is high. Adults survive spawning and may return to spawn again.

After spawning they migrate rapidly to brackish water, where they regain strength and weight quickly as they resume feeding. The young hatch around March, and they are probably carried by the current to the lower reaches of the rivers or into brackish water, where they spend their early years.

Sheefish are excellent eating and are

Ken Alt, Alaska Department of Fish & Game biologist, holds a big sheefish taken on the upper Kobuk River. The shee was caught for autopsy purposes with a gill net and seine, with the help of Eskimos in the area. (Amos Burg, Alaska Department of Fish & Game)

eagerly sought by Alaskan Eskimos of the Selawik, Noatak, Kobuk, Kuskokwim and lower Yukon areas. Flesh is white and delicately flavored.

Successful fishing for sheefish requires a knowledge of migration timing and location of wintering grounds. The following waters are in Alaska. Sheefish taken on summer feeding grounds, such as Minto Flats (near Fairbanks), Holitna River and the Selawik-Kobuk River areas fight better than fish taken on the spawning grounds in the fall (see fishing maps).

Most sport fishing for sheefish requires extensive travel by plane and riverboat. Sheefish can be taken at the mouths of clear-water tributary streams of the Yukon River throughout the summer, with the Melozitna, Howitna and Ray rivers providing fine fishing; but the Koyukuk River at Hughes and Allakaket provides the best fishing on the Yukon system the last two weeks of September.

The Holitna River in the Kuskokwim system at Sleetmute is a favorite in July. The sheefish of the Minto Flats population are available to anglers in the lower reaches of the Tolovana and Chatanika rivers in June and July, and on the upper Chatanika River spawning grounds in September.

The big ones are found in the Selawik-Kobuk country. Tuklomarak River (a small river entering Selawik Lake), Selawik Lake, Selawik River and the Kobuk River villages of Kiana, Ambler and Kobuk are all excellent.

Tackle for sheefish is usually medium-action spinning gear or bait-casting gear, and line of 10- to 15-pound-test. Various spoons, such as Dardevles, Hot Rod or Nebco, usually produce best results. During their feeding periods sheefish are caught close to the surface, and a fly rod with bucktails is efficient at such times.

Great Northern Pike

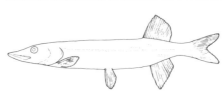

REPRINTED FROM ILLUSTRATED KEYS TO THE FRESH-WATER FISHES OF ALASKA

Esox lucius is the only member of its family found in Alaska—the pickerel and muskellunge are absent. The pike ranges from Alaska Peninsula streams

that feed into Bristol Bay northward to the Arctic coast and throughout the Interior. An isolated population of pike is found in the Ahrnklin River, 10 miles southwest of Yakutat, as well as in ponds in that vicinity. This range roughly parallels the range of the lake trout in Alaska.

Yukon Territory has some of the finest northern pike fishing in Canada. They are also found in British Columbia and Northwest Territories.

This long, slim, predatory fish with the large mouth and formidable teeth is one of the most voracious of freshwater fishes. Commonly found in sluggish brown-stained streams and lakes, it is also found in clear-water lakes, and even in fast waters along with various trout and even grayling. Color is greenish-brown, but this varies with the waters the fish is found in.

Pike spawn in shallow, marshy areas almost as soon as the ice goes out. They ascend small streams to marshy areas and move into the shallows of tundra lakes. Eggs are tiny, and a large female can lay several hundred thousand of them. Eggs hatch in about 2 weeks. Young pike start feeding on microscopic aquatic life, and by the time they are grown they'll tackle almost anything they can swallow—their own young, mice, muskrat, ducks and other creatures wandering too close.

Pike will strike almost any bright, moving lure. Sometimes pike concentrate in a slow-moving river hole, and they can be taken out of the same hole by the dozen—a fish almost every strike.

Bait-casting rods and spinning outfits are the most popular pike equipment. The current record pike for Alaska is a 38-pound fish taken from Fish Creek near Tanana in 1978 by Rhoda Edwards. There undoubtedly are larger pike in Alaska, and anglers like to use line of at least 12-pound-test in fishing for these hard fighters.

A must in pike fishing is a wire leader, for the sharp teeth of the fish will quickly sever monofilament or woven lines. Another highly desirable tool when pike fishing is a pair of long-nosed pliers for removing hooks safely. Bare-handed hook removal from a pike

Pike caught at Minto Lakes, west of Fairbanks, Alaska. (Jim Rearden)

is dangerous, for their needle-sharp teeth can inflict serious injury.

Various plugs, spoons, spinners and bucktail flies are effective pike lures. Pike are ever predacious, and anything that moves as if it might be food will tempt it into striking. They have been known to strike at canoe paddles and at fingers trailing in the water from a paddled boat.

Large numbers of pike are taken by Fairbanks, Alaska, sportsmen who travel to Minto Lakes, west of that city about 30 miles. The Tolovana River near Minto Lakes is also good (see fishing maps).

Other good Alaskan waters include the Innoko River in the Yukon drainage, Lake Minchumina and Kantishna River not far from Mount McKinley National Park, Selawik Lake on the Arctic coast, and the Kobuk River.

Some top Yukon waters for pike are Teslin (Nisutlin Bay), Squanga, Tagish, Marsh, Dezadeash and Pine lakes, and the Yukon River. Tatchun, Frenchman and Ethel lakes contain some real lunkers.

Fresh-water Ling

Lota lota, also called the lawyer, fresh-water cusk, eelpout, lush, or burbot, is found in most Alaskan drainages from the Copper River in Southcentral Alaska north and west to the Bering Sea and the Arctic Ocean. It is also common in northern British Columbia, Yukon Territory and Northwest Territories.

This is the only fresh-water codfish and, in common with other cods, it is an excellent food fish. It is a homely, somewhat sluggish species, brown-mottled on top, with a white belly. The head is somewhat compressed dorsally. Two features distinguish this fish from other fresh-water fishes of the North Country: near the tip of the chin on the underside is a single prominent barbel, or "whisker," and the fish has two dorsal fins.

Burbot live in streams and deep lakes. They spawn in late winter or in early spring—in much of Alaska spawning time ranges from February to April, and it takes place under the ice. Most burbot taken by anglers are under 10 pounds. The current Alaska record for burbot is 24 pounds, 12 ounces, for a 43-inch-long fish caught in Lake Louise in 1976 by George R. Howard.

Burbot are caught with hooks baited with cut fish or chunks of meat. Most burbot are taken by fishing through the ice, in water that is from 10 to 50 feet in depth. Best fishing is in 15 feet or less, in weedy bays and inlets.

Good burbot fishing in Alaska can be had in Big Lake and Nancy Lake along the George Parks Highway; Lakes Louise, Susitna, Leila and Spruce along the Glenn Highway (see fishing maps); and several lakes along the Denali Highway. They are also found in Paxson Lake, Summit Lake and Fielding Lake on the Richardson Highway.

Whitefish

Whitefish and ciscos, both in the whitefish family, are found in Canada and Alaska, sometimes in great abundance. These fish, a subfamily of the salmon family, are excellent eating and can provide good sport. Legal methods of take include spearing in some areas of Alaska.

The current Alaska sport-caught record whitefish weighed 7 pounds, 2 ounces and was caught in 1978 in the Tolovana River by Glen W. Cornwall.

There are probably six, perhaps more, species of whitefish in Alaska and Canada. Ranges and characteristics of these fish sometimes overlap, and even scientists are not in agreement on them.

Almost all whitefish species are found in brackish and fresh-water lakes and both slow- and fast-moving streams.

Round whitefish

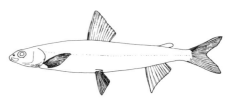

The round whitefish (*Prosopium cylindraceum*), however, is usually a stream fish, and not found in estuaries. It is most abundant in streams with gravel bottoms. In Alaska it is distributed across the northern slope of the Brooks Range, through the Brooks Range, on the Seward Peninsula and the drainages of the Yukon and Kuskokwim rivers. It is also recorded from Crosswind Lake near Gulkana. It is likely that it is found also in Southeastern Alaska, from the Taku drainage north.

Pygmy whitefish

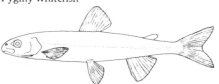

The pygmy whitefish (*Prosopium coulteri*) is reported from the Bristol Bay region and Southcentral Alaska. It is also abundant in British Columbia and Yukon Territory.

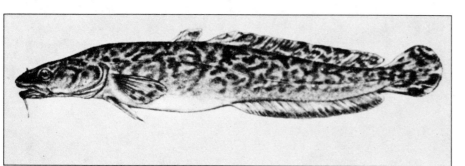

The ling cod isn't too attractive but is an excellent food fish.
(Courtesy of Alaska Department of Fish & Game)

Arctic cisco

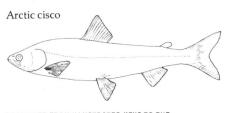

REPRINTED FROM ILLUSTRATED KEYS TO THE
FRESH-WATER FISHES OF ALASKA

The arctic cisco (*Coregonus autumnalis*) has a coastal distribution in Alaska from Demarcation Point through the Beaufort, Chukchi and Bering seas to the Bristol Bay area. It is primarily a fish of estuarine areas and is seldom found far inland.

Least cisco

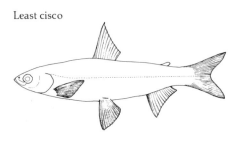

REPRINTED FROM ILLUSTRATED KEYS TO THE
FRESH-WATER FISHES OF ALASKA

The least cisco (*Coregonus sardinella*) has the same general Alaskan distribution as the arctic cisco, but it is also widely distributed throughout the Interior. It is especially abundant in lakes where it is important in the diet of pike, lake trout, burbot and sheefish. The least cisco is usually found in water of lower salinity than is the arctic cisco. This fish may weigh more than 5 pounds and measure more than 15 inches. This species ranges into Yukon Territory, Northwest Territories and northern British Columbia.

Broad whitefish

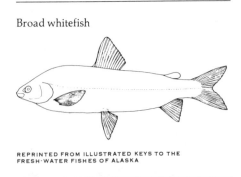

REPRINTED FROM ILLUSTRATED KEYS TO THE
FRESH-WATER FISHES OF ALASKA

The broad whitefish (*Coregonus nasus*) is widely distributed in Arctic Alaska and Canada. In Alaska it is

found in the Chukchi and Bering Sea drainages, in the Yukon River and its tributaries, including the Porcupine and Koyukuk rivers. It is widespread in the Minto Flats region of the Tanana River, but apparently rare upstream. It is common in the entire Kuskokwim River. It is absent from the Copper and Susitna river drainages. At Minto in Interior Alaska this fish averages about 5 pounds.

Humpback (Alaska) whitefish

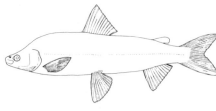

REPRINTED FROM ILLUSTRATED KEYS TO THE
FRESH-WATER FISHES OF ALASKA

The humpback whitefish (*Coregonus pidschian*) is the most widely distributed of any whitefish in Alaska and northern Canada. In Alaska it is found over the North Slope, the Chukchi and Bering Sea drainages, the entire Yukon and Kuskokwim river drainages, the Bristol Bay area and also the Copper, Susitna and Alsek river drainages. It is found in many different habitats, and these environments have been responsible for the variation found within the species. It is found in brackish water, lakes, slow-moving streams and fast- moving streams. It has both anadromous and landlocked populations.

The subsistence catch of this species on the Kobuk River averages slightly less than 2 pounds. Lengths of more than 21 inches have been recorded for

this species taken in the Chatanika River near Fairbanks, Alaska.

Whitefish have small mouths, weak or even absent teeth, somewhat large scales, usually whitish or silvery on the sides and below, darker on the back. They have a large adipose fin.

In Alaska whitefish may be caught with a spear, using a lantern to locate and to confuse the fish (at night, while wading or drifting through shallow water in a riverboat), or they may be taken with flies or single eggs. (Check regulations on the spearing. This is a sport of the Arctic-Yukon-Kuskokwim areas.)

Whitefish spawn in the fall, and the eggs incubate in 4 to 5 months, the first ones hatching in March or April. By June the tiny whitefish fry are dispersed in pools.

Whitefish may be caught through the ice during winter, or they may be taken during ice-free months.

Regardless of the time taken, the feeding habits of whitefish dictate the type of terminal tackle that must be used to catch them. Whitefish feed primarily on larvae, pupae and adults of aquatic and terrestrial insects, plus fish eggs. The most important insects are the midges, Dipterid (true) flies, mosquitoes, stone flies, mayflies and caddis. Midge larvae are the most important to some species of whitefish.

These foods are generally tiny. The fish are delicate feeders, and they shy away from visible leaders and heavy hardware.

Lightweight tippets and flies tied on small hooks—No. 16 and No. 18—are most effective in fishing for whitefish. Wet flies are effective and, occasionally, whitefish feed heavily on hatches, at the surface, and will readily take a delicately cast dry fly.

A humpback whitefish. (Jim Rearden)

A fly rod is the most effective tackle for whitefish. In Alaska the whitefish is used largely for subsistence, and very few sportsmen bother to fish for it. This will change as location and habits of this valuable and sporty fish are discovered.

Eulachon [Candlefish]

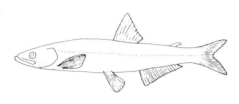

REPRINTED FROM ILLUSTRATED KEYS TO THE FRESH-WATER FISHES OF ALASKA

Thaleichthys pacificus, commonly called hooligan by Alaskans, is a smelt that is so fat at the time it runs into rivers to spawn that when dried, and a wick drawn through it, it will burn like a primitive candle.

It is a small, slender, white or silver anadromous species, having the adipose fin and general structure of the trout or salmon family. Adults, on migration into streams, may be 8 to 14 inches long.

The hooligan run is a sign of spring, and the run may last only a few weeks. Extremely abundant in some years, eulachon are dipped from the water with larger hand-held nets, or, at times, short lengths of fine (1½- to 2½-inch) mesh gill nets are tied to the end of a long pole, and it is swept through the water (the fisherman walking down the bank, following the fishing net until it is pulled from the water, the fish picked out and fishing started upstream again.)

They are found in Southeastern Alaska around Haines, and in the Chilkat River during May. Elsewhere in Alaska, in May and June in the Lower Cook Inlet area and in June in the Upper Cook Inlet; and also in the estuary areas of the Nushagak in Bristol Bay and in the lower Kuskokwim River during June.

These tiny fish are excellent eating. Bag limits are measured in pounds, and you deep fry them whole, without cleaning. Most Alaskans eat them whole, bones and all.

SALT-WATER FISH

Of interest to sport fishermen are the halibut, sablefish, Pacific cod, tomcod, whiting or walleye pollock, various rockfish, including the red rockfish and the black rockfish, turbot (arrowtooth flounder) and sole. (The salmon species are covered separately at the beginning of this chapter.)

Pacific Halibut

Hippoglossus stenolepis is the largest fish in Alaska that an angler is likely to hook. Weights of more than 400 pounds are known, and sport fishermen commonly catch fish of 150 to 200 pounds. A 440-pounder taken at Point Adolphus, Southeastern Alaska, in 1978 by Joar Savland is the current state record for a sport-caught halibut.

Found in bays, lagoons and coastal waters from Ketchikan to Bristol Bay

A day's catch of halibut from a charter out of Homer Spit on the Kenai Peninsula in Alaska. (Sharon Paul, staff)

from May through September, halibut readily take bait and are increasingly popular with sport fishermen. Fish depths from 20 to 40 fathoms.

Rods used for halibut are heavy, from 6 to 8 feet long. Star-drag reels

are most popular, with 50-pound-test monofilament line. Some sport fishermen use 80-pound-test line with 80-pound-test wire leaders—halibut have sharp teeth that can fray a leader in a hurry.

Lead weights of from 4-ounce to 8-ounce size are used, and baited hooks (size 9/0 to 12/0 are popular) are on the end of an 18-inch leader. Fishing is right on the bottom. Rod tips should be lifted frequently to reposition the bait and to attract feeding halibut.

Bait most commonly used is herring, but any oily fish will do. Salmon makes excellent halibut bait, and another top bait is octopus.

Halibut feed slowly along the bottom, taking any live or dead (if it is fresh) food they can find.

It's simple to fillet a halibut, then cut off the fins, and you have a boneless, sweet, white-meated fish.

You'll do best fishing from a boat for halibut, although a few are caught from deep-water docks. Don't bring a really big halibut into a small boat unless you are positive it is dead. Pacific halibut are strong, and many a fish has pounded planks loose, knocked fishermen over and tossed items of all kinds overboard. Commercial fishermen commonly shoot halibut in the head with a pistol before boating them. A gaff is a necessity, and it should be a strong one in order to hold a heavy halibut.

Rockfish

ADF&G

Belonging to the genus, *Sebastodes*, which includes 50 or more species found from California to Attu, on the tip of the Aleutian Islands, rockfish are the best known of the near-game saltwater species that are taken by sport fishermen.

The red or scarlet rockfish is commonly called the red snapper in British

Columbia and Alaska because of its superficial resemblance to the true red snapper of the Atlantic. The red rockfish of Alaska is excellent eating.

The red rockfish is usually found along the edge of steep drop-offs where depths might plunge from 40 to 60 fathoms to 150 or more. Use herring for bait and drop right to the bottom, pulling up a little bit to get the bait just above bottom.

When these fish are pulled from the depths the change in pressure often kills them, and their eyes protrude. They'll tug vigorously until the change of pressure kills or immobilizes them. Weights to 25 or 30 pounds are known.

The black rockfish, which is sometimes called black bass or sea bass, often is a pest to commercial salmon trollers. It is plentiful along kelp beds and rocky shores, usually facing the sea. It will strike plugs, spoons and spinners and it will take bait. It is an excellent eating fish.

Cleaning rockfish is a bit different from halibut—a lot more bones and not so much meat recovery. Look out for the sharp and slightly poisonous spines of the dorsals of the rockfishes (also on the tips of the gill covers of most species).

Best method is to hold the fish by the tail with pliers (and gloves); with the fish's back to you make a cut to the backbone just behind the head, then flatten the knife blade along the backbone toward the tail and carry through to the tail. Do the same on the other side and trim belly and fin portions away from the two side fillets. Check for additional bones you may have left, especially from the big dorsal fins, but there will be a few from ventrals and pectorals.

It's a simple matter then to take the edge of a piece of skin in the pliers again, lay the knife blade flat through the flesh to the skin and sweep the knife blade thus along the skin to the other end of the fillet.

Rockfish goes well in casserole dishes or baked, but deep-fried has its followers, too.

Other Species

Sablefish is among the other marine species that sometimes get attached to the sport angler's hooks. It is also called the black cod, but is not a cod.

Codlike appearance has earned its incorrect name. The gill cover of this fish has a black lining, and there is no barbel (chin whisker). Adults caught in deep water reach a length of 3 feet, but immatures caught in salmon waters are usually only 10 to 20 inches long. They are edible fish, but no trophy. Adults are excellent when smoked.

The Pacific cod, which is brown or gray, with a long barbel (chin whisker), has 3 dorsal fins. Anus is located below second dorsal fin. Grows to 3 feet and is excellent eating. It is no trophy.

Pacific tomcod, which grow to about 12 inches, are olive green on the back, with a small barbel on the lower jaw. Anus is directly below first dorsal fin. Eskimo fishermen take these fish by jigging through the ice for them. They are edible, but no game fish, and certainly no trophy.

Sole are common throughout Alaska and northern British Columbia. Several species of these are characterized by a rounded tail, rather than the widely flared tail of the flounder or turbot. Excellent eating. Usually less than 20 inches in length. Another bottom feeder.

Sculpins offer more fright than fight.
(Dolores D. Rogusska)

Sculpin, or Irish lord, has a large head with eyes placed high. It has large pectoral and anal fins. There are numerous spiny protrusions on all fins—handle with care. Edible. Length to 2 feet.

Arrowtooth flounder (turbot)

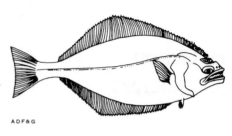

ADF&G

The arrowtooth flounder or turbot, is a brown flatfish (halibutlike in shape), with a large mouth that extends behind a line drawn through the eyes. Edible, but soft-fleshed when cooked. Up to 2 feet in length. Bottom feeder.

Walleye pollock (whiting)

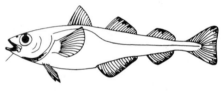

ADF&G

The walleye pollock, or whiting, is an olive green to dark brown codlike fish, with large eyes and a projecting jaw. Barbel is minute or absent. Anus is located below the interspace between first and second dorsal fins. It is edible, but no trophy. Length to 3 feet.

Shellfish

Shellfish, which include crabs of various species, clams, shrimps and scallops, are abundant along the British Columbia and Alaska coast. Paralytic shellfish poisoning is known to occur in blue mussels and in hardshell clams in some areas and for that reason we do not recommend utilizing these species. Alaska health officials have indicated they eventually plan a program to monitor hardshell clam beaches for toxic clams. Until they do, the attitude of the state is that no hardshell clams are safe to eat. Despite this, residents in some parts of the state who are familiar with local conditions use clams and blue mussels for food.

Cook Inlet razor clams. (Jim Rearden)

The razor clam, which occurs widely in Alaska and British Columbia, has long been a prized food. Best digging is on minus tides of spring and fall. A sport fishing license is required in Alaska for razor clam digging, and limits are set for most beaches (consult sport fishing regulations).

Top beaches for razor clams in Alaska are found near Cordova; on the east and west sides of Cook Inlet (from the Kasilof River to Ninilchik on the east side, at Polly Creek on the west side); and Swickshak beach south of Cape Douglas on Shelikof Strait. Razor clams are also found in many places south along the Alaska Peninsula.

Scallops are generally beyond the reach of sport fishermen. Even commercial fishermen need specialized equipment. Further, scallops are found in 20 to 30 fathoms or more, in specific locations. Nevertheless halibut fishermen often find scallops clamped to their longlines, and it might be possible for a scallop bed to be located, and a means found of consistently catching this delicious seafood.

Shrimp are found in great abundance all along the British Columbia and Alaska coast. Most coastal boat owners have a number of shrimp pots, which are light and relatively small, and have favorite places to catch shrimp. Several species occur. Largest is the spot, which may be 18 inches in length from end of its long feelers to tip of tail. This is the one found mostly among rocks in fairly deep water—from 15 to perhaps 40 fathoms.

Humpback shrimp and coonstripe shrimp are found to be most abundant on mud bottoms in from 10 to 30 fathoms.

Shrimp pots can be devised from plastic frames, metal frames, old tires, 5-gallon cans or anything that can keep shrimp inside once they are enticed through a 2- or 3-inch-diameter tunnel.

Fresh bait is a must with shrimp. Herring is usually used. Hanging bait—fresh fish of almost any kind—from the top of the pot will attract more shrimp than a punctured bait can alone. Both are commonly used.

Most effective shrimp pots seem to be those used by commercial fishermen that measure 2 to 3 feet on a side and are covered with burlap. Shrimp seem to want to seek dark places and are more willing to enter a darkened pot than one that has no covering over it.

See "Pot and Ring Net Fishing for Crab and Shrimp," page 80.

Fresh shrimp are deheaded—a quick snap removes the head and all the innards—and the tails are boiled in salt water until they float. Eat with melted butter or hot sauce of your choice.

Three species of crab (king, Dungeness and tanner) are abundant in Alaska. Dungeness and king crab are found in the tidal waters of British Columbia.

Dungeness crab are more often found in shallows and are more easily caught by the sportsman than the deepwater-loving king crab. Dungeness crab are frequently found in shallow salt-water lagoons, in the shallows at the heads of bays (especially in the fall) and in depths to 30 and 40 fathoms.

Dungeness, which generally average 2 pounds in weight, can be taken in pots or ring nets. See "Pot and Ring Net Fishing for Crab and Shrimp," page 80.

Another method of taking Dungeness is to cruise about slowly with a boat in shallow water, searching the bottom for crabs. When they are found they can often be scooped up with a dip net.

Dungeness crab should also be cleaned before cooking, in the same manner as is the king crab, described earlier.

Editor's note: *Many disagree with the cleaning before cooking theory and argue that the "whole thing cooked" adds a richer flavor. It also eliminates risk of too much salt if some is added to the cooking water, as it should be.*

Tanner crab inhabit deeper waters than do the Dungeness and are found associated with king crab. They can be taken in small pots or in ring nets. In weight they resemble the Dungeness, with crab up to 4 pounds sometimes being taken; their average size is much smaller. However, they are spidery and have long, compressed legs. Their meat is denser than that of either the king crab or Dungeness.

King crab can be purchased "from the boats" in season in many Alaska ports. (Sharon Paul, staff)

The king crab is the largest. Found from Southeastern Alaska to the Bering Sea, this huge crab (spreads to 6 feet, weights to more than 20 pounds) can be taken with pots and ring nets. Sportsmen and subsistence fishermen take them from deep inside waters of Southeastern Alaska, Prince William Sound, Kachemak Bay on Lower Cook Inlet and near Kodiak. Average size of males caught is 6 or 7 pounds. See "Pot and Ring Net Fishing for Crab and Shrimp," page 80.

Subsistence fishing (that is, crabs taken for personal use, not for sale), is legal throughout Alaska. Usual requirement is that the buoy marking the pot must have the name or initials of the owner on it. Best to make local inquiries, for regulations change from year to year.

King crab should be cleaned before cooking. Hold the crab with its head facing away from you, grasp it by the legs, and hold the edge of the shell (at the head) against a board, a rock or a barrel, and pull down, forcing the shell off the animal. Clean out insides, including the gills. Break crab in half, shaking out the dark and yellow substance in the body meat, and boil in salted water for 15 to 20 minutes. Eat with melted butter or cocktail sauce. Once again, many argue that the crab should be cooked whole, then cleaned.

Broiled King Crab Legs on the Half Shell—In our house we say this is absolutely the best way to serve king crab.

1—These four legs show top and bottom sides of four typical leg sections—a king crab has six legs and two

claws, one much heavier than the other, but very little body meat—the glob of meat at the body end of the leg is all the "body" there is and is called a "knuckle."

2—Break each section of the leg apart, carefully, and only when fresh or thawed from frozen, using care to pinch between joints and hold meat from pulling out with tendons. (Warning: king crab spines are sharp, and if your hands and gentle handling are not sufficient, don protective gloves when you're butchering.)

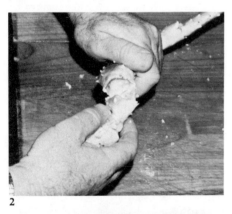

3—Next, turn bottom side up (the light colored, flattest side) and with a pair of poultry shears or similar—light ones with points are best—cut down each side, and lift off the now upper piece of shell.

4—Presto, you have a nice leg section with tendon removed lying in the remaining shell ready for broiling. You'll note that after you have similarly cut each leg section there are three proper leg joints of diminishing size to each leg, plus a knuckle, and the tender little morsel in the very tip of the leg. You may succumb and eat this as you go, but it is a bright piece of red to doll

up a salad or cocktail. For that you use the knuckles—the erstwhile "body" meat. By judicious use of the shears you can open the rest of claws (the big one takes a bit of bearing down to break through) for one more split "leg" section and the balance for the bowl of body meat.

5—Push out the knuckle meat with a forefinger. Bigger knuckles lend themselves nicely to knocking the meat loose by rapping the knuckle against

the lip of the bowl. In either case, you may have to first tear loose a restraining piece or two of shell membrane to make it easier to break the meat free.

6—Now the cooking: you have leg sections sitting ready to broil in their own fat, and a bowl full of pure knuckle meat for inclusion in the salad or cocktails, or whatever dish calls for the meat of the crab at this meal or another.

The leg sections to be broiled call for a simple sauce of melted butter (no oil thinning or additives) with a dash of garlic powder, a touch of lemon juice and a bit of dried parsley flakes. Place leg sections in appropriate broiling tray, brush well with butter sauce, then place under broiler a few inches away. Leave only a few minutes—most fish and shellfish suffers more often from overcooking—and as soon as the meat begins to bubble and brown, pull the tray out of the oven. The crab is ready to serve simmering in its own juices, on an appropriate platter.

Serve a bowl or two of extra butter sauce at the table . . . and provide a bowl or two for empty shells disposal. Toasted garlic buns, a tossed green salad, a bit of macaroni and cheese, plus a good Chablis or Pinot Chardonnay well chilled makes a meal—if you have enough crab.

In ordering, ask for frozen leg sections (not canned), and let thaw at room temperature for four to five hours. If time is not available, an hour or two in cold water will do the job, but the meat seems better thawing at a slower pace, and use just after it has thawed. Do not refreeze, and hopefully you will get crab that has had continuous frozen storage of not more than three months. For Alaskans near fishing centers, the fresh product is of course that much better—but any good king crab, fresh or frozen, broiled as we have described is true ambrosia. □

FROM PERSONAL EXPERIENCE

"The one that got away . . ."
Taken at a campground near the Anchor River on the
Kenai Peninsula in Alaska. (Sharon Paul, staff)

ALASKA'S CURRENT FISHING HOT SPOTS

Warren Tilman fishes for grayling in the Richardson Clearwater, a small tributary of the Tanana, east of Fairbanks. (Jim Rearden)

By Jim Rearden, Outdoors Editor, ALASKA® magazine

The big news in Southcentral Alaska for the 1979 season was the opening, announced in December, of specified upper Cook Inlet streams for the taking of 13,100 king salmon.

Cook Inlet's king salmon were so badly depleted in the early 1960's that both commercial and sport fishing were closed. Over the years—and especially during the last 3 years—these fat, silvery, broad-tailed, speckle-backed salmon have increased so that an opening was announced for some streams in the Susitna drainage, from late May until July 6.

Three of the streams, opened for four weekends only, mostly in June, are on the highway system. Others, accessible only by small plane, were opened continuously from late May to July 6. A catch quota was set for each stream.

The biggest quota, of 7,000 fish, was for the Deshka River, a relatively quiet, clear to brown-stained meandering river about 150 feet across at its confluence with the broad muddy Susitna. Nearby Alexander Creek and farther upstream Lake Creek each had quotas of 2,000.

Smaller quotas were set for Montana Creek and Willow Creeks, which are

open downstream from where the highway crosses, and the Little Susitna, which can only be fished efficiently by floating it. Put in at the Houston Bridge and come out off the Burma Road, about a 3-day trip.

For the first time a punch card was required of fishermen taking salmon and steelhead in the entire Cook Inlet basin, including the Kenai Peninsula. Total catch allowed was 5 king salmon, 2 steelhead (for the Kenai), 25 silver salmon and 25 in the aggregate of pinks, chums and red salmon. That's 57 salmon and steelhead.

Can't make it to Cook Inlet streams in May or June? How about heading for Valdez on the northeast shore of lovely Prince William Sound for silver salmon? They're there in numbers in late June and July. The catch rate for this top-quality sport fishery is unusually high. And there isn't a brighter, more lively, harder-hitting fish for its weight (7 to 15 pounds) than a fresh sea-run silver salmon.

Or, if July isn't convenient, try Cook Inlet streams for silver salmon in early August. The 3-day float trip on Little Susitna is good, or fly from Anchorage to the Deshka River. The Deshka usually has top-quality silver salmon fishing in August, plus rainbows and, in even-numbered years, pink salmon.

Feel like something really special for

midsummer, June through the middle of July? Charter a small floatplane from Anchorage, or take a scheduled flight to King Salmon or Dillingham and charter the small plane there, and head for the Agulowak and/or the Agulukpak rivers of the Wood River Lakes. The Agulowak is a clear gravel and rock-bottomed stream 4 miles long that connects Lake Nerka to Lake Aleknagik; the Agulukpak, also clear, runs 2 miles from Lake Beverley to Lake Nerka. They're often called "the second and third rivers," and they are almost too good for enjoyable fishing. The problem is you catch lively, fat, tackle-smashing char with virtually every cast. After a time your wrist tires, your back aches and you get bored with catching fish. Many of the fishing guides in the Bristol Bay region where these streams flow won't take clients to these two rivers until the last day of their trip, for after a fisherman has tossed his lure into the outlet of either the Agulowak or the Agulukpak he's spoiled and hard to please.

The fat and strong char concentrate at the outlets of these streams where they feed on the myriad red salmon that migrate to sea, and they eagerly slam into lures that may or may not resemble their primary food.

Bristol Bay, into which the waters of these two fabulous streams flow, is the world's greatest producer of sockeye salmon. Sockeye aren't often sought by sportsmen, for anglers haven't learned yet how to tempt them into hitting a lure; these fish seem fully occupied with thoughts of getting upstream to their spawning grounds. However, the deep, pure and clear gravel, rock and sand-bottomed lakes which rear Bristol Bay's red salmon also support vast numbers of char, lake trout, rainbow trout, grayling and even northern pike, and these are the species that sportsmen seek.

There is another species here in Bristol Bay's great arc of fish that excites sportsmen—king salmon, the same silver-scaled giant found from California north. Two outstanding Bristol Bay streams where sportsmen seek and catch these muscular, broad-tailed giants are the Naknek River and the even better Nushagak River. In recent years some sportsmen have been nailing lots of king salmon on the Nushagak near the village of Portage Creek, about 30 miles upriver from Dillingham.

Or, a good midsummer float, with top fishing available after a short air charter from Anchorage, is the Talachulitna River in the Susitna basin. The clear Tal has plenty of rainbows, some grayling, Dolly Varden and, in late July or later, pink and silver salmon. The Deshka River, also on the west side of the big and dirty Susitna River, makes a good float and can be reached on a short charter from Anchorage.

Air taxi operators in Anchorage offer package trips, including inflatable boat and camp gear, to these two rivers. They'll drop you off at the head of the stream and make an appointment to pick you up at a designated spot downstream a few days—or weeks—later.

Or, if you would like to drive and hike to good spring or summer fishing where you won't have to compete with other fishermen, drive from Anchorage up the Glenn Highway in late May to September. After you pass Eureka, virtually any clear-water stream you cross offers good fly fishing for grayling. Best bet is to leave your car near the bridge where the Glenn crosses a stream and hike at least a mile upstream or downstream. If one doesn't produce grayling, the next will, and this holds true all the way up into the Copper River drainage.

If Southcentral Alaska fishing isn't possible, try fish-loaded Southeastern Alaska. Best bets for fishing in the 125 by 400 miles of deep, green, island-dominated Southeastern Alaska include mid-March to September (best from mid-May until mid-June) salt-water fishing for hungry king salmon. Kings aren't taken in fresh-water streams of Southeastern Alaska — All streams here are closed to the taking of this great brute of a fish.

When you get a needle-sharp hook imbedded in the mouth of one of these ocean-fresh, powerful kings, you've got to have good fishing gear and you'd better hang on, for you're in for a fight. Herring trolled or drifted with huge flashers to attract salmon to them are most popular. Local hot spots include Bell Island near Ketchikan, salt chuck near Craig, Scow and Pybus bays near Petersburg. Saginaw Channel and Tee Harbor near Juneau, Sitka Sound and, 150 miles north of the inside waters, Yakutat Bay.

There are no highways connecting the cities in this great waterland. Boats and the regularly scheduled state ferries, called "the marine highway," and floatplanes are the most common ways to get around.

After the king salmon fishing has tapered off, along come the silver salmon, which are available from July to September— but most abundant in August. Hot spots are Clarence Strait and Tongass Narrows near Ketchikan, Duncan salt chuck near Petersburg, and Doty Cove north to Berners Bay in the Juneau area. Try Port Banks on Baranof Island from August to early November, with shiny spoons, or even flies.

Herring or large spoons are normally best bait for silvers in salt water. Flashers are frequently used for attractors. These powerful fish average 10 to 12 pounds and may exceed 20 pounds.

Sea-run cutthroat and Dolly Varden are available in Southeastern Alaska waters from May to October, and they'll hit almost any small lure; most popular are small spoons, salmon eggs and flies. Hot spots include Duncan salt chuck near Petersburg, outlets of Chilkoot Lake at Haines, Nakwasina Passage and Katlian River near Sitka, Castle River near Petersburg, Salmon Bay Creek near Wrangell, and Bostwick Inlet or Wasta Creek near Ketchikan.

The small 3- to 5-pound black-spotted pink salmon attract many

A hefty halibut caught in Sitka Sound in late June. (Sharon Paul)

anglers each summer from July through August, with hot spots at Mountain Point, the mouth of Lunch Creek near Ketchikan, and Auke Bay and Lena Cove near Juneau.

Perhaps Alaska's best sport fishing for halibut is found in Southeastern Alaska. This big, white-meated bottom fish is available from May to September, and their numbers peak in the inside waters in August. Preferred baits include octopus and herring. Many are caught on spoons trolled near bottom. Halibut of more than 200 pounds are not unusual, so don't try to fish with light gear. The Alaska record for sport fishing weighs 440 pounds and was caught in 1978 at Point Adolphus on the north end of Chichagof Island.

Rockfish are found in abundance in some waters of Southeastern Alaska. Best fishing is where the Gulf of Alaska washes the outside beaches of islands, or rock piles. It's best to fish deep, up to 600 feet, for these fish. They'll hit almost any lure or bait. One hot spot is at Point Retreat, about 20 miles northwest of Juneau.

The Situk and Italio rivers at Yakutat are favorite fresh-water spots for silver salmon in early fall. The fall run of steelhead, especially in the Situk, is one of the best in Alaska. It peaks in October and November.

Spring runs of steelhead, good about April, are found in Klawak and Eagle creeks and Karta River, all on Prince of Wales Island.

Fresh-water hot spots for cutthroat trout and Dolly Varden include Hasselborg and Thayer lakes on Admiralty Island, and Turner Lake off the Taku River on the mainland near Juneau.

Chilkat Lake near Haines has excellent cutthroat and Dolly Varden fishing.

If Southeastern or Southcentral Alaska aren't possible for you, perhaps you can try the Interior or Arctic Alaska, a vast, mostly unpeopled land with long, cold winters and short, warm summers, where some of the best fishing in Alaska is found. The variety of species isn't as great as elsewhere in the state, but the fact that few fishermen ever cast the many waters of the Interior and Arctic has a certain appeal.

The most common and widespread species—and the most popular—is that great little country bumpkin of a fish, the high-dorsal-finned grayling. His taste in lures is catholic, and he'll leap for a dry fly, dart after a spoon or spinner or suck in a wet fly—when he's in a feeding mood.

If grayling aren't feeding, wait a few hours or a day and their mood will change; the time will come when it will seem as if you can't get enough lures into the water to satisfy their voracious appetites.

Look for grayling in clear streams that flow into the great, dirty Yukon River or the equally muddy Tanana River. They're in the Kobuk, the Noatak and in virtually every other decent-sized clear stream of Arctic Alaska.

Want to try something different in the way of fishing? Try for the sheefish, that outsized cousin to the whitefish and distant relative of the salmon. This white-fleshed, large-scaled fish found only in the North can be taken during summer from the Holitna River, which flows into the Kuskokwim River just above Sleetmute. You'll have to charter a floatplane or use a riverboat to get there, but the trip will be worth it for the scenery alone. Sheefish are found in good numbers in the Kobuk River above the village of Kobuk. In September sheefish arrive in the neighborhood of Hughes on the Koyukuk River, one of the huge clearwater tributaries of the Yukon, where they annually spawn and where there is superlative fishing.

Sheefish range to 50 pounds or more; most are 10 to 20 pounds. When you've hooked one, you know you've got a powerful swimmer at the end of your line—this leaping, running, splashing fish is impressive. Spoons and spinners are best lures.

Char are found only along the coast of this Interior and Arctic region, but they are char like no others found in Alaska. Perhaps the best fishing and the largest char in Alaska are found in the Noatak River, Kivalina River or Wulik River, all streams that flow seaward north of the Seward Peninsula. Alaska's record char of 17 pounds, 8 ounces was taken in the Wulik. Eskimo fishermen, gill-netting for char for the table, probably take fish this size or larger every year from all three of these rivers.

If you'd like to try for some of the colorful lake trout found in the Arctic, charter a floatplane from Bettles to Chandler Lake, which lies in a high, treeless pass of the vast, wild, arctic Brooks Range. Or try Old Man or John lakes. These are the three top lake trout lakes of the region. The water is deep, cold and scarcely fished.

Best spot in Alaska's Interior for northern pike is Minto Lakes, a 20-minute hop by chartered plane from Fairbanks. Fish range to 20 pounds or more, and they hit spoons of almost any kind. Be sure to use a wire leader, for the pike's sharp teeth will quickly part anything else.

These are the fishing spots across Alaska that currently are most likely to produce fish. Each region offers its own special atmosphere and its own kind of fishing. Each offers a special kind of fishing adventure for resident and visitor alike. □

Red's Lake, a small lake holding pike, in the valley of the Chandalar, in the Brooks Range. (Jim Rearden)

SMOKING YOUR FISH

Alaskans and Canadians are blessed with runs of five kinds of salmon, plus steelhead (sea-run rainbow trout) and a variety of other fish that lend themselves nicely to smoking. There are several methods for smoking fish. The choice of method depends largely on whether the fish is to be eaten within a few days or weeks, whether it is to be canned, the amount of time you wish to spend on the smoking process, and the degree of flavor desired.

The following offer a variety of methods with explanations as to which process may best suit your personal needs.

Smoking Fish in the Bush

Story and photo by Ruth D. Edmondson
Reprinted from ALASKA® magazine, September 1971

Editor's note: *If you are dropped off by floatplane, or hike in several miles to a USFS cabin or wilderness camping spot, there will be no facilities at hand for preserving your catch. These areas generally afford the best of fishing and you may find yourself with more fish than you can eat— even staying within the legal catch limits.*

The following excerpt offers a solution found by one party when faced with this problem.

We had plenty of groceries. We didn't expect a plane to pick us up for several days. We couldn't eat all the fish we could legally catch. We wanted to take some home. Three-fourths of our group did not really care for fresh fish, although they admitted that pickled fish, smoked fish or salt fish were another matter.

By the end of the day we hatched the idea of smoking our catch. A fire bed was dug and forked stakes were driven into the ground to support cross members strung with fish. We used alder for firewood, then piled leafy branches over the entirety to keep the smoke enclosed.

The salmon were filleted and the backbone removed to within 2 inches of the tail. We cut them across to skin depth every 3 or 4 inches, sprinkled them with table salt, leaving it on overnight to help toughen the skin and meat.

Rainbow trout and grayling were eviscerated but otherwise left intact,

A firebed was dug, forked stakes driven into the ground to support cross members strung with fish.

just as you would buy them for fancy prices from mail-order houses.

The fire was started, and fish were strung on sticks and placed on stakes. The blaze was damped and the alder branches heaped around. A plastic sheet spread over the mound helped hold the smoke within our primitive fish preserver.

All was well as long as the fire received continual attention. Fresh wood and water were supplied as necessary to keep the flames and heat

down. There was no thought of complete curing; the object was to smoke-dry and seal the outer flesh in order to preserve the catch until it could be returned to the city and the freezer.

The experiment, for that is really what it was, kept the fish from spoiling, and the alder smoke gave it an added flavor. The primitive smoker was a delicious success. In other, more difficult circumstances such a technique could be an important survival aid.

Smoking Salmon for Canning

Condensed from Bulletin No. 31,
University of Alaska Extension Service, College, Alaska

Dress fish as usual. Split dressed fish on either side of backbone, removing the backbone. Remove gills but leave the bony plates to support the weight when hanging in the smokehouse. Rinse with fresh water to remove blood, slime and waste material. Score the fish, cutting several slits in the skin to improve salt penetration.

In a clean plastic container or crock mix a saturated brine solution: 6 cups of salt to 1 gallon of clean water.

Editor's note: *Place a potato in the container, add salt and watch the potato. When it floats you have the right amount of salt.*

Immerse the fish in the brine and let stand for 30 minutes to 1½ hours, depending on size of the fish or thickness of the pieces. The sides from a 15- to 20-pound fish must be brined approximately 1 hour.

Remove from brine and rinse lightly with fresh, cold water, just enough to remove salt from surface. Drain well. Blot surface with clean paper towels and let dry until surface is dry and shiny. Moving air will do this in 15 or 20 minutes.

If you wish to use dry salt or mild cure fish for smoking, the fish must be freshened by placing in cold running water overnight, or for approximately 15 hours after brining. Drain and dry as above.

There are two methods of smoking salmon—by cold smoke or by hot smoke. A light cold-smoked flavor is best for canning because the canning process intensifies it. Any nonresinous wood, such as alder, may be used for smoking.

Cold Smoke

Smoke 4 to 7 hours, depending on the size of the fish, in cool, dense smoke (not over 100°F) or until the surface is light brown.

Hot Smoke (kippered)

Smoke 3 to 5 hours, depending on the size of the fish, gradually raising the temperature of the smokehouse from 160° to 190°F, or until fish are cooked and have a light brown surface color.

If you wish to can smoked fish, the next step is to cut into can-height pieces.

Pack as for plain salmon, omitting salt. One-half pound flat cans are preferred. If desired, add a tablespoon of vegetable oil per can.

Follow directions for use of pressure cooker. Exhaust same as for plain salmon. Process ½-pound flat cans for 90 minutes at 240°F (12 pounds pressure).

I Smoke Salmon

By Helen Blanchard
Reprinted from ALASKA® magazine,
September 1971

When I see a salmon I do not see the scales or fins, nor do I envision a trophy mounted on our wall. Rather I see chunks of bright orange, tantalizingly delicious fish, smoking on racks—fish ready for eating, fish ready for sandwiches. I can even envision the finished jars of smoked fish standing in rows on my cupboard shelves, assuring me of gourmet meals until next fishing season.

We use wood from crab apple trees that are plentiful on Gravina Island near Ketchikan, where our homestead is located. Some use alder, but I like the sweet, mild, fragrant smoky odor and taste we get from apple wood.

Smoking fish is a simple, leisurely occupation that leaves me free to work in the garden after I get the wood charred and some coals to dry off and glaze the fish. After this I can tell by watching the smoke coming from the smokehouse when the wood needs replenishing.

Getting our fish is simple, too. My husband does some sports fishing and we use fish he catches. I also "fish" by informing friends that I will smoke their fish for half. This is a sure-fire way to "catch" a steady supply.

The fish I put up in jars only get a few hours of smoke; we like them mild. This clears the racks for finishing the other half of the supply of fish for the friends I smoke for.

Caution: When canning fish (even smoked fish) always use a good pressure cooker with an accurate pressure gauge and process 90 minutes at 12 pounds of pressure. Never use the water bath method for canning fish because of the danger of botulism.

Directions for Smoking Salmon

Fillet salmon (any species) or steelhead; cut into 4-inch squares, 2 inches thick. This way all the fish are uniform in flavor. Fish halves can be smoked if preferred. Use uneven pieces and backbone for canning.

For each 5 pounds of fish, sprinkle with the following mix (adjust to suit individual taste):

5 teaspoons salt
3 teaspoons raw sugar
¼ teaspoon black pepper

Let stand overnight. Drain. Place fish chunks on racks in smokehouse, skin side down, over glowing coals and charred wood in order to dry and glaze. This takes about an hour. Then smother the glowing coals to a heavy smoke with green chunks of apple wood or peeled alder.

For quick-kippered fish, ready in about 8 hours, use low rack, 18 inches from fire.

For longer smoking, use middle rack, 30 inches from fire. After first day of 8 hours of smoking, smoke about 2 hours each day for 7 to 10 days. The fish will become dry and hard-smoked.

Use top rack, 48 inches from fire, 3 to 4 hours to cold smoke for canning.

Our smokehouse is constructed of poles covered with handmade cedar shakes. It measures 4½ feet on each side, and is 6 feet high. The fire pit is built of rock filled with beach pebbles directly under the racks.

The racks are the full width of the smokehouse, 2 feet wide, constructed of 1-inch board frames covered with 1-inch mesh chicken wire. The smokehouse is lined to 2 feet above the fire pit with aluminum roofing sheets to prevent sparks from reaching the shakes.   □

GREAT BEAR
AND
GREAT SLAVE LAKES,
NORTHWEST TERRITORIES

Story and photos by Hank Andrews

Larry Helin of Detroit hefts a king-size lake trout taken from Great Bear. The weight of the fish is unknown.

Sportsmen who seek new and different thrills in fishing should toss a look toward Great Slave Lake and 200 miles farther north to Great Bear Lake, both in the Northwest Territories. Increasing numbers of anglers are flying to both lakes to fish for lake trout, and some sportsmen are going even farther north to seek arctic char. Some remarkable fish of both species have been taken in this area.

Fishermen often still find ice on Great Bear early in July, so the fishing season is short. There are deluxe lodges at Great Bear and fishing trip packages are offered from Winnipeg and Edmonton. A typical 8-day package fishing trip to Great Slave or Great Bear costs $1,200 to $1,400.

Most anglers who visit Great Bear or Great Slave seek lake trout, and many fish of more than 40 pounds have been taken in both. Great Bear and Great Slave are each more than 10,000 square miles in area. Great Bear is the larger;

it is a bigger lake than Lake Erie or Lake Huron of the Great Lakes.

Contrary to their deepwater dwelling habits throughout most of their range, the lake trout at Great Bear stay fairly near the surface even in midsummer because water temperatures average between 40°F and 45°F. In some shallow bays the water may be warmer.

Anglers find that no lead line or heavy weights are necessary to catch lake trout, and this enhances their fighting ability. Often fish can be taken by trolling heavy spoons that weigh 2 or 2½ ounces. Many fish are taken on Dardevle spoons or Hofschneider Red Eye spoons. Various other spoons also work, and these can be obtained at the fishing camps.

Some fishermen at Great Bear troll heavy spoons until they catch one or two lake trout, and then they cast again in the same area. In casting, one should use a 7/8-ounce spoon and let it

sink until it is from 20 to 30 feet deep before retrieving. Very often you can look into the clear water and see half a dozen lake trout chasing your bait.

Fishing can be superb or it can be very slow in Great Bear. Some fishermen use spinning tackle with 8- to 10-pound-test lines.

Fishing at either lake can be an unusual and refreshing experience to visitors from the south. At noon most fishermen schedule a shore lunch on a rocky island or shore. Days are long and some fishermen become so enthralled that they fish for 24 hours straight. Although both lakes are vast, much fishing can be done in protected bays or near islands.

Fishing camps at Great Bear offer fly-out trips to northern rivers for arctic char. One lodge features fishing in the Tree River. Dick Kotis, president of the Fred Arbogast Bait Company in Akron, Ohio, fished the Tree once and returned talking to himself. The fishing

was superb, he told me, and he rates it as one of his top fishing experiences. Char of 15 pounds are often taken, and some of these fish top 25 pounds in the Tree, he said. Fish are caught on wet flies or with spinning lures. The fish do not jump much, but they do make sensational runs for freedom.

The long days, haze-free skies, little rain and relief from the heat of southern regions combine to add zest to fishing.

While most anglers get only lake trout in Great Bear, some grayling can also be caught. Northern pike are also present. A fly-out trip from one lodge takes fishermen to Great Bear River for arctic grayling. These fish are easily taken on flies or on small spinner baits.

Fly fishing will also take lake trout; streamers or bucktails are favorites. Fly hatches can be observed in bays with gravel bottoms and feeding trout can be spotted on calm days.

Fishing at Great Slave is similar to that of Great Bear, with lake trout being taken at depths of 15 feet or more. Great Slave also holds grayling, northern pike, whitefish and ciscos. Some scattered walleyes are also found here.

Many anglers who fish the Far North in lakes such as Great Bear and Great Slave do not realize that the huge lake trout grow slowly—some reach 50 years of age—because the harshness of the environment in this region limits their food supply. Lake trout of 15 pounds or more often range in age from 20 to 30 years, and this means that a replacement fish for one of this

Above — Guides use huge nets to land big lake trout, like this 20-pounder, at Great Bear Lake. Angler is Harry Eyler of Cleveland, Ohio.
Right — The late Wynn Davis, former fishing editor for Outdoor Life *magazine, walks off with an arctic char he caught in the Tree River.*

size must exist here for the next 20 or 30 years.

Lake trout in Great Bear do not spawn until they are about 16, and they reproduce only every second or third year once maturity is attained, according to the Canadian Fisheries and Marine Services with headquarters in Winnipeg. At Great Slave, lake trout spawn usually at about 12 years of age.

Spawning occurs in late August and September. The young hatch the following June and spend the next few summers in shallow inshore areas.

Because of the delicate balance of life for these fish, efforts are being made to maintain a population of trophy trout that are 15 pounds or larger. Fishermen are urged to put back small fish, and some anglers are being urged to use barbless hooks to make it easier to release fish.

Also, anglers are urged to handle fish gently and to avoid grasping them by the eyes or gills.

This is much different from the early days of the fishery. In the 1960's anglers brought in great strings of fish almost daily. Now they are urged to release lake trout that are under 15 pounds unless the fish is injured or bleeding heavily.

Since catching a truly big fish seems to be the magnet that draws anglers to this last northern frontier of fishing, this attempt to preserve the big ones makes a lot of sense. The fact that fishing pressure is increasing is part of the reason; there are now at least 12 major lodges located on the two big lakes, and they lure some 2,000 fishermen annually.

Anglers are advised that even though some great catches are made, there are days when fishing is slow. You may not catch a fish of more than 15 or 20 pounds—or you may land a 40-pounder.

First-time visitors often forget that they are heading for subarctic areas when they go to Great Bear and Great Slave. The Arctic Circle passes over

Left — *Weighing in his lake trout, angler discovers he has taken a fish of more than 40 pounds while at a Cameron Bay lodge.*
Above — *Hank Andrews, an Ohio outdoor writer, likes Great Bear Lake fishing so well that he has been there three times. Here he holds a 20-pound and a 10-pound lake trout.*

the northern part of Great Bear, and summers can be quite cool at both lakes. Good rain gear is usually needed, not necessarily for rain, but to shield you from the spray of your boat on a windy day. Windbreakers also work well as rain gear, and the wind does blow here. Long underwear and woolen shirts are ideal summer wear for these lakes.

Insect repellent, for black flies and mosquitoes, and a sun-shield lotion, for lake surface glare during long summer days, are good items to bring. Sunglasses are a must.

Most visitors are amazed to find that Great Bear is not only cold, but exceedingly clear, with visibility as far as 80 feet. The lake is very deep, with the bottom at 1,300 feet in some areas.

Great Slave is as deep as 2,000 feet in the region of Christie Bay, although much of the lake is shallow. Great Slave can be reached by highway from Edmonton over the Mackenzie Route, which also goes into Yellowknife, the capital city of the Northwest Territories. Grimshaw, Alberta, is the starting point. It is 292 miles from Grimshaw to the Alberta-Northwest Territories border. Yellowknife is 330 miles farther north over graveled roads. The Mackenzie River is crossed via a free government ferry in the summer, and in winter traffic crosses on the ice. Each spring and fall during breakup and freezeup there is a 2- to 6-week period when traffic comes to a halt. Campsites and picnic tables have been established along this highway,

and there is a visitor center at the 60th parallel where drivers can learn road conditions. This center opens around May 22 and closes September 7. Camping permits are issued at this office.

Fishing camps at both Great Bear and Great Slave are deluxe and offer excellent meals. Many of the camps offer motel-type rooms with two beds in each room. Some even offer private baths.

Few people are aware of the vastness of the Northwest Territories, which occupies all of Canada north of the provinces, with the exception of Yukon Territory. The Northwest Territories includes the Queen Elizabeth Islands and the islands in Hudson Bay and Hudson Strait, James Bay and Ungava Bay, and it includes one-third of the total area of Canada. It has more than twice the area of Alaska. There are thousands of lakes in Northwest Territories, many of which have never been fished by sportsmen.

Some of these untouched lakes may have great fishing potential, but for now, for my money, it's hard to beat Great Bear and Great Slave lakes. □

Editor's note: *For information about lodges, guides and other facilities in this area write TravelArctic, Yellowknife, NWT X1A 2L9.*

SOUTHEASTERN KING SALMON

By Rupe Andrews

Along our Pacific coast of North America, Southeastern Alaska stands above all others for its king, or chinook, salmon. The irregular coastline, with its numerous bays, fjords and vast kelp beds, harbors huge quantities of forage fish for the ever-hungry kings. To witness a school of kings herding a school of herring around a kelp bed is enough to give the average salmon angler the memory of a lifetime.

The official world record king salmon taken by any means is a 126½-pound fish caught decades ago in a commercial fish trap near Petersburg, Alaska. In the summer of 1977 Howard Rider of Juneau broke the world record for sporting tackle in salt water by landing a slab-sided, 91-pound giant in the Chatham Strait area near Angoon, Alaska.

Commercial trollers tell of retrieving their troll gear in areas around Kuiu, Kupreanof and Prince of Wales Islands with leaders snapped and rubber snubbers broken off by large kings. Just thinking about the possibilities of setting the steel into a big king can start any Southeastern salt-water angler recounting tales of the one that got away and similar stories, all of which are, of course, true.

King salmon fishing is restricted to the salt water in Southeastern Alaska by regulation and logistics. The four largest producing fresh-water systems (Alsek, Stikine, Unuk, and Taku rivers) are all unfishable glacial rivers. These four systems annually receive estimated spawning escapements of 10,000 or more king salmon.

Angling for kings in Southeastern is always an adventure. In addition to occasional icebergs and incredibly beautiful scenery, the region abounds in a variety of water birds, marine mammals and game animals, such as brown bear and Sitka blacktail deer.

Several years ago, while trolling for kings north of Juneau along the famous "breadline," I had the good luck to hook a medium-sized fish. It was an early spring morning and the shoreline was glistening with herring spawn that covered rocks, seaweed and even empty clam shells. I had seen a number of sea lions chasing the schooled and spawning herring but hadn't paid much attention to them since they are common.

However, after several good runs of my hooked king, I sat up in my 16-foot open skiff when a large male sea lion made a pass at my fish. Pumping the rod hard, I brought the king to the side of the skiff. It wasn't ready to net, but I had the uneasy fear that I was about to share my catch — most likely the whole fish. As the salmon passed by the side of the skiff, I grabbed the landing net handle with one hand and held onto the rod with my other. I got lucky and that king centered right into the net, a mere 5 to 6 feet ahead of the sea lion. I muttered a few observations about the poor manners of that particular sea lion and sea lions in general as I dumped my fish into the skiff.

I was about to congratulate myself when the incident began to get out of control — the sea lion started to climb aboard. I don't know what a full-grown sea lion weighs, but it was a lot more than my skiff could handle. I frantically grabbed my fish "priest" — a short piece of shovel handle used to administer last rites to salmon. Furiously I beat on the sea lion. Down he went. Up he came. I beat some more. Down he went and swam off a few yards. That's when I decided to leave. The warm engine fired on the first pull, and I left the sea lion and the incident behind.

There are a number of successful methods and gears for taking king salmon. Most anglers troll for kings, but many anglers anchor off the end of a reef or island and "strip fish" in a riptide. The movement of the tide gives action to the bait or lure. Kings readily take all sorts of trolled lures, from whole herring to plugs and plastic-skirted hoochies. The most effective, and therefore the preferred method, is to troll a herring coupled with a dodger or flasher between the herring and the lead weight. Kings are deep feeders and leads of 6 to 8 ounces are commonly used. A good tip is to troll slowly. Old-timers who remember the real hand-trolling days, when Norwegian outboards (oars) were used, say that one had to row slowly to make a good payday.

There are probably as many ways to rig a herring as there are fishermen. They all work, as conditions vary. Perhaps a plug-cut herring or a strip (fillet) of herring will be a high performer. I think the real secret, if any, is that the angler must have confidence in what he is using.

Any number of good artificial plugs are on the market and they will also take kings. Again, there is a time and a place for plugs as well as for various techniques.

In recent years the hoochie, a plastic-skirted lure resembling a small squid or bait fish, has become popular. Hoochies are manufactured in an incredible assortment of colors. Color is very important. Successful trollers keep switching hoochies of various colors until fish begin striking. When fish stop striking, they start changing lure colors again. Translucent, shiny skirts are available for use under the hoochies and probably add an extra 10% to 20% to the chance of success.

Hoochies should be fished with a dodger or flasher, which further increases the chance for a strike. Dodgers and flashers are made in several finishes, but I recommend a bright chrome and brass combination. It pays to carry a little metal polish while fishing to keep dodgers and flashers as bright as possible at all times. Dull flashers are poor salmon attractors.

A good salmon-trolling rod of 7½ to 8 feet in length coupled with a trolling reel that has a good star drag, with at least a 250-yard capacity, is ideal. Fill the reel with 20- to 25-pound-test line;

you're asking for trouble if you use lighter line.

You'll need an assortment of trolling leads ranging from 4 to 12 ounces. If you're going to use herring, you will also need a supply of good 5/0 single hooks. If you have problems tying knots, there are herring hookups available that are pre-tied, ready for fishing. In my opinion these prepared trolling setups are worth the money for the time saved in changing baits.

Probably the most important aspect of king salmon fishing is determining when and where to fish. Many anglers swear that low tide is the best time. Start fishing one hour before low slack and fish through the slack for a couple of hours on the flood side. Apparently the changing tide influences feeding behavior of kings.

Kings often frequent kelp beds and other shallow areas adjacent to rocky, beachless areas to crowd forage fish or push them against the rocks, where they can't escape. These areas are good producers of kings if you can troll in close. A fathometer is handy when trolling close to the beach and will save a lot of gear from being lost on the bottom. One of the most affordable items to come along to help the salmon troller determine how much line he has out is multicolored monofilament line, marked every 10 feet by a different color.

Marine charts are available in most bookstores, sporting goods stores or ship chandleries in Southeastern Alaska, and they are helpful in navigating. A lot of time can be saved in finding areas that will produce king salmon by asking local residents, biologists in the local Fish & Game Department office or marine or tackle shop workers. Alaskans are friendly and will generally share such knowledge.

Good sources of information on the availability of charter or rental boats include local chambers of commerce. Contact the Alaska Department of Fish & Game, Public Communication Section, Subport Building, Juneau, Alaska 99801, for answers to questions on license fees, best season to fish specific areas for kings and for information on regulations. Good king fishing can be had in the vicinity of virtually every Southeastern city, but some are better than others at different seasons.

Lodges that offer outstanding fishing opportunities for king salmon are

Most Southeastern communities hold annual salmon derbies with kings taking many of the prizes. The weigh-in here was at Sitka in June 1978. (Sharon Paul, staff)

found adjacent to Ketchikan, Angoon and in Glacier Bay National Monument. Local travel agents can provide details on these.

Boats, tackle and frozen and fresh bait herring are available in all of the larger Southeastern coastal communities. If you own a boat that is easily trailered and if time is not a factor, try taking the Alaska Marine Highway (ferry system) that puts into port at a number of top king salmon fishing areas. By trailering your own boat, you not only have the convenience and flexibility of using your own equipment, but you also can bunk aboard your own boat in the small-boat harbors, assuming your boat is the average 18- to 24-foot cabin cruiser.

A lot of kings are taken from 14- to 16-foot open skiffs while day fishing, but a cabin cruiser is more comfortable. More often than not it is raining in Southeastern, and king trolling is much more enjoyable if you can get out of the rain from time to time.

No matter how you go about it, be assured that king fishing in Southeastern Alaska is great fun and a true adventure. To feel the surge of an Alaska king salmon as he strips off line by the tens of yards is to experience one of the great thrills of Alaska angling. □

Editor's note: *Rupe Andrews is Director of the Division of Sport Fisheries, Alaska Department of Fish & Game, at Juneau.*

The weather couldn't have been better at Atlin Lake.

Atlin Lake for Lakers

Story and photos by Chris Stall

Atlin is an out-of-the-way sort of place. Not a place to which fishing people throng—they seem to just trickle into Atlin. Way up there in the northwest corner of British Columbia, the sleepy, happy little town of 50 or so single-story log and frame buildings hugs the east shore of Atlin Lake. Perhaps a hundred people live there in summer, and they are friendly in a quiet sort of way. Ask for directions or for assistance and that's what you'll get; but ask where the lake trout are biting and you won't catch sight of a straight answer.

Most visitors arrive by auto. Tired of eating dust and dodging potholes on the Alaska Highway, the knowledgeable few turn south at Jake's Corner, Mile 865.3, seeking a day or two of respite. Balmy weather moderated by cooling breezes off the immense Juneau Icefield to the southwest makes relaxation come easy in this serene, uncrowded, unhurried corner of the world, and in the lake there are lake trout.

The villagers will prepare fine foods for you at reasonable prices; they will equip you with whatever you need or want in the way of deepwater trout gear; they'll put you into an outboard for a few bucks an hour and send you out onto their beautiful lake with stories of 30-pound lakers singing in your ears. Then all you've got to do is find the fish for yourself.

This could be a bit of a problem on an 80-mile-long, albeit fairly narrow lake. I was lucky enough to find myself on Atlin Lake, recently, in the company of one who knew the lake well. Thus I relate the tale of our 6 hours on Atlin Lake in the hope of guiding those who may be less familiar with the area.

Four of us arrived in Atlin from the south by airplane, a method I heartily recommend. Our flight originated in Juneau, which happens to be where we live. Joe Shaw, a Juneau realtor, had called earlier to ask if I'd swap a day of trout fishing on Atlin Lake in exchange for my services as pilot. I looked up from my typewriter keys, at which I'd stared unproductively for days, and spied a blue sky. Writing is so easy to put aside for a day!

After a phone call to arrange for airplane rental, the trip was set. By 9 o'clock I was at the Juneau airport and had just checked the plane when Ron Bolton, a city planner, arrived. Then Joe drove up with his partner Roy Varni. We loaded fishing gear and took off for a breath-taking scenic flight across the 1,000-square-mile Juneau Icefield, birthplace of a dozen major glaciers that grind down valleys into Alaska and Canada. After 30 minutes of sightseeing, Atlin Lake came into view. I followed Llewellyn Glacier to the southern tip of the lake, losing altitude, and in 15 minutes I planted the Cessna 182 onto Atlin's 2,500-foot gravel airstrip. In 3,000 hours of trying, I don't think I've made a more lovely and impressive 45-minute flight. And in Atlin, even the customs inspector was pleasant.

At 10 o'clock Joe took the helm of our rented 18-foot Lund; he has a small vacation house in Atlin and has fished the lake many times. The 20-hp motor moved us over the lake's quiet surface grudgingly but proved an adequate trolling motor. We went straight across the lake from town and fast-trolled along the shore around the northern tip of Teresa Island in about 40 feet of water. How can you tell the depth of the water in Atlin Lake? In 40 feet of that water you can still see lake bottom—it's that clear.

Joe hooked into one almost immediately, using a large yellow spoon with black diamonds about 30 pulls out from the end of a hefty salmon rod.

Characteristically, the fish didn't put up much resistance until it neared the surface, then it fought hard but briefly before Joe flipped it into the boat. It was a nice, fat 6-pound lake trout.

I have lived in Alaska for 8 years and I'm still not used to the way things are done in this "last frontier." Here you just don't hunt with anything smaller than a .375 H. and H. magnum and you don't go fishing with a light spinning outfit. These guys were trolling lures bigger than the fish I sought in my Westchester County youth of little lakes and quiet canoe rides with hula poppers. Here the fish might weigh 30 pounds, and they feed deep. My friends discussed their sinkers in terms of ounces while I lay in the bow soaking up the warmth and natural attractiveness of the surroundings—my idea of a very pleasant day.

We plowed north about halfway up the west shore to Atlin Lake's sole outlet stream, which was actually the extreme upper end of the Yukon River. Walking and casting from shore, Roy Varni caught many lithe grayling here, and he was using—hallelujah—spinning gear which had magically materialized from rod cases. I experimented with a couple of Scandinavian lures which kept the fish away. Ron and Joe were equally unsuccessful. Roy caught the only fish and wouldn't share the secret, but I was oblivious, lovingly turning the delicate crank of my little Garcia reel.

It was then that Roy revealed that the picnic lunch he had promised to bring along was still in Juneau. We all felt faint, having worked up healthy appetites in the course of the morning, but Joe made a quick decision as we piled back into the Lund. Being June, he would skip all the spots that he knew very well were "good in September" and head directly for Red Rock.

Near an outcropping of crimson sandstone on the east shore a few miles north of town there is a point of land, and offshore from that point there resides, it would appear, a school of lake trout. Joe found the school, made repeated passes, then thick and fast they came at last. Roy and Ron each landed a pretty laker and Joe pulled in three. The fish averaged about 4 to 5 pounds and looked like they'd do for supper, the thought of which was increasingly on everyone's mind. Amid shouts of "Pass the hamburgers now,

Left — Joe finds the lake trout and hauls in the first one unassisted. Below — The day's catch — 30 pounds of lake trout in less than 6 hours.

Roy," and "I'll have mine with lettuce and tomato, Roy," we headed back to town, where exquisite "mushroom-burgers," a specialty of the local restaurant, got everyone into fine shape to enjoy the flight back to Juneau.

It rained steadily in Juneau all through July, as is its wont when the moisture-laden air currents pile up against the Coast Mountains' west side. Just on general principle most people don't relish the idea of fishing in a downpour. Not so very far on the other side of the mountains, Atlin remains warm and arid. While we didn't cross paths with that legendary 30-pounder, we did at least catch 30 pounds of lake trout in less than 6 hours. I find myself planning a return trip to Atlin and for some of these same reasons, you might keep the sleepy little hamlet in northwestern British Columbia in mind also. □

How to Catch Trophy Rainbows

Story and photos by Mel Allen
Reprinted from ALASKA® magazine,
May 1972

Alaska has an abundance of large rainbow trout. They are not particularly hard to catch, once you learn how. But the feeding habits of large rainbows are different from those of smaller 'bows. Fishermen accustomed to taking smaller rainbows are often unsuccessful in taking the lunkers that Alaskan waters offer.

About 90% of the food taken by a big rainbow is found below the surface. Fundamentally the big 'bows are seldom insect feeders. The old adage of "big fish, big appetite" really holds true for these fish.

The larger a rainbow grows, the greater his appetite, and he turns to fish eggs, smolt, fry, plus any number of available bait fish. The smaller the rainbow, the more surface and/or insect life it seeks.

Aside from feeding habits, which are somewhat unpredictable, big rainbows are generally lazy. The big 'bow is most likely to be king of the hole or the run. He isn't worried about food because he follows it. He also doesn't worry about being eaten by others.

You sometimes see small rainbows flitting, dashing and plunging about feeding or sometimes in flight from an enemy. But you seldom see a big rainbow in the water unless he is spawning in small water, feeding in clear water or chasing your lure.

The feeding habits of the big rainbow are punctuated by speed and decisiveness. But between sporadic and infrequent feedings he sometimes won't move a foot to inhale the most enticing lure in Alaska. However, if you work the lure only inches from his snout, that's another thing altogether.

Since you can usually spot him in his lie, what technique will insure better probability of a catch? I think the best method is to learn where the big ones hang out and then learn how to fish for them. Chances are you'll end up fishing fairly deep and/or swift water, and you must fish it systematically. Cast closest to you and work on across the area you think might hold a big one, covering it adequately.

Monster rainbows like big water—water either deep, swift, possessing shelter or a combination of all three. If he is found in small water, there are important reasons why. Evaluate these reasons and you'll usually determine that the fish is seeking colder water, looking for food or moved by migratory or spawning urges.

Fast white-water runs, riffles, fast moving stretches, underwater falls, drop-offs and the like are typical big rainbow lies. They all offer a high-oxygen supply desired by the big pinksides.

You may also encounter strikes from the big ones in the most turbulent water, just as long as it is broken by depressions, rocks, logs, boulders or bends in the river. These are "comfort spots" for the big ones, and they serve as holding or resting places.

Often a single rock will provide needed refuge for big fish. Also the confluence of two streams is often a haven for the big boys. This may be a junction of cold and warmer water, with bountiful food supplies, plus highly oxygenated water.

The wise angler realizes that every variation of the flow requires specific fishing techniques for presenting the lure or bait. You can be sure that the larger the water, the more complex the current or flow. Generally smaller streams give away their secrets much more easily.

The biggest mistake made by most of us is that we rarely fish deeply enough for "Mister Big." Even when we do manage to get the lure or bait down to the fish, the presentation is often too brief, or worse yet, it is not worked properly enough to fool the big ones. Monster rainbows don't grow big by inhaling everything they see.

As a rule, the deeper, swifter and bigger the water fished, the more problems you will experience. This shouldn't discourage you; remember what you are after and stick with it.

Since principles are what we are evaluating, I'll not discuss the type of rod and reel to be used; I simply use the tackle best suited for the job at hand, trying to match water conditions.

Regardless of whether you are using a fly rod, a spinning rod or even a casting rod, there are three techniques or retrieves used by fishermen who consistently catch the big ones. Such a fisherman bottom-bounces, jigs and flutters his lure, depending on which is most effective that day. He'll cast into deep holes, swift runs, wide and deep water, and he seldom gets skunked. In doing all of this he will try spinners, flies, Wobble-Glos and Spin-N-Glos.

Bottom-bouncing is simple. The spinner (or other lure) is retrieved and allowed to bump and tap the bottom or protruding rocks. The main rule is to keep the lure on the bottom with the best action possible for the lure used. If you have to make a sacrifice, then give up a little bottom-bouncing for action. If a lure isn't worked properly, no matter what strata is fished, there is little chance of hooking your prize.

A fly is kept down by a sinking fly line plus a bit of lead wire weight wrapped around its hook shank. An upstream cast is made, the fly sinks, the retrieve or haul is started.

If you have chosen the Wobble-Glo or Spin-N-Glo, your problem is slightly different. Since these are good steelhead and salmon lures, they also work well for big trout. They are designed to be fished in a current where the flow can cause a wobbling or spinning action.

The object of these lures is to keep them wobbling or spinning while allowing the rigs to drift downstream, bottom-bouncing the entire drift. An experiment is needed to determine the exact amount of lead weight needed to allow a good drift yet a constant lure action.

Jigging is similar to bottom-bouncing, but it requires rod tip action. You can use the conventional lead jig, heavy spinner, or spoon. Jigging is hopping or jumping the lure off the bottom and then letting it fall back after a reel or two. Cast upstream, let the lure sink, then rapidly raise and lower the rod tip, and your lure will actually jump off the bottom and then sink again. The tip does the work.

Jigging sometimes drives big trout nuts. It seems to be most effective in deep holes or runs where the upper current is difficult to penetrate. I have found that just because the current is swift on the surface, it isn't necessarily fast on the bottom or in between.

The flutter method is probably the least known technique I have mentioned, and it is a killer and may work when all others fail. It is even superior to bait at times.

The secret of the flutter method lies in lure action, and only certain plugs, spoons and some spinners will do the trick. Pick out floating or sinking plugs that wiggle, rubber-skirted lures or bucktail lures with spinners or propellers. Spinners must have a narrow blade in order to reduce drag. Since no two lures act the same, you may need to observe and feel their actions before deciding on the best.

Here's how it works. Select, say, a sinking plug. Cast upstream and let it sink to the bottom. Take in slack. Now lift the rod tip as if to snatch the lure off the bottom. Rod pressure should be quick and sudden enough to make the lure wiggle normally or flutter as it is snatched off the bottom. Let it sink and repeat the snatch-settle, snatch-settle procedure the entire retrieve. That's all there is to it. With a little practice you can flutter spoons and spinners as well.

Sometimes rubber-skirted or bucktail lures are best because they give off a pulsating or breathing action. Also spoons are generally easier to flutter due to their ability to half-roll or wobble naturally. Less tip action is required to flutter spoons, so lighter tackle can be used with spoons.

With a surface wobbling plug, fluttering can be accomplished by adding lead weight about a foot and a half in front of the plug, using enough so it will sink to the bottom.

The choice of lures is important. You should attempt to match the lure to the water being fished. Use bright colors in discolored or murky water.

Spinners are deadly and probably the biggest producers of fish. Different sized and shaped blades are designed to meet different water conditions. Blade width and thickness will determine the depth that can be fished. The narrower the blade, the less water resistance and the closer it swings to the spinner shaft. This allows a much deeper penetration and better retrieve in fast water. You can call these blades willow leafs.

In contrast, the wide, almost round blade referred to as the Colorado swings slowly due to heavy water resistance. Consequently, it is better fished in slow, shallow or still water. A

Right — *Floyd Griesinger holds a 14-pound rainbow he took from Lower Talarik Creek, bottom-bouncing in deep water at the outlet.* Below — *The author with a 14-pound, 3-ounce rainbow he caught on a French-type spinner, using the bottom-bouncing technique in Lower Talarik Creek.*

slow-spinning blade lifts the spinner off the bottom in swift water and is almost useless for bottom-bouncing or fluttering under these conditions. The French, Idaho, Indiana and Bear Valley blades seem to strike a happy medium in that they spin about 45 degrees from the spinner shaft. These blades can be effectively fished about anywhere if properly worked. Remember that each blade size, shape and thickness brings a cumulative effect. Learn to match the water and the blade—it will increase your chances of tying into that lunker.

Spinner retrieves are important. Most good spinner fishermen say the spinner is most effective when the blade is revolving. Strive to keep the spinner deep but moving as slow as allowable to maintain blade swing. With practice you can feel the blade action as it revolves or strikes objects. If you are worried about snags and losing spinners, cut off one hook, or better yet, replace the treble hook with a single hook.

Here is the rule of thumb I use: the deeper and swifter the water, the longer but narrower the spinner blade to be used. The opposite works for shallow or calm water. A rounder blade pattern and its size will depend on the depth of water and sizes of fish desired—big spinner, big rainbow.

Try an effective streamer fly pattern 6 inches behind your spinner when fish are hitting short. This works well in lakes and while trolling.

Another good trick for catching trophy rainbows is to use bass plugs. Several years ago I was fishing the Naknek River with Jim Kinne. Three days of our 5-day trip were accented by 35-knot winds and sporadic rainfall. We couldn't properly fish spinners

due to the wind so we broke out a box of 4½-inch Bomber bass plugs. We landed and released more than 20 rainbows that weighed between 5 and 9 pounds. Those plugs were the only lures with good action to get down to the fish; we were digging rocks and rolling stones over with these metal-lipped plugs.

Since rainbows and steelheads are the same species, practically the same lures that are effective for the salty species also catch large rainbows. The ever-popular Spin-N-Glo and Wobble-Glo are no exception.

Some of Alaska's big rainbow waters are now designated as single-hook areas. Many lures have to be modified before they can be used in these areas, but it seems to me that a single hook holds larger fish better. Besides, the fish is less likely to be injured and can be released if desired.

I have used all of the techniques I have described here to catch the big pink-sided lunkers. You too can use these techniques, or devise others, that will consistently hang big rainbows on the end of your line. □

Pot and Ring Net Fishing for Crab and Shrimp

By Jim Rearden, Outdoors Editor, ALASKA® magazine

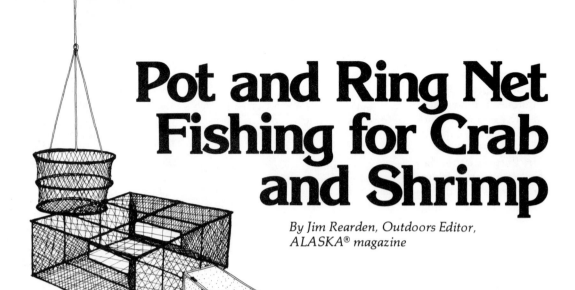

Illustration shows from top: a ring net, a crab pot and the smaller shrimp pot, the most commonly used traps for catching shrimp and crab.

Several species of crab and at least three species of large shrimp are commonly found along most of Alaska's 34,000 miles of coastline. Many Alaskans fish for these delicious seafoods under the subsistence regulations of the state, which are available at Fish & Game Department offices.

Crab and shrimp are caught in pots (also called traps) or with ring nets. Commercial fishermen use pots almost entirely, for they are more efficient. Ring nets are efficient only when crab or shrimp are abundant. Occasionally ring nets are available for rent at boat liveries or at large public docks where fishermen can fish over the side.

Ring nets vary in size and in the size of the webbing. Most are made up of two or three graduated-sized steel rings of ½-inch round stock welded into about a 3-foot-diameter ring. Webbing is tied across the bottom ring. A slightly larger ring is then fastened about a foot above that, and a third, even larger ring is sometimes fastened above that, with webbing attaching the three rings together and forming a tapered open-ended cylinder.

A bridle is tied to three points on the top ring. Bait, which is usually fresh or frozen herring but can be anything that attracts crab or shrimp, is tied to the center of the webbing before the ring net is lowered to the bottom by a rope attached to the bridle. The rope is slacked so that the two (or three) rings lie flat on the bottom, where the crab walks across them to reach the bait.

After the net is left on the bottom for a time, it is quickly lifted to the sur-face. When it is lifted, the webbing attached to the top ring (or top two rings), which is connected to the bottom ring, forms a barrier, or an open-ended cylinder, to help keep the crab in the ring net as it is lifted. Water pressure from rapid lifting, however, is the main force that keeps the crab or shrimp in the ring net; the animals simply cannot swim fast enough to get away from the rising net.

King, Dungeness and tanner crab are easily caught in ring nets, and when they are abundant, several good ring nets with buoys on the lifting lines can keep a fisherman in a small boat busy baiting and lifting them. When fished from a dock, the lifting line is tied to a rail or cleat.

Ring nets used for shrimp fishing are made with finer-mesh webbing than those used for crab, and are fished in the same manner.

The three common edible species of crab found in Alaskan waters are king, Dungeness and tanner (the latter marketed commercially as snow crab). Most subsistence fishermen and virtually all commercial fishermen use pots that are designed to be most efficient for the species sought.

King crab are usually found in deep water from the Bering Sea south throughout Southeastern Alaska. Commercial fishermen catch them in giant pots that may measure 7 or 8 feet square, 3 feet high and weigh up to 600 pounds or more when empty. They are fished as deep as 100 fathoms (600 feet).

Many Alaskans use home-built king crab pots that measure as little as 4 feet square, 2½ feet high and are used successfully in depths of 20 to 50 fathoms. "Sport" crab pots, consisting of two 26-inch or larger rings, with supports, netting and tunnels, may be purchased at sporting good or hardware stores in most coastal towns.

Knowing where to fish for king crab is half the battle. Commercial fishermen often seek underwater gullies, using a fathometer, and set their baited king crab pots there. Subsistence fishermen familiar with the area they are fishing do the same. Some fishermen believe king crab prefer a gravel bottom to one that is muddy or weedy. Most subsistence-fished king crab pots are fished in about 30 to 40 fathoms, although frequently crab may be found in 15 or 20 fathoms.

Bays that are open to the sea or to larger bays seem to provide best fishing. Often king crab are found on the side of a bay exposed to prevailing winds and currents — probably because these forces carry food to feeding crab. Avoid fishing too close to the mouths of streams where fresh water pours into the sea; king crab can't survive in fresh water, and they avoid places where fresh water mixes with the sea. However, during salmon runs all species of crab may congregate near the mouths of spawning streams where they feed on the carcasses of spawned-out salmon that are washed into salt water.

Lightweight sport-type pots may be pulled by hand. Many pleasure boats owned by coastal Alaskans are equipped with small hydraulic-powered pot pullers, miniaturized versions of the hefty ones used by commercial boats. Battery-powered anchor winches are sometimes used. Another variation is to use a small four-cycle gasoline engine of about 4- or 5-hp with a built-on winch head and fastened to the deck of a boat. The line to the pot is hauled through a pulley at the end of a davit.

Size of the line used for hauling pots depends upon the weight of the pot and the method of hauling. For power hauling, a strong small-diameter line is fine, but if the pot is to be pulled by hand, a line large enough to get a good grip on is a must. Sinking line should be used, with a large enough buoy to

Left — On good days 10 to 20 king and tanner crabs crowd the subsistence pot owned by Rose Anderson and her husband of Old Harbor. (Rose Anderson)
Above — Removing king and tanner crabs from a homemade pot. Pot was fished overnight in 40 fathoms and produced 16 king crab that averaged about 5 pounds. (Jim Rearden)

Above — The dark purplish color of the common red king crab shell turns brilliant red when cooked. Here Audrey Rearden of Homer drops half of a king crab into boiling water. (Jim Rearden)

support it. Floating line may lie on the surface, especially at low tide, as a trap for boaters who cruise past, or it may get wrapped in the propeller. When that happens you lose a pot, and a boatman may wind up drifting without power.

Minimum size for most crab pots is about a 3/8-inch line.

Bait is important. It is usually placed in a perforated plastic container, with a tight-fitting lid, and is hung by a line from the top of the pot so that it is about in the center. Herring is most often used, for it is oily and continues to attract crab for some time. Salmon is top-quality bait. If you can't find good bait, buy a can of salmon, punch holes in it and tie it inside the pot. The value of the crab you catch will probably exceed whatever you paid for the can of salmon.

Whatever you use, all bait must be fresh. King crab are fussy about how long the foods they eat have been dead—spoiled and smelly bait repels king crab.

Commercial king crab fishermen use "hanging baits," as well as bait in the perforated 2-quart size or larger plastic bait cans. Hanging bait is simply a freshly killed fish hung by a cord inside the pot. The crab enters the pot and feeds on hanging baits, and this seems to attract other crab. Often a pot with a fine-mesh web around it will trap live fish—greenling or Irish lords. Both make good hanging baits. Fresh salmon heads make superb bait.

Crab move constantly, and as long as the bait is "working" (releasing oils and scent) it will attract crab. Thus, up to a point, the longer a pot is fished, the more crab it is likely to catch.

Top-quality king crab throughout most of Alaska can be caught from August until January or February. King crab molt annually, and after the molt the new shell remains soft for some time and the crab meat is poor in quality. After the new shell becomes hard and a crab has filled it, the crab reaches top quality for eating. However, the molting period (late February to April or May in much of the gulf area of Alaska) is not precisely the

same each year, and hard-shell crab that are full and fat may be caught at any time. During the molting season and for a few months after, discriminating subsistence fishermen return to the water any crab that aren't full. When the shell of a crab leg is rubbery and easily bent and can be dented in with light finger pressure, the crab has just completed a molt and will be stringy, thin and poor eating.

Commercial fishing is stopped during the molting season and for a period after that, until crab have regained their hard shell and full condition.

Tanner crab are taken in the same areas and by the same methods as king crab. Tanner crab were tossed back into the water during the first years of the king crab fishery; there was no economic method of extracting the meat. Only when king crab stocks dipped to a low was commercial use of tanner crab developed. Hence the first years of fishing for tanner crab were done with modified king crab pots. Then pots developed by Japanese fishermen for tanner crab were used, and in one form or another this type of pot is still used by commercial fishermen for taking tanner crab. The typical pot for tanners, as used by commercial fishermen, is pyramidally shaped with a plastic chute leading from the flat top into the pot. Crab, attracted to the pot by the bait inside, climb the sides of the pyramid and slide down the plastic-lined entrance. Once inside the pot they cannot easily climb the slippery sides of the plastic chute.

Also, standard king crab pots, home-built pots designed for either Dungeness or king crab, or modifications of various types, will catch tanner crab.

Tanner crab are much smaller than king crab, but they may be considerably larger than a mature Dungeness. A really large tanner crab measures about 2½ feet, leg tip to leg tip, and weighs 4 to 5 pounds.

Tanners, like king crab, are a deepwater species, although they are often abundant in shallow water. While tanner crab and king crab may be found in the same areas, really good king crab areas produce few tanners and really good tanner crab fishing areas produce few king crab.

Baits and fishing techniques for tanners are very much like those used for king crab. Most subsistence fishermen use the same pots for both species and fish generally the same areas at the same depths and use the same baits. Often pots will contain both species after it has been fished for about a day.

Dungeness crab are found along the West Coast from mid-California into the Aleutians. They are medium-sized crab for a commercial species but smaller than the tanner and king crab. Males occasionally grow to 10 inches across the carapace (the dorsal shell), although legal size for commercial fishermen throughout most of the

Above — A 4- to 5-pound male king crab. Its spiny shell requires gloves for handling. Wristwatch in both photos is for scale. (Jim Rearden)
Right — A Dungeness crab, the familiar crab in most West Coast fish markets. This crab weighed about 3 pounds and was caught in a king crab pot that was fished in 40 fathoms. (Jim Rearden)

crab's range is 6 or 7 inches (6½ inches in Alaska). The females are scrawny, with little usable meat, and seldom reach 6 inches across the carapace— most subsistence fishermen toss them back.

Dungeness crab are caught in shallower waters than either king or tanner crab, although it isn't unusual to catch all three species in the same pot. Best-producing areas for Dungeness seem to be along sea-facing sandy bottoms from 10 to 30 fathoms, although these crab are found in a wide range of depths and bottom types.

Fresh bait, usually herring, is important in catching Dungeness crab. The standard commercial pot used for Dungeness fishing is round, and diameters of 42 inches, 48 inches or even 60 inches are used. These pots are about 14 inches high and meshed with stainless steel wire.

In Alaska each Dungeness pot must have two circular escape rings of 4-3/8 inches minimum diameter on opposite sides of the pot so that pots that are lost will not continue to trap crab and hold them.

The average commercially caught Dungeness crab weighs about 2 pounds.

Many coastal residents of Alaska keep a crab pot or two continually fishing. Rose Anderson recently wrote *ALASKA*® magazine about how she and her husband, who both teach school at Old Harbor on Kodiak Island, fish for crab.

Every other day after school they take their 13-foot skiff for a 15-minute run down Sitkalidak Strait where they keep a crab pot.

Between them they pull the 50 feet of line until the 35-pound sports-type pot appears. On good days they average 10 to 20 crab. What they don't return to the water or don't use they share with friends.

Once the pot is aboard they untie the bottom opening and sort out the crab they want to keep, tossing the rest overboard.

They usually butcher the crab in the boat, cutting the legs from the body and the gills from the legs.

The bait container is rebaited with leftovers from their kitchen, usually salmon or meat scraps. The pot is then returned to the water until the next visit.

Most subsistence fishermen who take crab prefer to clean them at the shoreline, where wastes can be disposed of and the part to be cooked can be washed.

Break king crab into two sections before cooking. Dungeness may be cooked whole by dropping the live crab into boiling water. Cook in boiling sea water or salted fresh water for about 18 minutes for king crab, from 15 to 20 minutes for Dungeness or tanner crab..

After cooking, drop the cooked sections into cold water to cool the pieces rapidly.

Meat can most easily be removed by cutting the legs open with heavy scissors or shears. See photos on page 64.

Shrimp that can be taken in pots in Alaskan waters include the spot, often called the prawn, which is the largest, and measures up to nearly 12 inches in body length; the coonstripe, somewhat smaller, with maximum body size of about 5 inches; and the sidestripe,

which is similar in size to the coonstripe.

Spot shrimp are most often caught in rocky areas where there are underwater ledges or cliffs, often at depths to 40 or 50 fathoms. Coonstripe shrimp, probably the most common of the larger prawn-type shrimp in Alaska, like mud bottoms and may be caught in depths from 10 to 30 or more fathoms. Sidestripe shrimp also like muddy bottoms but may also be found where the bottom is smooth and sandy.

Shrimp pots commonly used by subsistence fishermen are made of welded steel frames of from 3/8- to 5/8-inch stock. They are rectangular—from 1½ by 1½ feet square and 2½ feet long to

Left — A pan full of fresh-caught coonstripe shrimp. (Jim Rearden)
Above — A 3-pound tanner crab, caught in a king crab pot at 40 fathoms. Long spindly legs are typical. Wristwatch is for scale. (Jim Rearden)

much larger sizes—with a tunnel in each end projecting into the pot and a side panel that can be opened to bait the pot and remove the shrimp.

The best results are gotten by pots with burlap or some other close-weave material around the frames to provide a dark environment. Pots covered with such material will outfish uncovered pots.

Shrimp pots fish better with hanging bait, and any oily bait that is fresh attracts shrimp. Herring is the most commonly used in Alaska because of its availability.

Shrimp are territorial creatures, and once a small pot (1½ by 1½ by 2½ feet) has caught 4 or 5 pounds of shrimp, no more will enter. Thus larger

pots, left to soak longer, catch more shrimp. Shrimp pot fishermen with smaller pots try to pull them at least once every 24 hours. Once bait has lost its freshness and oil attractiveness, shrimp will manage to slowly find their way out of the funnels.

Shrimp are easy to prepare for cooking. Simply snap their heads off and leave the tails, or bodies, to be cooked. Once they are cooked, they are easily peeled—and the white meat is ready to eat.

To cook shrimp, drop the headed shrimp into boiling sea water or salted water. They will immediately sink. When they float to the surface they are cooked and ready to be scooped out and cooled.

Subsistence regulations for crab and shrimp in Alaska are simple with generous limits:

Shrimp may be fished for with pots year-round, with no limit. The pot buoy should have the name and address of the owner who is fishing it, with the word "subsistence."

King crab subsistence fishermen south of 60° north latitude, which includes Cook Inlet, all of Southeastern Alaska, Kodiak, the Alaska Peninsula and the Bering Sea south of Nunivak Island, are limited to six crabs per person per day. In Southeastern, the king crab subsistence season is closed from April 1 to June 30, and when the season is open, only males 7 inches or larger in width of shell may be taken.

Dungeness crab may be taken year-round without limit throughout the state except that in Southeastern Alaska and in the Yakutat area there is a daily bag and possession limit of 20 crabs per person per day of crab that are at least 6½ inches across the carapace. Further, spears and gaffs are illegal for taking Dungeness crab in commercial fishing districts 1 and 13. Pots left unattended longer than 2 weeks must have the bait and bait containers removed and all doors secured fully open.

Tanner crab may be taken without limit, year-round and in all of Alaska except in Southeastern Alaska and Yakutat waters, where the possession limit is 30 crabs per day and pots left 2 weeks or more must have bait cans removed and doors secured open.

Buoys for all subsistence-fished crab pots must have the name and address of the owner written on them, with the word "subsistence." □

ALASKA STEELHEAD FEVER

By Loren Pitchford (Photos courtesy of the author)

Winter steelheaders in Alaska are infected with a fever. They're the fishermen who continually stare at calendars and whose eyes sparkle whenever they eyeball the weekends in September, October and early November. Their home calendars have big red circles drawn around all these days, none of which denote birthdays, wedding anniversaries, vacations or things that normal folks wish to be reminded of.

They also take their fishing gear off the shelf when everyone else is putting it away. Finally, steelheaders are the fishermen who love to stand knee-deep in ice-choked Alaskan streams, flailing the water for fish that usually won't cooperate.

Those infected with Alaska steelhead fever have a common bond with duck hunters, for both pick the worst time of the year and the least favorable weather to pursue their favorite sport. When it's raining buckets or the snow is falling, you can count on them being out in force.

For their efforts they usually catch little more than a cold or the first stages of pneumonia. Nevertheless, their numbers seem to be increasing as the infection spreads. They've even developed quaint little sayings among their select group — sayings like "Don't let any ice grow under your feet" or "Here's hoping that the stream is pea green and the sleet is always at your back."

Last fall I asked a semifrozen steelheader what kind of a fish the steelhead was.

"I can tell you about one, mister," he replied. "It was the biggest, toughest fish I ever saw. Meaner than an alleycat and twice as fast. I'd been fishing for almost six hours without a touch, and my hands were getting a bit numb. Well, then it happened. When I set the hook to him he came out of the water like he was going to leap clean up on the bank. It was a sight like I ain't never seen before. About three feet of shining silver with a crimson stripe down his side. Then he was gone, and I never saw him again."

"You mean, that's all there was to it?" I asked.

"Why sure," he replied, "what else would you expect?"

"Well, I figured you might want to get more than one fish on in six hours of fishing," I answered.

He responded quickly. "Naw, you can't expect more than that. What do you want, a miracle?"

With that he disappeared downstream, flailing the icy waters as he went. It was evident that this poor soul was in the more progressive stages of steelhead fever.

A biologist I talked with was more definitive in identifying this illusive fish. According to him, steelhead trout are the same as a rainbow trout with a biological name of *Salmo gairdneri*, which is harder to spell than it is to say. The steelhead is the one that

spends part of its life in salt water, whereas the fresh-water rainbow doesn't. Steelhead go out to salt chuck during the second year of maturity and return to the streams of their origin in their third or fourth years. Why they decide to return to ice-cold Alaskan streams in the fall, lay over during winter and spawn in the spring is beyond me, but that's what they do. Some genius attached the label "winter steelhead" to them, and that handle has remained.

When winter steelhead return from the ocean they appear similar in physical characteristics to salmon, with silver sides, white bellies and dark blue gray backs. After they have spent time in fresh water they darken and take on more of the fresh-water rainbow's characteristics, including the crimson red side stripes, pink coloration on the

If you're lucky, you'll end up with a beautiful native steelhead such as the one shown in this picture.

gill plates and dark spots along the upper body line and back.

Steelhead differ from salmon in their spawning cycle in that they fail to give up the ghost after they spawn; instead they spend another year in the ocean before returning to fresh water to repeat the spawning cycle. They do this for quite a few years, all the while increasing in size. This trait drives winter steelhead fishermen wild and may be one of the reasons they keep flailing the water year in and year out. They are hoping that someday a monster steelhead will finally attach itself to the other end of their frozen lines. The current Alaska steelhead record, caught in salt water in Southeastern Alaska, weighed more than 40 pounds.

I've found that if you hang around long enough with those who have been infected with steelhead fever, some method to their madness appears. Winter steelhead fishing does require the application of definite techniques.

Although steelhead are of the same genus and species as rainbow trout, when they return from the ocean into the fresh-water stream of their origin, all similarities stop. The fresh-water rainbow are usually hungry and will readily strike at artificial or natural baits that are properly presented; the steelhead will not. Steelhead have one thing on their minds when they return from salt chuck, and that is to get into action on the spawning grounds. Consequently, when a steelhead sees a flittering lure dance by, or an artificial or natural bait float by, its basic reaction is to attempt to destroy the object rather than devour it. The brighter the bait, the angrier the fish. Colors like flame orange, brilliant red, pearl pink or sunshine yellow painted over Okie Drifters, Corkies and Spin-N-Glos seem to infuriate this usually cautious customer. Glittering silver, brass or copper colors that are found on spinners and other lures are also apparently offensive to the steelhead. Old standbys like fresh salmon eggs, crawdad tails, worms (used mostly in other western states) and fresh shrimp are often enticing enough to be noticed and struck at.

There's more to winter steelheading than just the color and type of bait or lure, however. If you're not fishing properly, you can turn blue from the cold and cast until arthritis sets in and it will do you little good. I've seen a lot of fishermen that fall into this cate-

The author poses with trophy native winter steelhead in the 14-pound class.

gory. They usually have big arms, an empty stringer and few kind words.

Rule number one in steelhead fishing is to fish the bait on or near the bottom of the stream. That's where the fish are. Steelhead are far from stupid when they are in clear Alaskan streams. They're going to select areas for their base of operations that provide safety and relaxation. Like any good strategist, they change these bases frequently.

The safest area in any stream is on or near the bottom, where the natural coloration of the fish blends with the streambed, thus providing suitable camouflage. The best areas for relaxation and rest are behind obstacles that shield the fish from swift currents. If you can find such a place, you may find a steelhead.

Naturally, you have to be on a stream that has a run of winter fish. In Southeastern Alaska that includes such streams as the Karta or Naha in the Ketchikan area, or the Situk near Yakutat. If you are on the Kenai Peninsula in Southcentral Alaska you'll fish shoulder to shoulder with other enthusiasts on streams like Deep and Stariski creeks or on the Anchor and Ninilchik rivers. Karluk River on Kodiak Island is the only stream that supports steelhead runs on that island.

If you happen to fish one of these streams during the fall and early winter, your chances are less than 50/50

that you will tie onto this great game fish. To improve the odds, you should use a leader that is around 12 to 14 pounds test and attach it to heavier terminal line about 14 to 16 inches from your bait.

At the point where you attach the line to the terminal gear you should leave a drop line to which a 3/16-inch hollow-core pencil-lead sinker can be attached. Or you can use solid-core pencil-lead and surgical tubing that is attached to the terminal gear. The length of the pencil-lead sinker varies, depending upon the depth and current speed of the stream. Usually 1¼- to 2-inch lengths will do the trick. The object is to have enough weight on the line so that your lure or bait will bounce along the bottom.

Once you have located a spot on a stream that appears to offer steelhead a suitable place of refuge, approach the area with caution, keeping far enough away so as not to disturb your quarry. Cast your offering immediately above the place where you think the fish is lying. If you have the proper weight on your line, you'll feel it bouncing along the bottom, which means that your bait is in the same vicinity. If a steelhead isn't there, which is probably more than 95% of the time, you'll get good practice in casting. If he is there and happens to be in the mood for destroying something, you're in for a real experience. Set the hook and hang on. □

RIVERBOATS
ARE FOR SPORT FISHING

Author with the riverboat used on the Kantishna trip, described in text. Boat is 24-feet long, aluminum, with a 50-horsepower propeller driven outboard on a lift. Handle seen to left of outboard and control station is for raising lift. (ADF&G)

By Michael J. Kramer

Most riverboats in Alaska are flat-bottomed craft 16 to 24 feet, or more, in total length and 48 to 60 inches in bottom width. Stability and load capacity increases with greater width and length.

Alaska riverboats are used for hauling freight, transporting of people, hunting and, perhaps most popular for sport fishing. Boating fishermen cover more country in search of fish and can fish more remote areas thus generally catch more fish.

The two most popular materials for constructing riverboats in Alaska are wood and aluminum. Wooden boats are usually home-built and the sides and bottom are covered with fiberglass cloth and resin for strength, water-tightness and to reduce drag.

Wooden boats are used mainly in large, deep rivers where chances of running up on rocky bars is minimal; high-speed contact with rocks or gravel bars is hard on wooden hulls. The more popular and more durable all-aluminum riverboats (manufactured to Alaskan specifications) are more expensive, but they can be used with confidence in large, deep rivers as well as in shallow, rocky-bottomed rivers. Properly cared for, a good aluminum riverboat will last a lifetime.

Aluminum boats are not indestructible, but leaks and rents can be repaired overnight with aluminum patch kits available at hardware stores and boat shops.

The outboard motor to be used with a riverboat must be matched with the size of the boat and the load to be carried. If you are going to use a boat for fishing with a friend or two, a 16- to 18-foot-long boat with a 35- to 50-horsepower motor will do the job. If you plan to take your family, or four or five people plus camping gear, you'll need a 20- to 24-foot boat with a 50- to 100-horsepower outboard motor. This will give adequate horsepower to push all that weight (up to about 1,000 pounds) upriver. You won't break speed records, but if speed is important to you, motors with horsepower rates of up to 235 are available.

A motor lift is a good investment in Alaska if you plan to use a propeller on your motor. A lift is a hinged transom that allows the operator to lift the propeller (and the entire motor) away from the river bottom — and out of the water if necessary.

This is necessary when the boat hits a shallow riffle; it saves wear and tear on the propeller and will keep you from getting hung up on a bar.

A couple of years ago I made a riverboat trip with Steve Tack, a fellow fishery biologist, to survey the entire Kantishna River and its tributaries to

Lake Minchumina, which is the geographic center of Alaska. We didn't know much about the area so we allowed a week for travel and sampling of fish populations. We used a 24-foot aluminum riverboat with a 50-horsepower propeller-driven motor installed on a lift, which we launched in the Tanana River at the village of Nenana, about 55 road miles southwest of Fairbanks; three and a half days later we entered Lake Minchumina after traveling the entire length of the Kantishna River, with frequent stops to sample fish populations in various tributaries. There were beautiful clear-water streams along the way where we stopped to sport fish for arctic grayling. Grayling fishing was very good and we had to talk ourselves into completing the survey trip.

The entire journey covered about 270 river miles, and the rig we used was ideal. The rivers we traveled were

An outboard motor with a jet unit attached. Motor is clamped to a lift. (ADF&G)

wide and deep, although we did use the lift often when we found shallows, which are common in rivers like the Tanana and Kantishna that are dirty with glacier-ground silt. Once we had to hop out and drag the boat into deep water.

A few weeks later we traveled upstream on the Salcha River, 40 miles east of Fairbanks, in a quite different riverboat. We couldn't have successfully used the same boat used on the Kantishna trip because the clear-water Salcha is shallow with many rocky

A riverboat being used for a moose hunting and sport fishing trip on the Nowitna River, a tributary of the Yukon. Note extra outboard, normally carried by most riverboats on long trips, the large barrel of fuel, and the motor mounted on a lift. (ADF&G)

riffles. We had to use a shallow-water rig to reach popular grayling fishing holes, where we wanted to conduct a creel census.

On that second trip we used a 20-foot aluminum riverboat with a 65-horsepower motor and an outboard jet unit, which replaced the propeller. Such jet units enable a boat to travel in much shallower water than a propeller-driven boat, even with a lift. A jet-powered boat needs only three to four inches of water, while 14 to 15 inches are needed for a propeller-driven boat.

Jet-powered outboards are becoming more popular with Interior Alaska residents, despite the fact that they lose about one-third of the motor's horsepower and burn slightly more gas. Jet owners claim they make up for this by being able to take shortcuts through shallow side sloughs and by traveling more or less in a straight line rather than remaining in deeper water as must be done with a propeller-equipped outboard.

Riverboats are used extensively in villages along the Yukon, Kuskokwim, Kobuk, Susitna, and Copper rivers. Most boats in the villages are wooden, homemade, sometimes 30 feet long, with 3-foot-high sides and an upturned bow to break through waves, which are common in the windy areas of these rivers. Most riverboats, however, are 18 to 20 feet long. Commercially manufactured aluminum boats have become more common in river towns and villages in recent years.

The Kenai River on the Kenai Peninsula, south of Anchorage, has experienced an increase in the use of riverboats because of the sudden popularity of sport fishing for king salmon and the desire of fishermen to get away from crowds to get where the fish are.

The desire to get away is one of the most important reasons for riverboat ownership, whether it is for a week-long northern pike fishing trip in the numerous sloughs and creeks emptying into the Yukon River or simply a weekend trip after arctic grayling from Fairbanks up the clear-water Chena. □

How I Catch Kenai Reds

Story, photo and illustrations by Mel Allen
Reprinted from ALASKA SPORTSMAN®'s
Alaska Fishing Annual, 1970-71

Three fine Kenai reds taken by the author. Only in recent years have red salmon assumed importance as sports fish.

There are five species of salmon in Alaska and two of them—the king and the coho—have long been the accepted hook-and-line fish. Only occasionally would the red, the pink or the chum salmon interest the sports fisherman by hitting a lure.

For many years prior to statehood, and after statehood until 1967, most of the thousands of red salmon taken by fishermen (we won't call them sportsmen) in the Russian and Kenai rivers were taken by snagging.

In 1967 the Board of Fish & Game made snagging illegal on the Russian River and created a flies-only fishery. All fresh-water snagging is now illegal in Alaska.

Red salmon will take flies if they are properly presented, and when hooked in this sportsmanlike manner, the red is fully as great a fighter for its size as the king and the coho.

Mel Allen is a fly fishing expert. Here he tells how to fly fish for and catch the fine Kenai red salmon.

Red fever was epidemic. The time was right, for the first salmon run had started into the Russian River on the Kenai Peninsula. I decided to seek the only known cure, and shortly I was drifting flies through my favorite stretch of river.

Before I could make my second cast, a commotion started downriver, and I stopped to watch what I call the "happy angler's dance." A short elderly gentleman was jumping in and out of the cold water as he wrestled a red salmon and bellowed "fish on" at the top of his voice.

I drifted a pale pink and red streamer over the cantaloupe-sized boulders on the bottom, knowing that the river held a plentitude of 9- and 10-pound silver tackle busters. They were suspicious of human shadow and motion, but they were less chary of a well-worked fly.

Soon I too performed the "happy angler's dance" sans jumping into the river and stripping my tonsils. I deny that I talk to myself. If nearby fishermen hear me mumble, they're wrong. I'm clearing my throat.

My first catch of the year, somehow the one remembered most vividly, happened in typical fashion. Suddenly the fly stopped. I struck, Nothing happened. I thought I was snagged on bottom. I struck again and my line shot straight out of the water as a fish exploded into view in a geyser of frigid spray. The line hissed through the water and the fish turned and almost climbed the opposite bank. It skimmed, half submerged, across the river's surface, then sank from sight. I gave him line and he took it freely. He swirled and headed downriver, as if back to sea, bucking, leaping and eating into my backing. I applied pressure, but not too hard; for me the thrill of fishing is the battle, not the netting.

The whip of my 9-foot fly rod began to absorb the fish's energy as I slowly guided the salmon to a quiet pool. I then got my first close look at my first red of the year. After enjoying his trim beauty I carefully removed the hook and watched him swirl into the deep pool.

He was a free fish, and the realization struck me that I was the one that was hooked. If you've fished, you'll know what I mean.

(Editor's note: *The Russian River is the major clear-water tributary to the glacial Kenai River of the Kenai Peninsula. Two runs of red salmon hit the Russian each year, with an average total run for both of nearly 65,000 fish. The early run normally starts between June 5 and 10 and averages 18,500 fish. The second and larger run starts between July 15 and 20 and averages 46,500 fish.*

While the average sports catch for the two runs has been around 15,000, unusually large runs allowed a record harvest of 62,000 Russian River reds in 1978, still achieving escapement goals, according to the Alaska Department of Fish & Game. Peaks above the average may occur about once in 8 years if conditions are right.)

The 1966 season, the last in which snagging was permitted, saw a catch of 21,800. Alaska's Board of Fish & Game then wisely passed a regulation prohibiting the taking of red salmon in the Russian River by snagging and limiting lures to flies only.

A conservation emergency helped to produce better sports fishing during the early run of reds into the Russian River. King salmon reached a critical low point throughout all of Cook Inlet, and in 1964 a complete closure was imposed upon both sports and commercial taking of kings. This meant that a month was cut from the commercial fisherman's season, which allowed more of the early-run reds bound for the Russian River to reach their spawning stream.

When ocean fresh, the red salmon, or sockeye, is a greenish blue fish with silver sides and a white belly; sexually mature and ready to spawn in fresh water, it becomes a brilliant red with an olive green head. Like other Pacific salmon the male developes a "kype," or a beaklike jaw, and a noticeably humped back. Once they reach this stage they are thin and without appetite. Such fish should be allowed to spawn unmolested.

All Pacific salmon mature in salt water and return to the stream of their birth for spawning. Usually reds spawn in a drainage where there is a lake for the young to grow in. All Pacific salmon die after spawning.

By spring the fry hatch and move into a lake where they spend from 1 to 3 years before migrating to sea. After 2 to 4 years at sea a red salmon weighs from 3 to 10 pounds, and during its fourth to sixth year of life it returns to spawn in its natal stream.

While they are growing and maturing in salt water, reds feed voraciously, but once they enter fresh water on a spawning run, most authorities agree they no longer feed.

If so, why do they hit flies and spinners? No one really knows, but there is a theory that I like, that flies resemble food, and that reds strike from sheer instinct prompted by years of frenzied salt-water feeding.

When most sports fish are really feeding they'll normally hit a lure or a fly traveling at almost any speed, and some species are consistently caught with fast retrieves. Not so with reds. I maintain that reds are lazy. As a rule they are noncooperative when flies or lures are fished fast. I have found that you just can't fish too slowly for reds. Watch the rocks, though, because they'll gobble up your flies.

It is generally agreed that fish are color blind, or at least they can't see the same spectrum as humans. I have noticed that when salmon are hitting, the color of the fly doesn't make much difference. I believe that under certain conditions some flies and color patterns are more visible in the water and therefore more effective.

Water conditions, then, have a lot to do with how to fish and what fly to choose. If the water is high, rough and discolored, large bright flies are needed. Natural-colored flies must be hard for salmon to see in the discolored Kenai River, because they have never produced for me, and the fish god knows I've certainly tried them.

In fishing fairly clear water you have greater freedom in selecting the right colored fly. In my experience, the smaller and lighter-colored fly is best. Here the neutral-colored flies—the tans, browns and grays—can be used with good results. You don't have to use smaller hooks; just use less fly tying material. I prefer a No. 4 fly when clear-water fishing for reds.

Fish on the bottom. That's the best advice I have to offer. It may not be the cheapest, but it is the most productive.

None of the Pacific salmon are surface feeders. The area in a stream from the water's surface to a few inches above the bottom is usually as barren as an empty creel. Reds hug the bottom. Some biologists think that salmon can maintain a better sense of orientation, plus feel more secure, with a greater thickness of water overhead. Also, irregularities on the river's bottom—irregularities like rocks or logs—tend to slow the current and provide shelter for resting fish.

If you are to catch reds, the technique of reaching bottom with each cast has to be mastered. Never hesitate to cast upstream if swift and deep water makes it necessary. If the water is shallow, cast across and/or slightly downstream. Adjust the depth as required by varying how far upstream or downstream you cast. Normally it is more desirable to cast upstream since it allows increased drift, thus a better opportunity to entice a fish into biting. It also presents the fly as a natural drifting bait.

Bottom-bouncing is a familiar technique if you fish with spinners or use wet flies or streamers. It simply means putting the lure on the bottom and keeping it there throughout the entire drift. There are many ways of accomplishing this.

Fly fishermen can use sinking lines, thus eliminating the need for sinkers or split shot. It may be necessary to weight the fly. If so, use minimum weight. A sinking line, a weighted fly and an expert fisherman is a devastating combination for red salmon.

Spinning tackle is most difficult to use successfully with flies, not due to the difficulty in casting them, but for numerous other reasons. Fly weight must be adjusted to suit water conditions, and the angler must learn to cast lightly weighted flies. Most likely the greatest problem confronting a spin fisherman is the balance between line, sinker, rod and reel. He has to keep his line tight without pulling the fly off the bottom. Enough weight is needed to keep the inherent kinks out of the heavy monofilament line for good accurate casting, yet it must be light enough to keep from snagging every rock in the stream. When a spin fisherman masters these principles, he is usually successful in taking red salmon.

There are almost as many ways to weight a spinning line as there are fishermen. I have used all of those pictured with this article and feel that any of these methods is workable. I personally prefer the neoprene tubing steelhead-type rig, which is simply a short piece of neoprene tubing wired to a tri-swivel, with a small size of pencil lead stuck inside.

It is difficult to feel a strike when using a sinker; even with a fly rod it is difficult to know for sure when it is a sinker hitting bottom or a red salmon tapping a fly.

One of the most deadly methods in high or discolored water is to slowly work the fly, then let it drop back down the current by letting out line, either fast or slow, varying the action to reach different depths. Even holding the fly steady in one spot for a long time with the rod at a right angle to the current so the action of the rod tip holding the fly against the pull of the current is imparted to the fly is extremely productive. Although this is an old trout fishing trick, it works very well on all salmon.

Probably the most difficult part of wet fly or streamer fishing is knowing when you have a strike in time to set the hook. Even when fishing downstream, there is usually enough slack in

Fig. 1 — The productive yarn fly is used by many anglers. Fluorescent yarn is best; yarn should be combed before using.

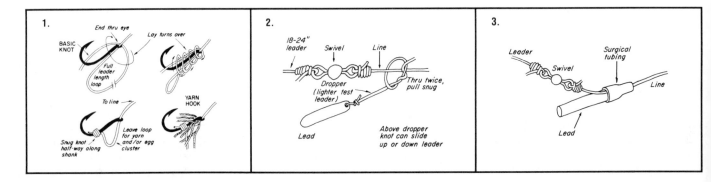

the line to give salmon some chance of spitting out the hook. The percentage of hooked fish per strike is far less in streamer and wet fly fishing than possibly any other technique of angling. It seems almost impossible on some days to hook a salmon.

All I can suggest is to fish and fish and fish and build up a sixth or seventh sense that will enable you to respond to every change, no matter how slight, in the way the line and fly drifts or acts. Every vibration, even if imaginary, and every flash or change in the water is important. When you strike without knowing why, and suddenly find your fly fast to a salmon, you are on the way to being a good red fisherman.

And when you can handle the upstream cast and feel the strike, you're in, man, you're in.

I feel that most red salmon fishermen cause too much movement of the fly. Don't work that fly—you'll pull it off the bottom, away from the fish. Use the natural drift method.

Red salmon running the clear Russian River are hard to see in the shadows or in the boiling water. It's hard to conceal yourself from them. This is why most fishermen work the holes, the deep runs and the murky water near the mouth.

Volumes have been written about the exact shade or color which is the best fly for use in certain waters. For red salmon, in my opinion, the attractor type of fly is best. They don't imitate anything but are designed purely for attraction. Almost any color will work on reds. Flies are interesting, pleasing to tie and use when one has time to experiment. But many patterns aren't necessary, or at least they haven't been for me.

It is my theory that salmon, when

Fig. 2-6 — All of these set-ups are excellent methods for getting flies on the bottom, where the reds are. A minimum of 18-inches between fly and sinker is a legal requirement in the Russian River.

they see a fly moving through water, can distinguish density (lightness or darkness) of a fly and its size. Using this theory, whether it be fact or not, has made it possible for me to catch more and larger trout as well as salmon. What I am trying to prove is that the fly itself may not be as important as its density and the way it is presented.

Effective density of a fly, and effectiveness of a fly size, can be altered by the color of water, depth, amount of sunshine, clouds, darkness and shadow. Consequently, to meet changes, you should adjust by altering color patterns to insure adequate visibility. I don't mean, necessarily, that you should use gaudy flies. Most fishermen have found that the basic colors of red, orange and yellow are best for the Russian. I agree that these flies work well, especially early in the season. However, I feel that white or a light color mixed with a brilliant or dark color plus being sparsely tied is far more efficient than a solid color. This, I maintain, is due to density contrast.

If you really want action, try fishing some fluorescent pink with red, blue, orange or even yellow flies. The pink seems to be better than white on early season reds, and my guess is it is due to its visibility in murky water. Also, light patterns seem to take more fish as the season progresses, perhaps due to clearer water. White and brown and pink and brown are real killers.

Two years ago on a fine sunshiny day I was on the Russian trying to catch some second-run reds. I started with orange, switched to red, then to yellow with no success. I finally tried a Muddler Minnow, a brown trout pattern well-known to western trout anglers. I was shocked—two casts and two reds. After thinking about it I decided that I had been fishing clear water about 3 feet deep and the bright patterns had been spooking the fish instead of attracting them. This made me

an advocate of the shaded and light patterns.

I finally lost the Muddler after catching and releasing nine reds.

I have often seen anglers cast into the glacial Kenai water with brilliantly colored flies to get strike after strike. This is no accident; the fish are using the murky water as concealment. In such water they can see the brilliantly colored flies.

I tie my own flies, but I don't try to tie perfect imitations. Instead I tie a few patterns that are easy and quick to make. I feel that in fly tying simplicity is best. I've used yarn on snelled steelhead hooks with good results. Hooks, of course, are important. Russian River reds are strong. I prefer the popular and strong steelhead hooks such as the Mustad No. 7970 in a No. 4 or No. 6 size.

I'm impressed with flies that have built-up bodies because they seem to give better results; my guess is it is due to their density. Practically any material can be used to mold a nice shapely body—silk floss, wool, fur and chenille are a few examples. Most of my coho flies have dyed wool bodies. If I fish murky waters, I use a dark, fluorescent wool to provide a better silhouette. If I fish clear water, I select a lighter color, such as yellow, pink or white for the body. Don't disregard fluorescent colors in clear water, though, especially if you tone them down by using light-colored hair wings. Density appears to be important.

It's a fair bet that when your salmon fly is properly drifted, regardless of type of fly, a salmon will grab it. You can argue about patterns, color and types, but a fisherman who most frequently does the "happy fisherman's dance" is the guy who spends his time on the stream learning how to present those flies on the bottom, and matching the fly density with water conditions.

That's the real secret in fooling reds. □

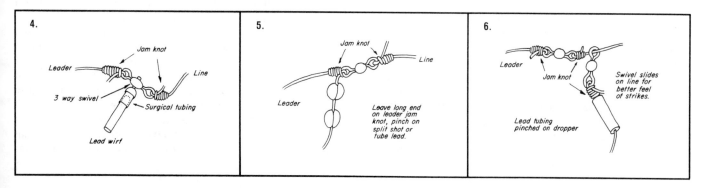

How to Avoid Bears While Fishing

By Dave Hardy

Four fisheries' biologists in hip boots trudged up a shallow stream that pours into Upper Russian Lake on Alaska's Kenai Peninsula. They were sampling riffles for the eggs of red salmon. Jim Browning towed the 14-foot skiff loaded with gear. Dave Nelson walked beside the skiff while Rance Morrison and Jim Friedersdorf waded behind. All were intent on their work.

Without warning a brown bear appeared in the stream. From 30 feet it charged with ears back and ruff erect. The spray flew as four angry paws splashed closer. Jim Browning fled, only to trip and sprawl face down in the creek. Rance and Jim surged to the side of the stream. Dave reached into the skiff and grabbed a 12-gauge shotgun, lifted it, fired, pumped and fired again. Another shot rang out as Rance placed the final bullet with his .44 magnum pistol.

The barren sow was dead, with shotgun slugs in the neck and under the ear. All thoughts of work ended as the biologists talked in trembling voices, the adrenaline filtering out of their systems. Soon they dragged the bear out of the stream and skinned her. By law the hide and skull of any bear killed in defense of life or property must be surrendered to the Alaska Department of Fish & Game.

The incident was later summarized in an official report by David Nelson. "There was no warning and no known provocation on the part of the individuals involved. I killed the animal at a distance of about 10 feet. At that time it was approximately five feet from another member of our group."

Sobering words. Although brown bears prefer to avoid people, that bear could have encountered any of the thousands of fishermen who blithely wander the banks of the Russian River. She chose instead a group of four armed men and died as a result.

No one will ever know why she charged. Very likely she was startled and was suddenly forced to choose between fighting or fleeing. Maybe she thought Jim was the sole intruder and saw the others only after she was committed to fighting. Maybe she fled in the only open direction, downstream between the dense, brushy banks. Maybe she had a toothache or had just gotten up on the wrong side of the alders that morning.

How bears behave is a subject of great interest. As a game biologist with the Alaska Department of Fish & Game, I have fielded many questions about bears. For starters I usually provide a copy of an ADF&G pamphlet called *The Bears and You*, which covers all the basics and is available free from the Alaska Department of Fish & Game, Subport Building, Juneau, Alaska 99801.

When I hike a salmon stream that's anywhere off the beaten path, I carry a weapon. I prefer a .375 H. and H. magnum bolt-action rifle, but others prefer a 10- or 12-gauge repeating shotgun loaded with slugs or buckshot. I once killed a big boar brownie with a .30-'06 rifle, which I consider the smallest gun that affords adequate protection. Pistols are better than nothing, mainly because an armed person acts with greater confidence when meeting a bear. (Let's face it though, even a .44 magnum, that most powerful of pistols, packs less wallop than a .30-30, the old favorite deer rifle.) The important thing is to be familiar with your firearm. You must be able to place your shots accurately and rapidly, which takes *practice*.

Two years ago a U.S. Forest Service fire patrolman stumbled onto a brown bear on a trail by a Kenai salmon river. At 25 feet the first shot from his .357 magnum revolver struck the bear in the eye. He then emptied his pistol into the critter and climbed a tree. That bear had to be dispatched by a nearby fisherman packing a .300 magnum rifle.

As a firm believer in the "umbrella principle," I know a bear will never show if I'm armed and ready. Good. That's all the more reason to pack firepower. Under Alaska law, a hunting license is not required for packing a gun in the woods. Canada does not allow handguns across its borders, however, so leave pistols behind if you are driving to Alaska.

Because bears usually leave unseen whenever they see or smell a person, visitors are often unaware that their paths have crossed a bear's. Even most bear encounters don't require any shooting. If you meet a bear and it stands on its hind legs and moves its head from side to side, chances are that bear is trying to figure out what it has come upon. Help the bear. Holler and jump up and down. Tell him you are human and smell bad and he'd rather eat a fat old king salmon. Blow a whistle. Clang a cowbell. Shoot off roman candles (except in fire season). Fire a shot into the ground. Do anything to convince the bear that you are not prey. Most of the time it will leave. Sometimes it will drop to all fours and run at you, then stop and raise up again. *Don't panic and run.* Redouble your efforts to tell it of your strangeness.

Bears' eyes distinguish movement well. They are not superior at recognizing form and color. If a bear can't smell you, then its ears are a main source of sensory input.

That's the trouble with fishing. Stream noises mask your sounds and winds that blow up or down the valley are wrong about half the time. Bear numbers are high along most salmon streams, and such streams commonly meander with lots of short reaches and bends. Banks are dense with vegetation, and visibility is curtailed. Both you and the bear are concentrating on your fishing. Sounds dangerous, doesn't it?

You can minimize the danger by

fishing so that the scents of soap or old fishing shirts waft ahead of you. Make noise. Sing. Whistle. Strap a bell on your belt. In really high-density bear areas, ADF&G salmon counters sometimes explode firecrackers every 100 yards or so. The idea is to do everything possible *not* to startle a bear at short range and to give it time to leave gracefully.

If you do see a black or a brown bear in the next pool and it hasn't seen you, back out of there very quietly. You both will appreciate the courtesy. If this happens several times, I suggest that another stream may be where you really want to fish.

Sows with cubs are especially dangerous. Young cubs often play in streamside brush while mama fishes. It behooves a fisherman to give a bear in a stream a wide berth. A startled squall from a cub is a frightening sound but not half as frightening as the crashing of brush made by its charging mother.

In the mid-1950's my father Mal Hardy, a U.S. Forest Ranger, took a party of timber buyers ashore on an island in Southeastern Alaska. They were only traveling a quarter of a mile, and he foolishly left his rifle in the skiff. As luck would have it they ran

into two small cubs and one very large sow in a small clearing; the cubs' squalls and the sow's bellow of rage sounded almost simultaneously. Before anyone could holler "bear," five men were up five trees, with the sow circling angrily, searching for an intruder to fight. After the sow left they climbed down and headed toward the beach, only to see a young single bear near the water. The lesson of always carrying a firearm was thus doubly reinforced.

Sometimes a bear that is startled at very short range will charge in your direction. If you are unarmed and on a narrow trail, your best bet is to dive headfirst to the side. Lock hands over your neck and lie face down. That "fight or flee" switch is one a bear can flip at anytime. It may actually be charging, but your act of vacating the field of combat allows it to retreat gracefully. If it decides to fight, then you are as well-protected as you can be, particularly if you have a pack-frame on your back. If you are armed, the choice of what to do in the situation is yours.

Bear sign can be easily seen, even by the greenest cheechako. Partly devoured salmon carcasses, bear tracks in the mud, gray and runny droppings laced with fish bones and a two-lane trail beside the stream all point to continual bear use.

Bear densities are greatest at streamside and decrease with distance from the banks. However, bears often wander into the brush and settle down for an afternoon snooze. Always exercise caution in dense cover near streams.

It is the height of foolishness to pitch a tent or sleeping bag on a streamside bear trail. When floating a river, choose sites on islands or in places that show little bear use. Make camp downwind from bear-use areas. Most rivers have favored fishing holes and long, relatively empty stretches between.

A friend and his companion once pitched their tents on a sand bar at twilight after a long day's float down a river. That it was the wrong sand bar became evident when a shaggy visitor strolled between their two tents early in the morning. At daylight they found

The author and a bear share a fishing hole along an Alaskan river. Fishing this close to bears is not recommended. (Hans Sandquist)

Sows with cubs are short-tempered. This sow lit into the intruding bear seconds after the photograph was taken, and might have chased the fisherman-photographer if he'd come as close. (Dave Hardy)

a heavily used bear trail not 12 feet away.

Fortunately that bear was not attracted to the freeze-dried foods they had stored in a plastic bag at the other end of the bar. From habit they had cleaned up all traces of supper, washed dishes and burned their trash. Since a bear depends on his nose to find foods such as garbage or carrion, it makes sense to obliterate odors in bear country. Food packed in double plastic bags stays dry and doesn't broadcast "come hither" odors. Suspending food from a tree limb away from camp is a good practice. It always takes a lot more line than you figure to do the job properly, so carry plenty. A cloth sack on the outside will strengthen the plastic. No food should ever be kept in the tent.

Not all bears are gentlemen. Black bears and subadult brown bears are often ignorant about humans, and sometimes they are like the mule that requires a 2x4 to get its attention — they are hard to convince. Several years ago Chip Dennerlein guided a party of fishermen down the Talachulitna River, in the Susitna basin. Into camp wandered a very dumb, very forlorn black bear. A yearling, his ma had kicked him out of the nest and he wanted a friend. Chip hollered and threw things at it. Nothing. He screamed and shouted. Nothing. Chip finally fired his .357 over the bear's head from 10 feet away. The bear jumped back several feet and gave him a reproachful look. After 15 minutes of watching the bear, Chip got mad. When the bear finally turned and started lumbering into the cook tent, Chip kicked his sturdy hiking boot, which moved the youngster's rump several feet past the door flap. *That* the bear understood, and scurried 20 yards to scratch his way up a tree. Soon it slid down and ambled off into the woods, looking back several times. That bear was unusual. For obvious reasons I can't recommend Chip's method.

That particular bear had the potential of becoming a panhandler or camp-ground bear, the most dangerous but least respected of all Alaskan critters. When bears enter campgrounds and root through garbage, people assume they are harmless. Not so. Those cute black bears are more unpredictable and more dangerous than a boar grizzly stalking the tundra. *Don't feed them.* Don't press close to photograph them. Sooner or later someone will make a false move and that someone will be hurt, and the bear will have to be destroyed.

It is unnatural for bears to subsist on hot dogs and peanut butter sandwiches. Bears and men are not natural companions, not the friends portrayed by the fictional *Gentle Ben* or *Grizzly Adams.*

The Alaska Department of Fish & Game will not, as a general rule, transplant a troublemaking bear. That animal has lost its fear of humans and poses a threat to anyone who ever meets up with it. Such bears are usually destroyed. The blame must rest on those who fostered the unnatural behavior.

One sure-fire bear lure is the odor of hot salmon glazed in brown sugar. From all appearances bears like smoked salmon better than humans. Smoking fish beside your camper is like sending an engraved invitation, asking a bear to visit your camp.

Bears are also attracted to fish entrails and scraps. Clean your fish at streamside and throw the offal into moving water. Many Lower 48 fishermen consider such behavior irresponsible. The reverse is true. Nature litters the bottom of streams with thousands of whole carcasses of spent salmon every year. The breakdown of their flesh helps fertilize the stream.

Here are my ten commandments for fishermen:

1. When fishing a back-country salmon stream carry the most powerful weapon you are comfortable with.
2. Make noise, and fish with the wind at your back.
3. Don't camp on or near bear trails.
4. Burn food garbage and pack out the remains.
5. Wash dishes, especially frying pans, after use.
6. Store food in plastic bags away from camp, preferably suspended out of reach.
7. Never leave food in your tent.
8. Clean fish at streamside and throw the offal into moving water that will carry it off.
9. Treat campground bears with caution. Don't feed or crowd them.
10. Respect bears.

Bears are beautiful animals that all too often catch the short end of the stick in their dealings with man. In Alaska's wilderness, the tableaux of salmon-chasing bears in crystal streams has long been maintained. It is man who is the intruder. Adopt my rules as your own and your intrusion will be minimal, your chance of conflict small. With luck you may see a wild Alaskan bear in its habitat. Such an encounter may well be a high point of your life. Good luck and safe fishing. □

Want That Fish Mounted?

By Cliff Jeska and Darrell Farmen
Photos by Cliff Jeska

The handling a fish receives in the field is the most important step toward a good fish mount. What to do is determined by how long you will be in the field and how far you are from your taxidermist. Basically there are three different procedures for taking care of a fish that is to be mounted.

Fish deteriorate rapidly, and this deterioration is accelerated if the fish is not kept cool and moist. After you have landed your fish, the first step is to kill it. Do not allow the fish to beat itself to death on the shore or in the boat. A knife blade pushed through an eye and back into the brain cavity is a fast, efficient means of killing any fish. Next take a few close-up color photos of the fish. The photos will aid the taxidermist in getting a good color reproduction on your mount.

The procedure you choose next is determined by how far you are from your taxidermist or how long you will be in the field. Procedure #1 is the simplest: put the fish on ice or wrap it in a wet cloth and put it in the shade. Do not leave it in the water or on a stringer. If you can get the fish to a freezer in a few hours, do it. Wrap the entire fish in wet paper towels, especially the fins, put it in a plastic bag and freeze it. It is best if frozen flat and not in some odd shape.

Follow Procedure #2 if it will be several hours before you can get your fish to a freezer. It will stay fresh much longer if internal organs and gills are removed. Don't cut it up the belly. Belly-cut fish are almost impossible to mount with good results. Instead, decide which side of the fish will be the show side. Choose the side that is in best condition (the side with fewer scales missing, fewer or no scars). Now, on the opposite, or nonshow, side, make an incision just below the lateral line, into the body cavity. The cut should run from the head to a point a few inches in front of the anus. Remove the internal organs by cutting them from the head. After this has been completed, the fish can be wrapped in wet cloth or put on ice. Ice will keep a fish fresh only for about two days. When you get home, prepare the fish for freezing as previously described.

Procedure #3 is the most difficult and should be used only if you are going to be in the field for several days and cannot get to a freezer and don't have enough ice.

The fish must be skinned, but before skinning it, you must make a pattern so the taxidermist won't have to guess how big it was. Place the fish on a piece of paper, show side up, and draw around the body (**photo #1**). Next, at the areas indicated in photo #1, measure or approximate the thickness of the body and mark it on the pattern. At those same points take circumference measurements and write them next to the corresponding thickness measurements (**photo #1**). Also note any physical characteristics of the fish on the pattern in the appropriate areas. Some descriptions of color patterns or shades can also be written on the pattern if you can't photograph the fish. Any other information about the fish or where it was caught may also be helpful to the taxidermist. Once this has been completed you can skin the fish.

The first step in skinning is to make an incision on the

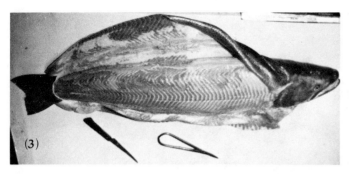

(3)

(7)

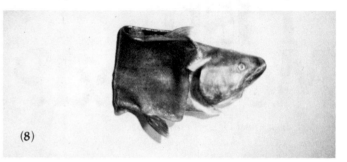

(8)

nonshow side from the head to the base of the tail. Make a T cut at the tail. Next, cut through the bone at the back of the gill cover (**photo #2**). Now cut the tip of the throat loose from the head. Peel and cut the skin away from the body, toward both the back and the belly. A dull knife works best for this since it is less likely to slice the skin. When you reach the base of a fin, cut or snip the fin roots from the body (**photo #3**). When the dorsal, anal, pectoral and pelvic fins have been cut free, move to the tail. Cut through the backbone as close to the tail as possible (**photo #4**).

Now lift the body from the tail end and carefully cut so the skin falls away from the body. Continue doing this until

(4)

(5)

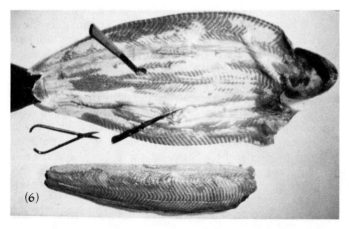

(6)

you have reached the head (**photo #5**). Next cut through the backbone at the head and remove the body completely. Before you cook the fish for dinner, check the skin. Remove any large pieces of flesh from the skin, being careful not to knock scales loose, for scales must be replaced one at a time if they are lost, so take care in handling the skin. This is more of a problem with salmon from salt water, which have loose scales, than it is with fresh-water fish (**photo #6**). Once this has been done the skin can be rinsed in water to remove excess blood and debris.

Spread the skin out, scale side down, and cover the entire skin with salt, spreading it evenly about one-eighth of an inch thick. Don't forget to salt the inside of the head. Put the skin in a cool, shady place for about an hour so it can drain. After the salt has removed most of the moisture, fold the skin over so it looks like a flattened fish (**photo #7**). Now carefully fold the tail toward the middle, then fold it again. Be careful to not fold it tightly or scales will be knocked loose. Continue folding the skin over loosely until you come to the head (**photo #8**). The skin can now be packed with more salt in a plastic bag or several bags. Keep the skin as cool as possible, in the shade and covered with a wet cloth. A skin so handled should keep for a week or more if it is properly packed in salt so excess moisture is removed.

When you return home, freeze the skin by placing the entire package in the freezer. When you take the fish to the taxidermist don't forget the pattern. Explain to him what you have done and tell him what you want him to do. He should not charge extra for mounting your skinned fish if you have done it properly and your pattern is fairly accurate.

If you have followed all the steps carefully, you can expect to end up with a lifelike trophy (**photo #9**). □

Cliff Jeska owns Silver Eagle Taxidermy in Anchorage, which he started in 1977 after working in three different taxidermy shops. In addition to skin mounts over styrofoam bodies, he offers fiberglass reproductions of fish.

Darrell Farmen is part-owner of D&C Expediters, Anchorage, which fleshes, salt-cures and dries, and ships to taxidermists, raw Alaskan trophies.

MAJOR FISHING REGIONS

Many lakes in Alaska offer good grayling fishing, such as this small lake 1 mile from Chitina, along the Edgerton Highway. (Sharon Paul, staff)

Southeastern Alaska

Compared with the main part of the huge peninsula that is Alaska, the Panhandle, or Southeastern Alaska, is a small region. It includes an area roughly 125 by 400 miles, and much of this is deep green and clear water, and straight up and down mountains, many of which rise directly from salt water.

Game fish are primarily salmon and trout, and both use the salt water and the numerous streams and lakes to complete their life cycle.

Geologically, it has been only in recent years that much of Southeastern Alaska has been freed of overlying glaciers. There are still glaciers here that flow down to the sea to drop their huge "calves" into the green water. Almost the only flat lands are a coastal strip south of Yakutat Bay in the north, and around river mouths and valleys, as left by retreating glaciers.

Between Lituya Bay and Glacier Bay, again in the north, some of the highest and most spectacular mountains in all of North America rise directly from the sea. Mount Fairweather, for example, stretches to 15,300 feet.

This is the wet part of Alaska, for it lies in the path of the great storms that come across the Gulf of Alaska. When the storms hit the glaciered peaks, they dump their load. There is well over 100 inches of precipitation in the southern section around Ketchikan, while at Yakutat, the northerly limit of Southeastern Alaska, annual average of precipitation is 133 inches.

With such abundant precipitation, there is little sunshine. Temperatures are moderate, and the residents live in rain gear without thinking much about the rain.

As a result of the moisture and mild temperatures, a lush and almost tropical flora is found. Below timber line is the so-called rain forest of western hemlock, Sitka spruce, red cedar and Alaska yellow cedar, jack pine and alder. Berries are found almost everywhere. Interspersed among the tall green conifers are open muskeg swamps where grasses, flowering plants and more berries are found. Deer use areas along the fringes of these openings.

Islands, big and small, dominate Southeastern Alaska: Admiralty, Baranof, Chichagof, Kupreanof, Kuiu, Prince of Wales, Revillagigedo, Zarembo and dozens of others. Admiralty, Baranof and Chichagof are brown bear country, where the huge bruins are famed for their size and abundance.

You don't drive a car to travel about Southeastern Alaska, for there are virtually no highways, except for short distances out of the villages and towns. Boats and airplanes are relied upon.

There is much life here. Sea birds flock on the waters. You glimpse deer along the beaches. Snow-white goats peer down at lowlanders from high on the rugged slopes. There are seals, and whales and porpoises. And fish. This land was designed for fish. They derive their energy from the rich waters, and come to the net or gaff fat and full of life.

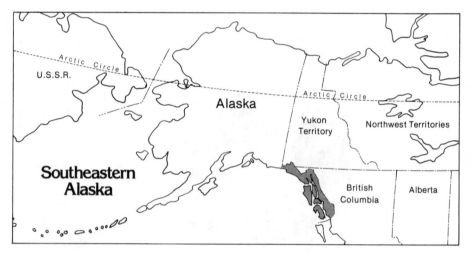

Watch yourself when fishing Southeastern Alaska streams. In summer few of them lack salmon, and where there are salmon streams, there are probably bears: perhaps black—which can be just as dangerous as a brown bear—or the king of bears, the great Alaska brown bear, grabbing salmon in his big jaws to walk ashore and pin it down with huge claws to rip the meat.

Travel in this green-clothed land of mountains and water is easy. You can quickly fly to Juneau, Sitka and Ketchikan direct from Seattle in a jet. There are scheduled flights from these cities to the smaller ports of Petersburg, Wrangell, Kake, Haines-Port Chilkoot, Klawock or wherever you want to go.

Or if you like water travel you can take one of Alaska's modern super

ferries out of Seattle, WA, or Prince Rupert, BC, and ride it to Haines or Skagway. You can take your car on the ferry or leave it. Hotel and motel accommodations are generally available throughout Southeastern Alaska. It is necessary to make reservations well in advance.

Best months for Southeastern Alaska fishing are from May to September, with July and August probably offering the most action in both salt and fresh water.

Within recent years fishing lodges and charter boat services have come into being in many locations in Southeastern Alaska. Consult *"The Guide Post®"* section, in the monthly *ALASKA®* magazine, $15. per year, to locate listings of guides, charter boats and accommodations. Also consult *The MILEPOST®*, $5.95, plus $.75 for fourth-class postage and handling or $2.50 first class, for information on accommodations and charter operators. Both publications are available from Alaska Northwest Publishing Company, Box 4-EEE, Anchorage, AK 99509.

You don't *have* to charter a boat or go to a fishing camp. You can fish on your own and make out fine. One of the finest deals available is to arrange for use of one of the 130 USFS cabins scattered throughout Southeastern Alaska. (See page 15.)

Warm clothing, preferably woolen, with good light rain gear and hip boots (or waders, your choice) is appropriate summer gear for Southeastern Alaska. Bring insect repellent. Southeastern Alaska does not have the mosquitoes of the Interior tundra, but they can be pesky. A pair of light cotton gloves comes in handy when you are fishing from a boat. The wind, usually wet, can get cold.

You'll want a variety of tackle if you want to sample everything from king salmon to the high-lake cutthroat. Heavy salt-water spinning gear is popular for king and silver salmon fishing. Trolling rods, salt-water type, with big star-drag reels are commonly used.

Lighter-weight spinning tackle is often used on cutthroat, rainbows and Dolly Varden. The fly-rod man will be in his element here, and a fairly heavy rod, perhaps 5 or 6 ounces, with a variety of wet and dry flies, will fit the fishing in most of the large or small streams of Southeastern, or they'll work fine in salt-water lagoons where the river and salt water join—where salmon lie, readying for the journey upstream, or where cutthroat trout, Dolly Varden and even rainbows grow fat and full of energy.

Southeastern Alaska has just about everything a sport fisherman can ask for.

Southcentral Alaska

Southcentral Alaska, for our purpose, includes Cook Inlet through Prince William Sound, and that vast arc south of the high-peaked Alaska Range.

Although this is an area about the size of Oregon—300 by 300 miles—it is not large by Alaskan standards.

This is the "populated" part of Alaska, with Anchorage as the metropolis. Half or more of Alaska's 400,000 population live in this varied region. This is where many of the state's highways are and where The Alaska Railroad runs.

While this is a "crowded" area by Alaskan standards, elsewhere it would be considered a virtual wilderness. Two of Alaska's great, silty rivers roll to the sea here—the huge, sprawling Susitna at the head of Cook Inlet, and the roily Copper, just east of Prince William Sound. Both have thousands

upon thousands of miles of clear tributaries, networks of rivers, streams, lakes, ponds, marshes, channels, sloughs. Both are rich in fish.

This is game country, too. The little but tough Sitka deer is found throughout Prince William Sound, which, incidentally, has more than a passing resemblance to Southeastern Alaska with its glaciers, fjords and heavy rainfall. This is also the land of the moose, with the Kenai Peninsula moose rated as the world's largest. There are brown bear, too, along the coastal streams of Lower Cook Inlet and the outer islands of Prince William Sound. Black bears are found in most of the area. Caribou roam the upper Susitna and Copper, wandering back

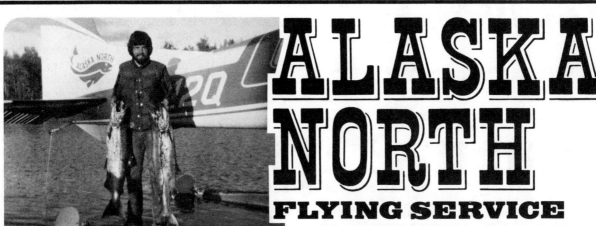

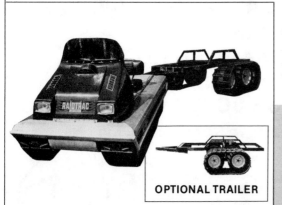
and forth across the rolling highlands that separate the two drainages. Goats ply their mountaineering trade around the great ring of rugged mountains that rim the heaving Gulf of Alaska. And in this great area are found the biggest of the white Dall rams.

But it's fish we're concerned with here, and fish there are. All five of the salmon home into Cook Inlet and Prince William Sound. This is about the northern limit of the steelhead's range, and a few of these silvery fish are found in streams of the southern Kenai Peninsula—Anchor River, Deep Creek, Ninilchik River, Stariski Creek. Try for them in late August, September or even October. You'll find many of these streams loaded with Dolly Varden at this time, too.

Move into the high lakes of the Kenai; perhaps you'll find the only grayling on the Kenai Peninsula.

Or charter an airplane out of Anchorage and fly to the Talachulitna River, a clear, gravel-bottomed beauty, and catch rainbows up to 5 pounds. If you're there in late July or August you'll get tired of removing spawning pink salmon from your hook, because in even-numbered years they are there by the thousands. There will be fewer on odd-numbered years.

If you want to sample a variety of rainbow trout fishing, try one of the canoe routes featured on the Kenai National Moose Range. There are dozens of lakes with connecting streams, all with colorful rainbows in them. Write to: Refuge Headquarters, Kenai National Moose Range, Kenai, AK 99611, for information.

To the east, in Prince William Sound, where the climate comes from the stormy Gulf of Alaska, you'll find an amazingly rich fauna and flora. Temperatures here rarely go below zero in winter or above 80°F in summer. Cordova is rainy; close to 100 inches falls in a year. Valdez is in the 60-inch bracket. Seward, on the western edge of the sound, is where the wind blows and where there is about 70 inches of precipitation annually.

This is Sitka spruce and western hemlock country, with dense alder patches near timber line. Cottonwood, birch, willow and other woody species are found. Grasses and berries of many kinds are abundant, especially on the Copper River Delta.

Streams of the sound are typically short and swift. They're great for

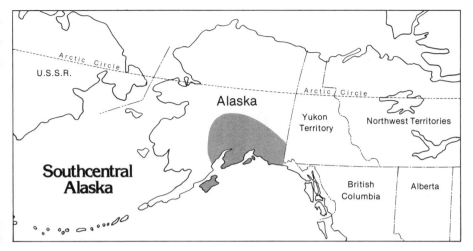

Southcentral Alaska

spawning pink and chum salmon, but not really the best type for sports fishing. *The* fishing in the sound is the clear green salt chuck, where the salmon school and the Dolly Varden follow. There are a few smooth-flowing clear streams there with cutthroat trout in them, but it is the most northerly point of the cutthroat range.

Fly over Prince William Sound on a clear, calm summer's day and you'll be treated to the most gorgeous sight imaginable. The water of the sound is often fairly calm, especially in the sheltered places. It is clear and deep. The islands are covered with magnificent conifers. There are great long beaches, mountains with huge glaciers. There are fjords, channels, lagoons and clear streams.

Follow the Copper River to its headwaters and you'll find a network of clear, gravel-bottomed rivers and streams that almost join a similar system of the upper Susitna. The streams are full of grayling. On the Copper side there are red salmon and king salmon. The lakes are full of lake trout, great potbellied, orange-fleshed fish of 20 to 30 pounds. The lakes are so numerous you can't count them. Timber line is at about 2,000 feet, and to the north loom the great peaks of the Alaska Range. It's a rolling land of vast distances. The air is brilliantly clear.

It's easy to fish Southcentral Alaska by using the fine paved highways that bisect it. Stop at stream crossings and go fishing. (It's usually not best right at the highway. Use the hour method. Leave the highway and walk up or downstream, as you wish, for one hour. Then fish your way back to your car. You'll find fish.)

Or, if you'd like to get away from the highways and the sound of trucks and cars and buy yourself a little piece of wilderness silence, stop at almost any of the major wayside lodges or any of the towns or villages in this huge area and charter a plane. Have the pilot fly you to a place that he knows about and leave you, with camp gear, with a date for his return. See pages 18-19 for approximate rates.

Or you can have one of the many Anchorage charter services drop you into the headwaters of one of the fine Susitna River tributaries—the Alexander, Deshka, Lake Creek or the Talachulitna—and you can use a kayak or a rubber raft to float the river, fishing as you travel. Your pilot can meet you at some point downriver.

Another variation is to climb aboard the daily train from Anchorage to Fairbanks and ask the conductor to let you off "where the fishin's good." He'll know. And the train will stop and let you off. You can stop the southbound train any day you wish to get back to Anchorage.

Many visitors drive via the Alaska and Glenn Highways and spend weeks exploring Southcentral Alaska, hiking for fish, or flying for fish. The variety is almost endless, and the fishing can be fabulous. Others fly from the South 49 directly to Anchorage and rent a car or a pickup truck with a camper and get to great fishing country in less time.

Spring, summer and fall clothing for Southcentral Alaska is about the same as you'd want for spring or fall months in coastal Oregon or Washington. Rain gear is occasionally necessary on the Kenai Peninsula during summer. The same is true for the valley of the Matanuska to the north. It is more frequently needed in Prince William Sound. Mosquitoes are bad in some areas, so have plenty of repellent.

Fishing tackle is up to the individual, depending upon what species you're after and how you like to fish. Light and heavy spinning gear is most popular and will handle the biggest of fish. Silver salmon, which start running in early August, are easily handled with light or medium spinning outfits, or even with a medium or heavy fly rod. Some of the waters in Southcentral Alaska, such as the Kenai River, are murky, but they hold plenty of fish. Fluorescent flies, bright "cherry bobbers," shiny and oversized spinners and other unusually visible lures will catch fish in such streams.

Most of the area away from the highways is virtually untouched. A short walk from the highway, a 15-minute hop in an airplane, and you will find yourself where the fish are.

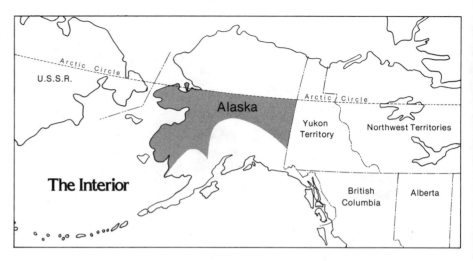

The Interior

The Interior – from Yukon Border to the Bering Sea

The Interior of Alaska is essentially a 250-mile-wide swath east and west from the Yukon Territory boundary to the Bering Sea.

Here Mother Yukon, Alaska's greatest river, flows southwesterly across the heart of the Great Land, dumping into the icy Bering Sea. The great muddy, twisted Tanana is born near the Canada-Alaska border, to the south of the Yukon River, and it parallels the Yukon until its heaving waters join it. Downstream, the Koyukuk crosses the Arctic Circle to add its clear, cold waters to the big river.

The great Kuskokwim River rises near Mount McKinley and for 350 miles more or less parallels the Yukon to also pour its waters into the Bering Sea.

These rivers drain virtually all the vast Interior between the arctic Brooks Range and the glacier-hung Alaska Range 250 to 500 miles to the south.

This is a land of water. There are huge lakes and great swamplands. There are murky waters and clear. Permafrost—permanently frozen ground—lies beneath much of this huge subarctic and arctic region, and the water can't seep into the earth. Instead it lies on the surface or flows across it, bound for the Bering Sea. Virtually all of the waters contain fish.

There is the grayling, the bread-'n'-butter fish of the North, with the familiar great sail on his back. There are slashing, toothy pike, voracious fish that catch and swallow half-grown ducklings. There are sheefish, fabled olive-silver-scaled fighters found only in the Far North, and rated by those who know them, among the finest sports fishes in North America.

And then there are lake trout, great potbellied, speckled beauties with

forked tails, waiting to break an unsuspecting angler's tackle. And that cousin to the eastern brook trout and the Dolly Varden, the arctic char, red-spotted, silvery fighters found in a swath across the arctic coast, in the wilderness of the Brooks Range and in the lower Yukon-Kuskokwim.

This is wilderness by any standard. There are more square miles of land per resident in this great reach of mountains, valleys, forests, rivers, lakes and tundra than in any other land under the American flag.

And more unfished waters.

Want to fish the Yukon River? You're not likely to catch anything in the Yukon itself; it's too muddy. But there are uncounted clear-water tributaries to the Yukon. There are many villages along the big river, and a few score of sportsmen do travel along the big river each year. But the very size of the Yukon is hard to grasp, and it has scarcely been touched by sport fishermen. Good fishing is available in every clear tributary that flows into the Yukon, from the Canadian boundary to the mouth.

Occasionally sportsmen fly to some of the streams that feed the Yukon, and once in a while those traveling down the Yukon may follow one of these upstream for a mile or so. But it is rare for any fisherman to go far up any of these streams—many of which are a hundred or more miles long.

The only other way to fish this region, besides using a riverboat to travel up or down the major streams, is to fly a bush plane to a selected spot, or series of spots. There are mail flights to virtually all villages in Alaska at least once a week, and the fare for such flights is seldom great.

Once at a village, the visitor will find

Alaskan hospitality at its best. Unless villagers are unusually busy in catching and drying fish or engaged in some other project, someone will most often be willing to hire himself and his boat out. And you can't beat local knowledge of where the fish are.

This is a land that is warm in summer and cold in winter, for it is sheltered from nearly all marine influence, except on the western or Bering Sea end. In the Interior, normally by October, ice in river sloughs will support a man.

The west end of our swath across the center of Alaska includes the Yukon-Kuskokwim Delta, which is a concentration of the rich soils washed downstream by the two rivers. This is flat country, lake country: from 30 to 50 percent of the delta is lake. In summer some of the world's greatest concentrations of ducks and geese and other waterfowl gather here to nest.

Fairbanks, the major city of the Interior, is connected to the south and east portions of the state by the George Parks and Alaska Highways, both good paved roads. The Steese High-

way leads northeast to Circle, AK, and the Elliott Highway leads northwest to Manley Hot Springs, AK. The North Slope Haul Road extends north to Prudhoe Bay, but is open to the public only as far as the Yukon River. These three roads are all well-maintained gravel roads. However, beyond this road system there are virtually no roads throughout the vast area that is the Interior.

This is airplane and boat country. Take a scheduled flight from Fairbanks or Anchorage to any of the major villages (Fort Yukon, Bethel, McGrath, Tanana, Koyukuk or any of a dozen others) and arrange to travel from the village either by airplane or by boat to the fishing area you want.

Don't go to any of the villages unless you are prepared to camp, for often there are no facilities to house visitors. Take a good tent and sleeping bag, cooking utensils and enough food. Food is costly and often scarce in bush villages.

July and August are probably the best months to fish this region, although you might find excellent

fishing variously from late May through September.

Take warm clothing, rain gear and plenty of insect repellent. Fishing tackle is your choice; you may have opportunities to catch fish weighing anywhere from 3 to 30 pounds.

Bristol Bay and the Alaska Peninsula

The Alaska Peninsula tapers off of southwestern Alaska and thrusts far into the North Pacific, eventually turning into the stepping stones that are the Aleutian Islands.

Bristol Bay, judged by most Alaskan fish experts to be the fishiest place in Alaska, lies hard on the northwest end of the Alaska Peninsula, where it joins mainland Alaska.

The craggy, glaciated 2,000- to 5,000-foot-high Ahklun Mountains lie to the north and west of The Bay.

HOW, WHERE AND WHEN TO CATCH FISH IN ALASKA
From Alaska Dept. of Fish & Game, "Alaska Sport Fishing Guide"

Fish Species	Best Bait or Lure	Max. Size	Time of Abundance				
			Southeast	Southcentral	Westward	Interior	Kodiak
ARCTIC CHAR	Spoon, Eggs	20 lbs.	Absent	June-August	June-Sept.	July-Sept.	Absent
ARCTIC GRAYLING	Flies	5 lbs.	July-Sept.	May-Sept.	May-Sept.	May-Oct.	Absent
BURBOT	Bait	30 lbs.	Absent	All Year	All Year	All Year	Absent
CHUM SALMON	Spoon	15 lbs.	July-Sept.	July-August	July-August	July-Sept.	July
CUTTHROAT TROUT	Bait, Spin., Flies	7 lbs.	May-Sept.	June-Sept.	Absent	Absent	Absent
DOLLY VARDEN	Bait, Spin., Flies	15 lbs.	May-Oct.	All Year	All Year	Absent	May-Oct.
BROOK TROUT	Eggs, Spin.	5 lbs.	May-Sept.	Absent	Absent	Absent	Absent
HALIBUT	Octopus, Herring	300 lbs.	May-Oct.	All Year	All Year	Absent	May-Sept.
KING SALMON	Herring, Spoon	100 lbs.	April-July	May-July	May-July	July-August	June-July
KOKANEE	Spin., Eggs	2 lbs.	May-Sept.	All Year	All Year	Absent	Absent
LAKE TROUT	Spoon, Plug	45 lbs.	Absent	All Year	All Year	All Year	Absent
LING COD	Herring	80 lbs.	All Year	All Year	All Year	Absent	All Year
NORTHERN PIKE	Spoon, Spin.	30 lbs.	Absent	All Year	All Year	All Year	Absent
PINK SALMON	Sm. Spoon	10 lbs.	July-August	July-August	July-August	Absent	July-August
RAINBOW TROUT	Flies, Lures, Bait	20 lbs.	May-Sept.	All Year	All Year	All Year	All Year
RED SALMON	Spoon, Flies	15 lbs.	June	June-July	June-Aug.	Absent	June-July
ROCKFISH	Herring, Spin.	20 lbs.	All Year	All Year	All Year	Absent	All Year
SHEEFISH	Spoon	50 lbs.	Absent	Absent	May-Sept.	July-Oct.	Absent
SILVER SALMON	Herring, Spoon	25 lbs.	July-Oct.	July-Sept.	July-Sept.	All Year land-locked	Sept.-Nov.
STEELHEAD TROUT	Spoon, Eggs	45 lbs.	April-June Oct.-May	May-June Aug.-Oct.	May-June Aug.-Oct.	Absent	April-May Sept.-Nov.
WHITEFISH	Flies, Eggs	10 lbs.	All Yr. Haines	All Year	All Year	All Year	Absent

(Bristol Bay is the only "The Bay" in Alaska. Say "The Bay" anywhere in the state and instantly anyone knows what you are talking about.) From the Ahkluns to The Bay drain shallow and clear streams, mostly through deep water-worn gorges. On the eastern edge of the Ahkluns exist perhaps the most scenic and most wondrously fishy system of lakes in all Alaska—the Wood River-Tikchik Lakes. They are deep, formed by glacier action. The longest, Lake Nerka, is 29 miles long. There in The Bay region, dozens of deep, clear, beautiful lakes of more than 2 miles in length exist besides the Wood River and Tikchiks. And there are hundreds of lakes that are less than 2 miles long.

The scenery isn't all that is great about the fine lakes in the great arc of Bristol Bay uplands. Almost all of these lakes are part of the greatest salmon factory in the world, for Bristol Bay supports the world's largest red salmon runs. Each year millions of silver-sided sockeye or red salmon return to The Bay to spawn.

The red salmon isn't of much interest to most sportsmen. They can be caught on occasion, with the right kind of wet fly fished close to the bottom of clear water. And they fight with all the fury packed into their torpedo shape. But sports fishermen have found but a few places where they consistently hit a fly.

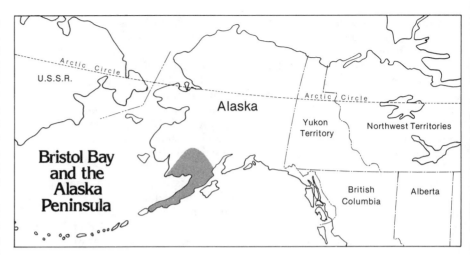

Bristol Bay and the Alaska Peninsula

Instead, sportsmen are interested in the vast numbers of rainbow trout, the countless grayling, the lake trout, the arctic char, the Dolly Varden and even the toothy pike found in various lakes and streams rimming The Bay.

South and east of the Ahklun Mountains, stiffening the south side of the Alaska Peninsula, runs the high-peaked volcanic Aleutian Range, which skirts Iliamna Lake, Alaska's largest, 75 miles long, 20 wide. Streams that run into Iliamna Lake and others nearby are generally regarded as the world's finest for rainbows. Alaska has declared the Iliamna Lake drainage a trophy fish area, giving it special protection. The idea is to catch fish for enjoyment—not food—and the limit

on the number of fish is sharply reduced in this area, as are methods of fishing. Helicopters are prohibited as transport for fishermen. (See Area 7 regulations in *Alaska Sport Fishing Seasons and Bag Limits*, for details.) Hopefully there will be fish for anglers yet to come.

The climate of The Bay is that of the Bering Sea. Summer temperatures are cool. July, the warmest month, averages fewer than six days with temperatures above 70°F at King Salmon, in the heart of the Bristol Bay country. It is a foggy, cloudy world, with cool winds and frequent rains. Much of the land is barren of trees except away from the salt-water shores. Trees run out rapidly when you travel south of Bristol Bay onto the Alaska Peninsula and into the Aleutians.

South and west is the Alaska Peninsula and Aleutians area. There are fish here, for the rivers on both the north and south sides of the peninsula hold salmon. These are mostly pinks, some reds, chum, a few silvers. Dolly Varden are the most abundant of the troutlike fish. Try the Meshik River any month from May to October, and you'll take big Dollies.

But the peninsula south of The Bay isn't a country that sport fishermen make a point of reaching. Why should they fly *away* from the finest fishing in Alaska, or perhaps the world? This the traveler would do by moving away from The Bay, with one exception: the Ugashik Lakes have in them, somewhere, a world record grayling waiting for some sportsman. The biggest grayling so far found in Alaska were in Ugashik Lakes.

There are various fishing lodges in the Bristol Bay region that offer complete "fishing packages" for the

sportsman. Or a daily flight from Anchorage to Iliamna, King Salmon or Dillingham will get him there quickly and from any of these points a bush plane can be chartered, and the pilots in these areas know where the good fishing is. Often you can arrange to use cabins at some of these lakes, or you can camp and arrange for your pilot to return.

Be prepared for rugged living if you're going to be in a tent, for sudden high winds are frequent. Fog and rain are normal. Temperatures in the 50's or lower can be expected in the warmest months. Insects can be bad, and there are brown bears, always dangerous, along all the streams and lake shorelines of this area.

Arctic Alaska

This is true wilderness where few fishermen have ventured. This region is almost 300 miles north to south and 600 miles east to west. Fewer than 10,000 people, mostly Indian and Eskimo, live in the entire area. Through the heart of this, Alaska's Arctic, sweeps the great Brooks Mountain Range, with clear, sweet streams flowing both north and south off its wild and lonely peaks. There aren't many trees in the high Brooks Range, and fewer yet on its north slope. There are bears and wolves and wolverine. Herds of caribou roam the land, and there are white sheep on the high grassy slopes of the mountains.

North of the Brooks Range the prairies roll gently north to the Arctic Ocean. There are almost countless streams, which wander somewhat aimlessly, and there are countless lakes. Here are grayling that have never seen a fishing lure, and arctic char in water that has never felt a rubber boat. There are lake trout that are often 15 or more years old.

This land fairly buzzes with summer life. There are nesting ducks and geese, shore birds, gulls, terns, sparrows, flycatchers. The cry of the arctic loon drifts across the land. Thick grass and herbs carpet the ground. Colors are delicate, and flowers are everywhere.

Mosquitoes are everywhere, too, until late August.

The great rivers that flow south and west out of the Brooks Range are the Kobuk and Noatak, both rich with

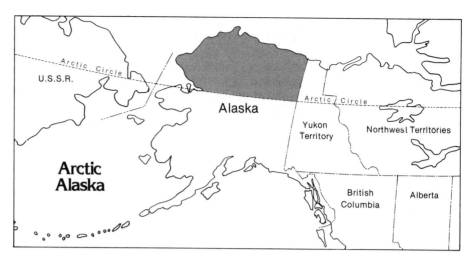

fish. Here there are grayling, sheefish, Dolly Varden, arctic char, salmon, whitefish. Neither stream has been fished much by sportsmen.

The Koyukuk River flows south out of the central Brooks Range, dropping from the mountains in a gentle winding flow, following across the great valley of the Yukon, to enter the Yukon 120 miles as the raven flies south of the Circle.

Farther east are the Chandalar, the Sheenjek and the Coleen, all lovely, rich river systems. All are wild, lonely, with sweet water, polluted only by wading moose or swimming bear. These wilderness streams start high in the Brooks Range, mostly in cold arctic lakes, then flow south to the Yukon.

This is a world of long winters and short summers, but the long daylight hours make up for the brief summer. For some weeks in June and July it never really gets dark, as the sun seems to circle around and around above the horizon.

During the summer the eastern Arctic can be warm, even uncomfortably so in sheltered valleys. Coastal streams and villages are cool, where wind blows fog off the ice pack in the Beaufort Sea.

Alaska's Arctic is a land where the average annual temperature is well below freezing. This froze the ground eons ago. It remains frozen year-round—permafrost it's called. If it weren't for the permafrost the Arctic

would be a dry, barren desert, for precipitation here is sparse. The frozen ground prevents water from soaking into the earth, and much of the land as a result is boggy, with myriad lakes, small and large. Plant life is luxuriant in summer, with grasses, herbs and flowering plants and shrubs of willow and alder, scrub birch, ground birch. Spruce forests are found along the south flank of the Brooks Range up to 1,500 feet or more.

Major jump-off points to Alaska's Arctic are Fairbanks and Anchorage. From the airports at both of these cities there are numerous scheduled flights to Nome, Kotzebue, Barrow, Fort Yukon and other destinations.

Secondary jump-off points for the central and eastern Arctic are Bettles Field and Fort Yukon; for the western Arctic, Kotzebue, Nome or Barrow.

A pleasant way to fish and to get to know the Arctic is to fly to Fort Yukon or Bettles Field, charter a small plane and have the pilot drop you off at the headwaters of one of the clear, gently flowing streams high in the Brooks Range. Take with you a tough inflatable boat, or a good kayak, and drift downstream, camping when and where you please, fishing as you go, enjoying the scenery, the wildlife and the superb fishing. You can arrange for the pilot to pick you up at some point downstream.

The Sheenjek is ideal for such a drift. The Alatna is another. The John was a wonderful stream a few years ago, but the discovery of oil in the central North Slope of the Arctic brought a winter road to the John River, and its scars remain.

If you want to try sheefish (see section on game fish in this book), this is the region to try for them.

Another way of enjoying the Arctic fishing is to have a bush pilot drop you at a good lake, with camp gear, so you can fish the inlets and outlet.

There are, too, a few Alaskan guides who specialize in guiding fishing parties. Arrangements can be made for short or long trips into various parts of the Arctic.

Good fishing is available at or near many villages, which are located mostly on rivers. There are scheduled airmail and passenger flights to virtually every village in Alaska. But accommodations are limited or nonexistent at most of the smaller villages, so the do-it-himselfer should have a sleeping bag, a small tent and a supply of food. Be sure the tent is mosquito proof.

At most villages it is possible to find someone who can be hired to take visitors on fishing trips in a boat. Few formal fishing guides exist in Arctic Alaska.

Warm clothing, hip boots or waders, with rain gear, is appropriate for fishing anywhere in Alaska, and this fits the Arctic. You'll also need plenty of insect repellent.

Choice of fishing tackle is up to the fisherman. Spinning gear is appropriate anywhere in the Arctic. The same equipment, with only a change in strength of line, will handle 1- or 2-pound grayling, or 30-pound sheefish or salmon. Fly fishermen will want a light fly rod, tapered line and leader, and a good supply of dark flies for grayling. They like mosquitoes, Blue Dun or Black Gnat, and sizes No. 12 to No. 16 are a good approach for starters.

Arctic Alaska is the least known and one of the most exciting areas of Alaska, and the fishing there can be superb.

Yukon Territory

Yukon Territory is a vast, rugged land (about 35 percent the size of Alaska), which is mostly wilderness, including everything from large plains in the north to what is commonly called the smallest desert in the world on the shores of Bennett Lake at Carcross in the southwestern corner. In between there are some of the highest mountain peaks in North America in Kluane National Park which borders on Alaska in the extreme southwestern corner of the territory, and includes Mount Logan, Canada's highest peak. There is also the Yukon River and its thousands of tributaries which make up one of the largest river basins on the continent.

Yukon summers nowadays bring about 300,000 visitors to the territory, most to visit historic gold rush sites. Attractions in Yukon Territory include wilderness hiking trips, gold panning, photo opportunities, gambling—Dawson City has the only legalized gambling casino in Canada, operated on Las Vegas rules—and, of course, fishing.

Summers are warm, with almost total daylight during most of June. Casual clothing is called for, including a woolen shirt or sweater or light ski jacket. Yukon nights, even in summer, can be chilly. A waterproof nylon shell to wear over a woolen shirt is a good combination for windy or rainy days, and cool nights.

Yukon Territory has hundreds of sparkling lakes and bubbling streams abounding with no less than 11 important sport fish species. Many of these waters are located along the highway system and secondary roads with others necessitating only a short walk to streams and lakes offering excellent angling possibilities. However, the best fishing is found in waters accessible only by air or backpack trip.

With a population of less than 25,000 there is little competition for visiting anglers in any waters of Yukon Territory. Turn off on that unmarked side road, even for a mile or so. It may lead to a clear mountain stream where the bottoms of the pools are literally black with grayling. Cast a fly or spinner into that unnamed pond beside the road where out of the corner of your

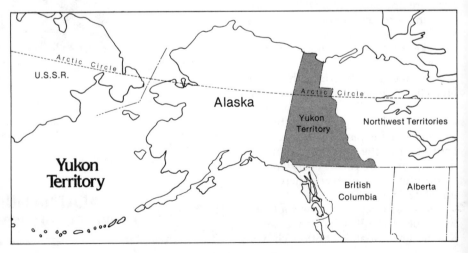

eye you thought you saw a fish rise. Don't be too surprised if you find yourself tangling with an acrobatic rainbow trout or a mean-mouthed northern pike.

Ask local residents where you might find some good angling. Yukoners are genuinely friendly people and a few pleasant inquiries over coffee in a highway truck stop could reward you with excellent fishing.

For the serious angler with a day or two to spare, consider a floatplane trip into a hidden wilderness lake only minutes away. Many of these mountain lakes have seldom been fished and most contain good populations of lake trout, grayling or pike. Charter operators are located in most Yukon communities. Their rates are reasonable for short hops and some may even provide a canoe and camping gear if you don't have your own.

There are guided river trips with canoes, riverboats and rubber rafts. Boat trips down the Yukon are popular, and several companies offer them. Historical tours, wilderness tours, and fishing lodges that feature fly-in fishing are popular attractions. Rates for fishing trips at comfortable lodges run from $100 to $150 a day, depending upon length of trip, and distance from highway.

A few canoe and boat rental sources include: Yukon Canoe Rental, 6159 Sixth Avenue, Whitehorse; Gold Rush River Tours, Box 4835, Whitehorse; Adventure Yukon, 510 Steele Street, Whitehorse; Bob White's Kluane Camp, Mile 1070, Alaska Highway.

For more information, write Department of Tourism and Information, Box 2703, Whitehorse, YT, Y1A 2C6.

Northwest Territories

More than twice the size of Alaska, this land reaches northward from the 60th parallel to the North Pole.

Two climatic zones divide the territories—the arctic and subarctic (the boundary between these bears no relationship to the Arctic Circle). A large part of Northwest Territories lies within the subarctic zone, including all of the Mackenzie Valley. Southern Baffin Island is arctic, and summers are cool, with July maximums around

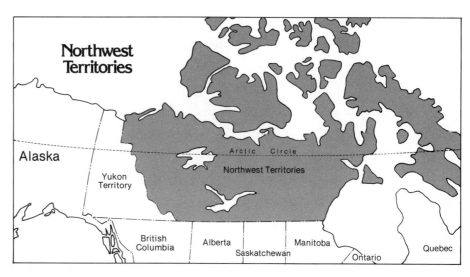

50°F, and minimums around 35°F. Long hours of summer sunshine compensate, and there is only 5 to 10 inches of rain during June, July and August.

Keewatin district, to the south of Baffin Island, is slightly warmer. Spring comes late here because of slow melting of ice. Frost-free period is only 40 to 60 days.

The Mackenzie Basin has intensely cold winters that average -20°F, with summer temperatures averaging about 50°F, July being the warmest month. The Mackenzie Basin is divided into two climatic zones (1) Southern Mackenzie Valley and Great Slave Lake, where summers are comparable to the prairie provinces, with the average July maximum about 69°F. Rainfall is light and the long sunny summer days are invigorating. (2) The Northern Mackenzie Valley and Great Bear Lake is truly the land of the midnight sun, where sunsets blend into sunrises. Nonstop summer activities are possible through much of June and July, and the climate is much the same as southern regions, but slightly cooler. Rainfall near the arctic coast averages about 2.5 inches.

There are only about 40,000 people in all of the Northwest Territories, and the land is virtually roadless beyond the Mackenzie Highway. This is a land where the bush plane is king, and there are scheduled flights to virtually every village and town. Planes range from Super Cubs, Twin Otters, to commercial jet liners. Small charter planes are available in most larger communities. Float-equipped planes are most common during summer, and there are literally thousands of clearwater, fish-filled lakes where they can land and drop off fishing parties.

Arctic and subarctic mammals are common in parts of Northwest Territories, including caribou, moose, mostly in forested areas and both black and grizzly bears. In Wood Buffalo Park there are about 7,000 wood bison. Another 300 are found in the Mackenzie Bison Sanctuary. Musk ox are found primarily in the arctic islands of the territories, but some may be seen in the Bathurst Inlet area and in the Thelon Game Sanctuary. There are between 9,000 and 12,000 musk ox in Canada's Arctic.

The wooded areas have wolf, fox, wolverine, mink, marten, lynx, otter, weasel, beaver, muskrat, rabbits and squirrels.

Birds are a familiar sight throughout the summer, for it is the breeding ground for thousands of geese, ducks, swans and shore birds. Most of these breeding grounds are inaccessible for the average tourist; however some of these species can be seen at coastal locations.

Eastern Northwest Territories is almost devoid of forest, but in the Mackenzie District there are areas of forested land, varying from scattered clumps of stunted conifers and birches to fairly heavy stands of poplar and spruce. The principal trees are aspen and balsam poplar, white and black spruce, white birch, tamarack and jack pine.

The northern coniferous section is a small triangle east of Fort Smith, where black spruce is the principal tree, with some jack pine and tamarack. The mixed-wood section is a small area along the Alberta boundary south of the west end of Great Slave Lake and the Mackenzie River. The Mackenzie lowlands section is the most important forest area of the territories, occupying low-lying plains in the basin of the Mackenzie River including lower portions of the Liard, Peel and Great Bear rivers. White spruce, poplars and birch are well represented; black spruce and tamarack occupy the swamps and jack pine is found in sandy areas.

The northern transition section is north and east of a line passing through the mouth of the Mackenzie River to Great Bear and Great Slave lakes. Poor climate, thin soils and poor drainage result in stunted trees.

The treeline for Northwest Territories runs from the northwestern corner, across the Barrenlands to the southeastern corner near Hudson Bay. North of this line there is no timber, although there is smaller plant life that is quite colorful in summer.

Tourism is growing in Northwest Territories, and nowadays about 20,000 visitors annually reach this land to spend time in about 28 communities. There are more than 70 lodges and outfitters.

Equipment needed for a trip into Northwest Territories on a fishing adventure should include a cooking stove if you plan to reach the arctic, for there is no wood. Much of the land is rocky, so an air mattress or at least a sleeping pad is a must. Mosquitoes and black flies are at their worst from early June to well into July, so a tent with a mosquito bar is also a must. In open areas, or on the water, bugs are not a serious problem. After sunset, or in marshy areas, insect repellents and headnets are needed in various areas.

Stores are found in almost every community, but selection is limited, and cost is high. Sometimes gas stations are 200 miles apart, so it's best to top off that gas tank when opportunity offers.

Linda Keezer watches her sons, Mike and Mark, try their luck in the Prophet River near Mile 245 of the Alaska Highway in northern British Columbia. (Edward Keezer)

streams, many teaming with trout, pike or grayling.

It is a land of huge lakes—Williston, Babine, Takla, Dease, Atlin, Marsh (half in British Columbia, half in Yukon Territory). It is a land of wild rivers, many of them huge roaring cataracts, others slow-flowing clear streams ideal for fishing. Some drain north into the Mackenzie River and on to the Arctic Ocean, like the Kechika, the Liard, the Muskwa. Others drain to the west and through the mountains into Southeastern Alaska—the Stikine, Iskut, Nakina and Taku.

While the best fishing is available with a floatplane, one can drive a car to top fishing, too. A good trailerable boat helps.

This is also big game country— moose, deer, bighorn sheep, mountain goat, cougar and both black and grizzly bears.

Best months are probably August and September, after the bad mosquito and fly months of June and July.

Fishing is good as long as the water is open, however. But good weather and lack of flies makes a trip much more pleasant.

This is warm clothing country, even during mid-summer. Nights can get cool, and prolonged rainy spells can occur. Insect repellent is a must. A pair of light cotton gloves is handy.

A variety of tackle can help make a fishing adventure in northern British Columbia a success; deep water tackle for lake trout that may weigh more than 30 pounds, or pike in the same range (be sure to use a wire leader for pike), and light fly or spinning gear for grayling, and smaller rainbow trout. You also might have to fish deep for big rainbows in some of the larger lakes and deep streams.

There are plenty of good places to camp along the highways. The number of fishing lodges is increasing, and often have boats and motors for rent, and can point a fisherman toward the best fishing in an area. □

Northern British Columbia

This is a wild land of few roads and rugged country. It lies in the rain shadow of the great coastal range that separates it from moist, stormy Southeastern Alaska. It is a land of cold winters and brief, warm summers. It is floatplane country, where the fisherman can be put off at literally any one of thousands of fishable lakes or

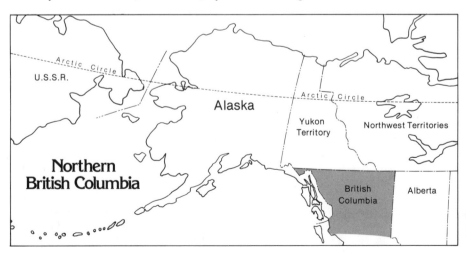

674 FISHING SPOTS

in Alaska, Yukon Territory, Northwest Territories and Northern British Columbia

KEY TO FISHING MAPS
Numbers correspond to area maps shown within the following
sport-fishing guide section.

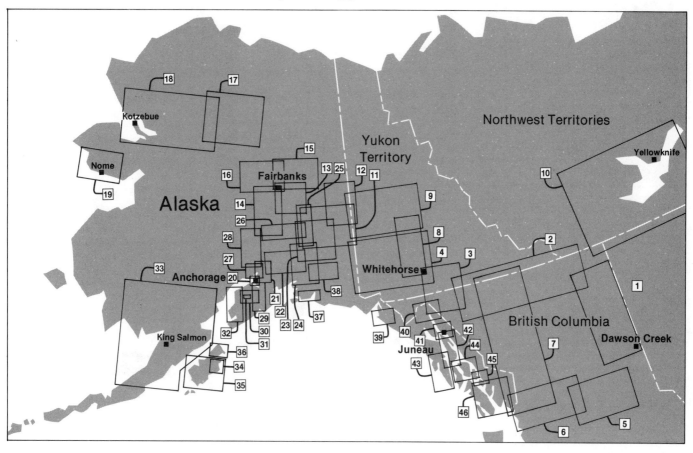

1. **Alaska Highway:** Dawson Creek to Fort Nelson, BC
2. **Alaska Highway:** Muncho Lake, BC, to Teslin, YT
3. **Alaska Highway:** Teslin to Whitehorse, YT
4. **Alaska Highway:** Whitehorse, YT, to Alaska/Yukon border
5. **Yellowhead Highway 16:** Prince George to Topley, BC
6. **Yellowhead Highway 16:** Topley to Prince Rupert, BC
7. **Cassiar Highway 37:** Kitwanga, BC, to Watson Lake, YT
8. **Klondike Loop:** Whitehorse to Pelly Crossing, YT
9. **Klondike Loop:** Pelly Crossing, YT, to Alaska Yukon Border
10. **Northwest Territories**
11. **Alaska Highway:** Alaska/Yukon Border to Delta Junction (Alaska)
12. **Taylor Highway:** Tetlin Junction to Eagle (Alaska)

13. **Alaska Highway:** Delta Junction to Fairbanks (Alaska)
14. **George Parks Highway:** Fairbanks to Broad Pass (Alaska)
15. **Steese Highway:** Fairbanks to Circle (Alaska)
16. **Elliott Highway:** Fairbanks to Manley Hot Springs (Alaska)
17. **Brooks Range:** Bettles Area (Alaska)
18. **Kotzebue Area** (Alaska)
19. **Nome Area** (Alaska)
20. **Anchorage Area** (Alaska)
21. **Glenn Highway and Palmer-Matanuska Valley** (Alaska)
22. **Glenn Highway:** Sutton to Glennallen (Alaska)
23. **Glenn Highway:** Glennallen to Tok (Alaska)
24. **Richardson Highway:** Valdez to Glennallen (Alaska)
25. **Richardson Highway:** Glennallen to Delta Junction (Alaska)
26. **Denali Highway:** Paxson to Cantwell (Alaska)

27. **George Parks Highway:** Wasilla to Willow (Alaska)
28. **George Parks Highway:** Willow to Broad Pass (Alaska)
29. **Seward-Anchorage Highway** (Alaska)
30. **Sterling Highway:** Mile 37.6 to Soldotna (Alaska)
31. **Skilak Loop Road** from Mile 57.7 Sterling Highway (Alaska)
32. **Sterling Highway:** Kenai-Soldotna to Homer (Alaska)
33. **Bristol Bay-Alaska Peninsula** (Alaska)
34. **Kodiak Area** (Alaska)
35. **Kodiak National Wildlife Refuge** (Alaska)
36. **Afognak Island** (Alaska)
37. **Copper River Highway** (Alaska)
38. **Chitina-McCarthy Road** (Alaska)
39. **Yakutat Area** (Alaska)
40. **Haines and Skagway Area** (Alaska)
41. **Juneau Area** (Alaska)
42. **Admiralty Island** (Alaska)
43. **Sitka Area** (Alaska)
44. **Petersburg Area** (Alaska)
45. **Wrangell Area** (Alaska)
46. **Ketchikan Area** (Alaska)

Most of the information on fishing spots and maps in Alaska, in this section, are taken from the
Alaska Sport Fishing Guide, courtesy of the Alaska Department of Fish & Game.

MAP NUMBER 1
Alaska Highway: Dawson Creek to Fort Nelson, BC

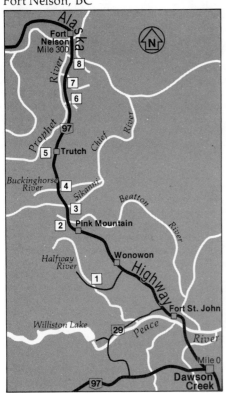

MAP NUMBER 2   Alaska Highway: Muncho Lake, BC, to Teslin, YT

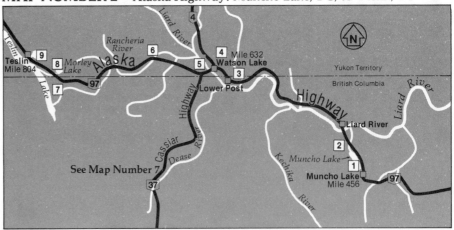

MAP NUMBER 3   Alaska Highway: Teslin to Whitehorse, YT

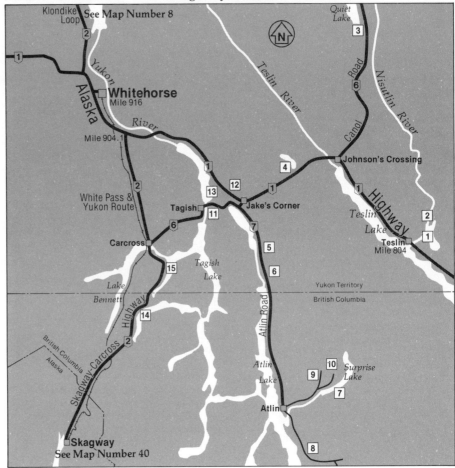

MAP NUMBER 1
Alaska Highway: Dawson Creek to Fort Nelson, BC

1. **HALFWAY RIVER**, access road at Mile 95. River roughly parallels the Alaska Highway at a 10- to 20-mile distance from Mile 50 to Mile 143. River is swift and not fordable. Dolly Varden to 11 pounds; rainbow 1 to 2 pounds; whitefish; grayling best in fall.
2. **BEATTON RIVER**, Mile 147. July through September. Dolly Varden; grayling; rainbow.
3. **SIKANNI CHIEF RIVER**, Mile 162. Grayling to 2½ pounds, early spring; whitefish to 2 pounds; northern pike; ling cod.
4. **BUCKINGHORSE RIVER**, Mile 175. Northern pike 3 to 4 pounds; grayling to 20 inches, June through September.
5. **BEAVER CREEK**, Mile 206.7. Northern pike 3 to 4 pounds; grayling to 20 inches; rainbow to 20 inches.
6. **PARKER CREEK**, Mile 246.9. Dolly Varden to 5 and 6 pounds; grayling to 1½ pounds.
7. **BIG BEAVER CREEK**, Mile 263.4. Dolly Varden to 5 and 6 pounds; grayling to 1½ pounds.
8. **JACKFISH LAKE**, Mile 279. On right 6 miles. July through September. Grayling; jackfish; ling cod.

MAP NUMBER 2
Alaska Highway: Muncho Lake, BC, to Teslin, YT

1. **MUNCHO LAKE**, Mile 456. June and July best. Grayling to 18 inches; whitefish to 12 inches; lake trout to 25 inches.

2. **TROUT RIVER**, Mile 466. May, June and August best. Grayling to 18 inches; whitefish to 12 inches.
3. **HYLAND RIVER**, Mile 605.9. Dolly Varden and grayling.
4. **WYE LAKE**, Mile 632. East of Watson Lake, BC, 0.25 mile. Stocked lake. Coho salmon and rainbow.
5. **LIARD RIVER**, Mile 642.4. Dolly Varden; lake trout; grayling; whitefish; northern pike. Catches fall off when river is high and muddy—often in summer.
6. **RANCHERIA RIVER**, access at Miles 689 and 710. Dolly Varden to 10 pounds, average 2 pounds; grayling to 2 pounds.

CAUTION: The Alaska Highway crosses the British Columbia-Yukon Territory border several times between Miles 734.7 and 776.3. Be sure you have the appropriate fishing license when fishing in this area.

7. **SWAN LAKE**, Mile 743.8. Trout and whitefish.
8. **MORLEY LAKE** and **RIVER**, Mile 796. Northern pike near mouth of river; rainbow at mouth of bay.
9. **TESLIN LAKE**, Mile 804. Lake trout average 4 to 6 pounds, but some up to 30 pounds; grayling to 4 pounds; sheefish to 20 pounds; whitefish, March through November; northern pike to 25 pounds.

Alaska Highway: Whitehorse, YT, to Alaska/Yukon border

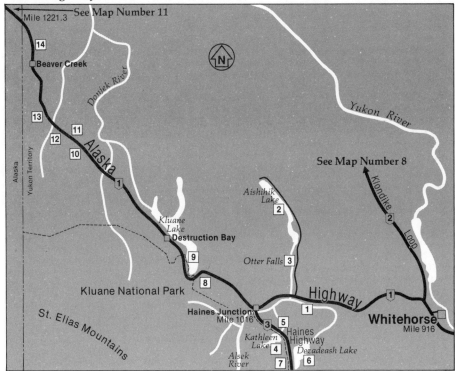

MAP NUMBER 3

Alaska Highway: Teslin to Whitehorse, YT

1. **NISUTLIN BAY,** Mile 804. Lake trout to 40 pounds; grayling; whitefish; sheefish; northern pike average 4 to 6 pounds, but some up to 30 pounds; salmon up to 50 pounds caught occasionally in these waters, but are in poor condition after traveling over 2,000 miles upstream.
2. **NISUTLIN RIVER,** Mile 804, flows into Nisutlin Bay near Teslin. Sheefish; lake trout; grayling; whitefish; northern pike.
3. **QUIET LAKE,** on Canol Road, 50 miles north of Mile 836. Northern pike; lake trout to 20 pounds; grayling 2 to 4 pounds, at northeast corner and in mouths of creeks.
4. **SQUANGA LAKE,** Mile 843. Year-round. Northern pike to 30 pounds; whitefish to 20 pounds; burbot to 6 pounds.

The Atlin Road from Jake's Corner

CAUTION: The road to Atlin crosses into British Columbia a few miles south of the junction. Be sure you have the appropriate fishing license when fishing these waters.
5. **LUBBOCK RIVER,** Mile 16 access road 2.4 miles to river. Breakup to mid-September. Excellent grayling fishing.
6. **SNAFU LAKE,** access road at Mile 17.5; **TARFU LAKE** and **MARCELLA POND,** access road at Mile 21.2; all have been stocked with rainbow.
7. **SURPRISE LAKE,** 12 miles northeast of Atlin, good road. May through August. Grayling to 2 pounds.
8. **PALMER LAKE,** 10 miles south of Atlin, good road. June and July. Grayling to 17 inches; pike to 8 pounds.

9. **LOWER McDONALD** and **McDONALD LAKES,** 12 miles northeast of Atlin, good road. Lake trout to 8 pounds; grayling to 2 pounds.
10. **GLADYS LAKE,** 34 miles northeast of Atlin, road rough in places. June through August. Lake trout to 30 pounds; northern pike to 20 pounds. Excellent game area.
11. **TAGISH RIVER,** Mile 865.3, west of Jake's Corner, 13 miles. River connects Marsh and Tagish lakes. June and July. Lake trout 5 to 30 pounds.
   NOTE: Bridge over river at Tagish will be replaced in 1979. Construction will close road from February to October. During this period access to Carcross from Mile 904.1 on the Alaska Highway only.

Alaska Highway (continued)

12. **JUDAS LAKE,** Mile 872. Follow vehicular trail 0.4 mile on right. If raining leave car at pulloff area, as trail is treacherous when muddy. Casting from shore is possible, but a boat is needed to get to the 3- to 5-pound rainbow. Lake stocked with coho salmon and rainbow.
13. **MARSH LAKE,** Mile 875. Excellent fishing for grayling and northern pike.

Skagway-Carcross Road (Klondike Highway 2) from Mile 904.1

14. **TUTSHI LAKE,** 35 miles south of Carcross on the new Klondike Highway 2. Excellent fishing for lake trout and grayling early in the season.
15. **WINDY ARM,** 10 to 15 miles south of Carcross. Good fishing for grayling and lake trout.

MAP NUMBER 4

Alaska Highway: Whitehorse, YT, to Alaska/Yukon border

1. **CRACKER CREEK,** Mile 988. August. Good for grayling at mouth of creek.
2. **AISHIHIK LAKE,** access at Mile 995.6. Public campground at Mile 6, boat launch at Mile 27. Road maintained for summer travel to Mile 26. Check road conditions, lake usually doesn't ice-out until late June. Excellent for lake trout 5 to 40 pounds.
3. **OTTER FALLS,** Mile 17 on Aishihik Lake Road. Good fly fishing for rainbow and grayling.

Haines Highway (Yukon Highway 3)

4. **KATHLEEN LAKE,** Miles 12 to 17. Public campground on lakeshore from Mile 16.6; boat launch. Grayling; silver salmon; lake trout 5 to 40 pounds.
5. **KATHLEEN RIVER,** Mile 15.6. Rainbow; grayling; lake trout.
6. **DEZADEASH LAKE,** Mile 28. Lake parallels highway for 9 miles. Boats available at lodge. *CAUTION:* Storms come up quickly on this mountain lake. Northern pike; lake trout; grayling. Good fly fishing where feeder streams flow into the lake.
7. **KLUKSHU RIVER SYSTEM,** access from Haines Highway south of Dezadeash to British Columbia border. *CAUTION:* Grizzly feeding areas; exercise extreme caution. **TAKHANNE RIVER.** Early July. Excellent king salmon fishing. **TAKHANNE FALLS,** grayling; Dolly Varden; rainbow; salmon. **TATSHENSHINI RIVER,** access from Mile 49. Steelhead; sockeye, chinook and coho salmon. **KLUKSHU LAKE,** 0.5 mile east from Mile 36. Spawning ground for salmon in August and September; lake trout; rainbow.

For south portion of Haines Highway see Map Number 40.

Alaska Highway (continued)

8. **KLOO LAKE,** Mile 1035.4. Grayling; lake trout; northern pike.
9. **KLUANE LAKE,** Miles 1054 to 1095. Longest and highest lake in Yukon Territory (153 square miles in area). Several lodges and fishing camps with boats and guides for hire. Grayling; northern pike; sheefish; lake trout to 50 pounds.
10. **EDITH CREEK,** Mile 1146.2. June and July. Grayling to 16 inches.
11. **KOIDERN RIVER,** Mile 1151.5. June and July. Grayling to 16 inches.
12. **PICKHANDLE LAKE,** Mile 1159. Northern pike to 20 pounds; whitefish; ling cod; best fishing from boat.
13. **MOOSE LAKE,** Mile 1176. Midsummer. Grayling to 18 inches; boat needed.
14. **MIRROR CREEK,** Mile 1214.5. Spring and July-August. Grayling to 16 inches. Small streams and culverts in area also good for grayling in May and June.

For continuation of Alaska Highway from Alaska-Yukon Territory border see Map Number 11.

MAP NUMBER 5 Yellowhead Highway 16: Prince George to Topley, BC

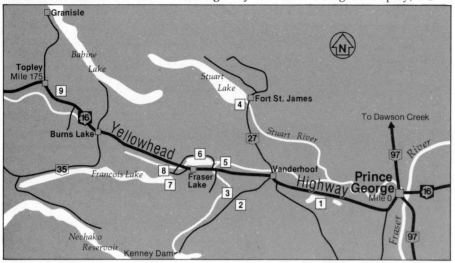

MAP NUMBER 6 Yellowhead Highway 16: Topley to Prince Rupert, BC

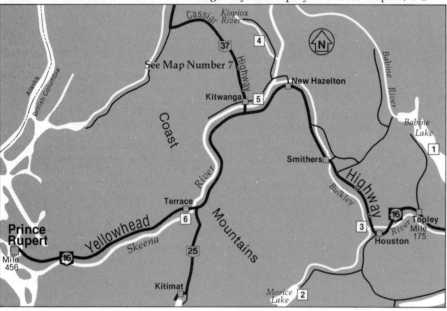

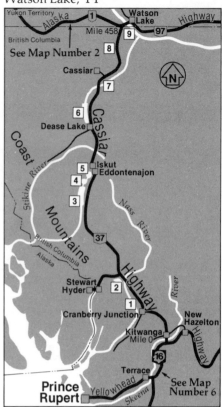

8. **STELLAKO RIVER,** Mile 102, south 7 miles on side road. River flows from northeast end of Francois Lake. Rainbow over 2 pounds; good fly fishing.
9. **BROMAN LAKE,** Mile 165. Spring and summer. Rainbows; char to 4 pounds.

MAP NUMBER 6
Yellowhead Highway 16: Topley to Prince Rupert, BC

1. **BABINE LAKE,** Mile 175, north of Topley 27 miles, on road to Topley Landing and Granisle. Rainbow 6 to 8 pounds; arctic char, May through November.
2. **MORICE LAKE,** Mile 194, west 52 miles from junction at Houston. Road follows Morice River to lake. June through October. Rainbow to 4 pounds; arctic char to 25 pounds.
3. **BULKLEY RIVER,** Miles 198, 221, 225 and other roadside pulloffs west of Houston. Spring and coho salmon to 24 pounds, spring to fall; steelhead to 25 pounds, late fall.
4. **KISPIOX RIVER,** Mile 278.4, north of New Hazelton junction 12 miles, and 10 miles north of Hazelton. Good steelhead stream from September to freezeup. King salmon, spring.
5. **SKEENA RIVER,** Mile 294 and at many access points west along highway. King and silver salmon; rainbow. Fishing is best when weather cooperates to produce low water level and little silt.
6. **SKEENA RIVER,** Mile 363. Terrace area boasts the world's record salmon caught on rod and reel—a 92½-pound spring salmon captured 4 miles west of the downtown area at Fishermen's Park.

MAP NUMBER 5
Yellowhead Highway 16: Prince George to Topley, BC

1. **CLUCULZ LAKE,** Mile 38.5. Very good fishing in spring; ice goes out first week of May. Good ice fishing December to March. Lake gets very rough when windy. Early spring and late fall. Rainbow to 3½ pounds; kokanee to 1½ pounds; arctic char to 57 pounds; whitefish to 5 pounds, anytime.
2. **NULKI LAKE,** 18 miles southeast of Vanderhoof on the Kenney Dam Road. Rainbow to 6 or 7 pounds, with 2-pound average.

3. **TACHIK LAKE,** 18 miles southeast of Vanderhoof on Kenney Dam Road. Rainbow 2 to 7 pounds year-round.
4. **STUART LAKE,** Mile 62, north of Vanderhoof 37 miles on Highway 27, near Fort St. James. Rainbow; lake trout; Dolly Varden; grayling; whitefish; kokanee; sturgeon.
5. **NECHAKO RIVER,** Mile 87.2 Yellowhead Highway. Early summer to fall. Rainbow; Dolly Varden.
6. **FRASER LAKE,** Mile 90, on the right westbound. Char to 25 pounds, early spring; rainbow averaging 2 pounds.
7. **FRANCOIS LAKE,** Mile 102. Side road leads 7 miles to northeast end of lake, where the Stellako River flows from the lake. Rainbow to 2 pounds; kokanee to 1 pound; char 4 to 20 pounds.

MAP NUMBER 8
Klondike Loop: Whitehorse to Pelly Crossing, YT

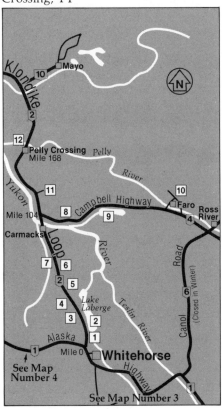

MAP NUMBER 9
Klondike Loop: Pelly Crossing, YT, to Alaska/Yukon Border

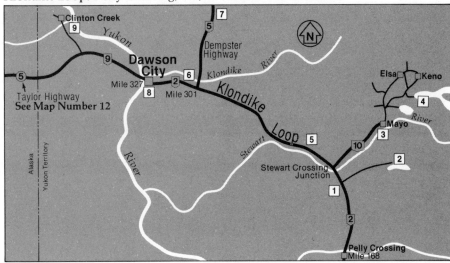

MAP NUMBER 7
Cassiar Highway 37: Kitwanga, BC, to Watson Lake, YT

1. NASS RIVER, Miles 72 to 86, north of Kitwanga. Salmon to 35 pounds; Dolly Varden to 5 pounds; steelhead to 20 pounds in fall.
2. MEZIADIN LAKE, Mile 99. Salmon to 35 pounds; Dolly Varden to 5 pounds; steelhead to 20 pounds in fall.
3. KINASKAN LAKE, Mile 230.5. July and August. Rainbow to 20 inches.
4. TATOGGA LAKE, Mile 246.1. Rainbow. Lodge with boat rentals and riverboat trips up the nearby Stikine River.
5. EDDONTENAJON LAKE, Mile 250. July and August. Rainbow to 20 inches.
6. DEASE LAKE, Mile 320. Good access to lake, small boats may be carried down trail through gravel pit to lake; unimproved camping area on shore. Large pike reported.
7. COTTONWOOD RIVER, Mile 362. Grayling 16 to 17 inches; Dolly Varden to 15 pounds. Nearby COTTON LAKE, Mile 356, also reports good fishing.
8. BLUE RIVER, Mile 397. May through September. Grayling to 17 inches; Dolly Varden to 15 pounds.
9. ALBERT CREEK, Mile 457. Good grayling fishing 1 mile north of British Columbia-Yukon Territory border. *Be sure you have a Yukon Territory fishing license.*

MAP NUMBER 8
Klondike Loop: Whitehorse to Pelly Crossing, YT

1. HORSE CREEK, Mile 12.6. Good grayling fishing at road side.
2. LAKE LABERGE, Mile 22.4. Territorial campground 2 miles to right; boat ramp. Lake trout; grayling; northern pike. *CAUTION:* Lake can become rough quickly when windy.
3. FOX CREEK, Mile 26. June and July. Excellent for grayling. FOX LAKE, Mile 35. Territorial campground. Good fishing for lake trout from shore at the campground; grayling excellent year-round.
4. LITTLE FOX LAKE, Mile 43. Lake trout 3 to 8 pounds, fish near the islands.
5. BRAEBURN LAKE, Mile 55.3. Lake trout to 12 pounds, July; grayling to 16 inches; pike to 30 pounds.
6. TWIN LAKES, Mile 71.5. Campground. Two small lakes, one on either side of highway. Lake trout; grayling; pike.
7. NORDENSKIOLD RIVER, Mile 98.5. River parallels the highway for several miles. Good grayling and pike fishing all summer.

Campbell Highway

8. FRENCHMAN LAKE, 25.5 miles east of Carmacks. Access road on north side of Campbell Highway leads 4 miles to lake, with small public campground and boat ramp. Trout; pike; grayling; best fishing at south end of this 12-mile lake.
9. LITTLE SALMON LAKE, 80 miles east of Carmacks, 22-mile-long lake with campground at either end. Lake trout; pike; grayling.
10. FISHEYE LAKE, 104 miles east of Carmacks at Faro. Short access road leads to campground. Rainbow.

Klondike Loop (continued)

11. TATCHUN LAKE, Mile 118.5. Side road leads east 4 miles to lake and picnic site. Good fishing year-round, but best in early spring or fall. Northern pike to 30 pounds.

TATCHUN CREEK. Grayling to 16 inches, June to October; salmon July through August.
12. PELLY RIVER, Mile 168, adjacent to village of the same name. Salmon to 5 pounds in July; chum salmon to 3 pounds in mid-August.

MAP NUMBER 9
Klondike Loop: Pelly Crossing, YT, to Alaska/Yukon Border

1. CROOKED CREEK, Mile 205.2. Grayling in summer.
2. ETHEL LAKE, Mile 206.5. Side road leads east 17 miles to lake and territorial campground. June to August best. Northern pike to 30 pounds; grayling to 3 pounds; lake trout 2 to 50 pounds.
3. STEWART RIVER, near Mayo 34 miles northeast of Klondike Loop junction on Elsa-Mayo Road. Salmon 5 to 10 pounds; whitefish 1 to 2 pounds.
4. MAYO LAKE, 42 miles beyond Mayo on side road. Mid-June to mid-August. Lake trout to 40 pounds.
5. MOOSE CREEK, Mile 229. Grayling.
6. UPPER KLONDIKE RIVER, Mile 301 near junction of Klondike Loop and Dempster Highway. Excellent grayling fishing.
7. BLACKSTONE RIVER and CHAPMAN LAKE, on the Dempster Highway. Arctic char ½ to 1½ pounds. This highway was completed to Inuvik, NWT, in late summer 1978. Very limited facilities; many fishing waters yet to be tested. Check on current road conditions and for fishing information in Dawson City before starting out.
8. TAILING PILE HOT SPOTS at Dawson City, Mile 327. Some ponds created by tailing piles in the Dawson City area have been stocked with grayling or rainbow; ask for details at the government liquor store, corner of Third and Queen streets, where hunting and fishing licenses are sold.
9. YUKON RIVER near Clinton Creek, 63 miles northwest of Dawson City on a side road. Grayling to 3 pounds, April; chum salmon to 12 pounds, August; king salmon to 40 pounds, July and August.

MAP NUMBER 10 Northwest Territories

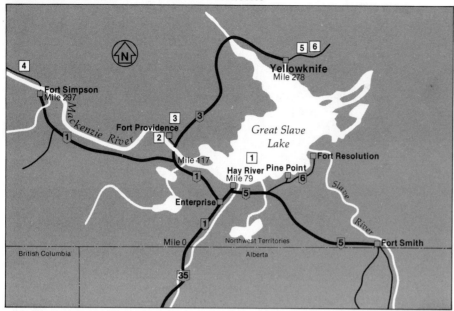

MAP NUMBER 11

Alaska Highway: Alaska/Yukon Border to Delta Junction (Alaska)

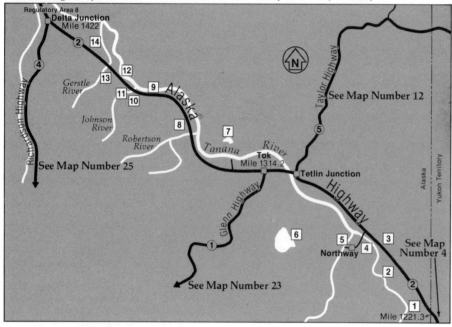

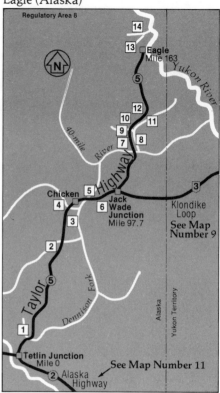

5. **PROSPEROUS LAKE,** 12 miles east of Yellowknife on the Ingraham Trail (Highway 4). Boat launch, picnic site. Lake trout; grayling; whitefish.
6. **PRELUDE LAKE,** 18.5 miles east of Yellowknife on short access road from Ingraham Trail. Public campground, tent and trailer sites, swimming, boat ramp, boat rentals, cabins. Lake trout; northern pike.

NOTE: Many remote lakes in Northwest Territories have resorts and many offer great fishing, far from the territories' limited road system. Lake trout to 30 pounds; northern pike 30 to 40 pounds, sometimes up to 60 pounds. Write to TravelArctic, Yellowknife, NWT, X1A 2L9, or stop at the Yellowknife visitor information center.

MAP NUMBER 11

Alaska Highway: Alaska/Yukon Border to Delta Junction (Alaska)

MAP NUMBER 10

Northwest Territories

1. **GREAT SLAVE LAKE,** accessible from Hay River, Pine Point, Fort Resolution, Fort Providence and Yellowknife, is an exceptional sport-fishing lake. Northern pike to 40 pounds; sheefish; walleye; pickerel; grayling. Record fish for the lake was an 80-pound lake trout taken in 1969.

2. **MACKENZIE RIVER,** access from Fort Providence, 3 miles northwest of Mackenzie Route (Highway 3); guides, cabins, boats and air-charter trips available. Grayling; northern pike; pickerel.
3. **MARIAN LAKE,** in Fort Providence area. May and June best. Pickerel; jackfish 5 to 6 pounds; whitefish 2 to 4 pounds all season. Other fishing spots in the area include **MOSQUITO CREEK,** pickerel 5 to 6 pounds and **SLEMMON LAKE,** lake trout 6 to 40 pounds.
4. **AKALI LAKE,** reached by a 70-mile road from Fort Simpson. Jackfish; pickerel 3 to 7 pounds.

1. **SCOTTIE CREEK,** Mile 1223.9. Grayling to 14 inches.
2. **DEADMAN LAKE,** Mile 1249.4. State campground 2 miles on good dirt road. Northern pike to 2 feet, but skinny. Locals call them snakes.
3. **GARDINER CREEK,** Mile 1253. Grayling 14 to 16 inches.
4. **MOOSE CREEK** and **CHISANA RIVER,** Mile 1264, access from Northway Road. Drive across Tanana River and park. Trail follows riverbank downstream 1.5 miles to slough. Excellent fishing for northern pike to 8 pounds.

MAP NUMBER 13
Alaska Highway: Delta Junction to
Fairbanks (Alaska)

5. NABESNA SLOUGH, south end of Northway runway. Grayling to 3 pounds.
6. TETLIN LAKE, fly-in from Northway. Riverboat charter available. Northern pike to 15 pounds; grayling; whitefish.
7. LAKE MANSFIELD, accessible via fly-in or riverboat. Accommodations available; northern pike 30 to 35 inches.
8. JAN LAKE, Mile 1352, on right 0.25 mile. Rainbow 6 to 12 inches; silver salmon 6 to 16 pounds.
9. BERRY CREEK, Miles 1371 to 1374. Grayling to 14 inches.
10. LISA LAKE, Mile 1381.2. Access road south 0.7 mile to lake (winter road only). Excellent fishing for silver salmon and rainbow.
11. CRAIG LAKE, Mile 1383.7. Access road leads 1.3 miles to trail. Trail is 0.5 mile to lake. Rainbow; silver salmon.
12. LAKE GEORGE, Mile 1385. Accessible by riverboat, inquire locally. Northern pike; whitefish; burbot.
13. DONNA LAKE, Mile 1391. Access trail 3.5 miles to lake, excellent rainbow fishing. LITTLE DONNA LAKE, 1 mile farther, also excellent for rainbow.
14. DELTA CLEARWATER RIVER, Mile 1405. State campground 8 miles from highway. Boat needed for best fishing. Grayling; silver salmon; whitefish.

MAP NUMBER 12
Taylor Highway: Tetlin Junction to
Eagle (Alaska)

1. LOGGING CABIN CREEK, Mile 43. Pulloff. Grayling to 14 inches.
2. WEST FORK OF DENNISON RIVER, Mile 49. Pulloff. Grayling to 14 inches.
3. TAYLOR CREEK, Mile 50.4. Pulloff. Grayling to 14 inches.
4. MOSQUITO FORK RIVER, Mile 64.4. Use-site. Grayling to 14 inches.
5. 40-MILE RIVER, Miles 73 to 75. Road parallels river and crosses stream at Mile 75. Campground at Mile 75.3. Grayling to 15 inches; sheefish to 4 pounds.
6. WALKER'S FORK, Mile 81.9. BLM campground. Grayling to 14 inches.
7. 40-MILE RIVER, Mile 112.6. Late summer and early fall. Grayling; sheefish.

MAP NUMBER 14
George Parks Highway: Fairbanks to
Broad Pass (Alaska)

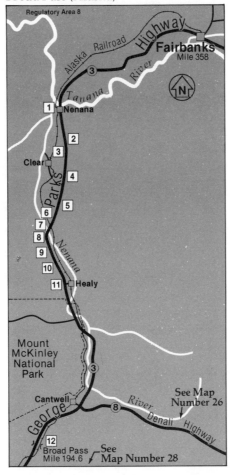

8. O'BRIEN CREEK, Mile 113.2 to 113.6. Stream parallels highway; good to excellent fishing. Several pulloffs.
9. ALDER CREEK, Mile 117.1. Excellent fishing. Grayling to 15 inches.
10. COLUMBIA CREEK, Mile 124.5. Smelt to medium size; grayling.
11. KING SOLOMON CREEK and LIBERTY FORK, Mile 131.5. BLM campground. Grayling.
12. NORTH FORK OF KING SOLOMON CREEK, Mile 135.8. Road crosses creek. Grayling.
13. AMERICAN CREEK, Mile 151.8. Road parallels stream at outskirts of Eagle. Grayling.
14. MISSION CREEK, Mile 161. Town of Eagle; trail leads 0.5 mile from town to creek. Grayling.

MAP NUMBER 13
Alaska Highway: Delta Junction to
Fairbanks (Alaska)

1. QUARTZ LAKE, Mile 1433.8. East of highway 2 miles on improved gravel road; boat launch. Rainbow; grayling.
2. 81-MILE LAKE, Mile 1441.5. Pulloff. Good grayling fishing.
3. SHAW CREEK, Mile 1442.7. Pulloff. Grayling, early spring and fall.

4. BIRCH LAKE, Mile 1462. Boat landing and beach. Good year-round. Rainbow; silver salmon.
5. HARDING LAKE, Mile 1477.5. State recreation area with boat launch; 89 camper/trailer units. Lake trout, large but scarce, year-round; northern pike; burbot; silver salmon. LITTLE HARDING LAKE, Mile 1477.5. Between Harding Lake and highway. Good winter fishing for silver salmon.
6. SALCHA RIVER, Mile 1479.2. Highway crosses river. Use foot trails along river to reach fishing areas. Boat required for best fishing. Accommodations available. Grayling; king and chum salmon.
7. LITTLE SALCHA RIVER, Mile 1483.7. Private, posted property surrounds river. Grayling. Spring and fall.

MAP NUMBER 14
George Parks Highway: Fairbanks to
Broad Pass (Alaska)

1. NENANA POND, Mile 303.4. Turn south on gravel road; campground. Silver salmon.
2. FISH CREEK, Mile 296.8. Road crosses creek; pulloffs. Grayling.
3. JULIUS CREEK, Mile 295.3. Go west 2 miles on pack trail; Clear Creek access via same trail. Grayling.
4. JULIUS CREEK, Mile 285.7. Road crosses creek; pulloffs. Grayling.
5. SEVEN-MILE LAKE, Mile 280.3. Go east on winter trail 7 miles to lake. Undeveloped use-site. Northern pike; whitefish.
6. BIRCH CREEK, Mile 272.5. Road crosses creek; spring fishing if water conditions correct. Grayling.
7. BEAR CREEK, Mile 269.4. Road crosses creek; spring fishing if water conditions correct. Grayling.
8. ROCK CREEK, Mile 261.2. Road crosses creek; spring fishing if water conditions correct. Grayling.
9. SLATE CREEK, Mile 257.8. Road crosses creek; spring fishing if water conditions correct. Grayling.
10. PANGUINGUE CREEK, Mile 252.5. Road crosses creek. Grayling.
11. EIGHT-MILE LAKE, Mile 251.2. Turn west on Stampede Road and go in approximately 8 miles. Lake is 0.25-mile from road; no use-sites. Grayling.
12. BROAD PASS LAKES, Mile 194.6. Several lakes in area of Broad Pass. Summit, Edes and Duck are the only ones named; most lakes easily accessible from highway. Grayling; whitefish; lake trout; burbot. SUMMIT and EDES LAKES, lake trout to 8 pounds.

See Maps Number 27 and Number 28 for south portion of George Parks Highway.

MAP NUMBER 15   Steese Highway: Fairbanks to Circle (Alaska)

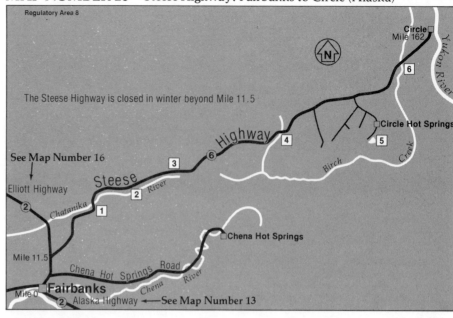

MAP NUMBER 16
Elliott Highway: Fairbanks to Manley Hot Springs (Alaska)

MAP NUMBER 15
Steese Highway: Fairbanks to Circle (Alaska)

1. **CHATANIKA RIVER,** Miles 29 to 39. Numerous pulloffs. Campground with boat launching site at Chatanika River bridge, Mile 39. Good grayling fishing all summer; salmon; sheefish, July through September; spearing for whitefish in October; northern pike; burbot.
2. **CHATANIKA RIVER,** Mile 47. Turn south on gravel road to undeveloped use-site. Good fishing throughout season. Grayling; northern pike.
3. **FAITH CREEK,** Mile 69.1. Road crosses creek. Pulloff. Grayling; northern pike.
4. **NORTH FORK OF BIRCH CREEK,** Mile 93.2. Pulloff. Boat launching for Birch Creek Wilderness Canoe Trail. Grayling, good all season; northern pike.
5. **MEDICINE LAKE,** Mile 127.8, turn right 8 miles to Circle Hot Springs, go directly across airstrip; 2-mile trail to lake. Lake connects with Crooked Creek which is navigable by canoe to Birch Creek. Northern pike; whitefish.
6. **BIRCH CREEK,** Mile 147.1. Road crosses creek. Undeveloped use-site and boat launch. Grayling; northern pike.

MAP NUMBER 16
Elliott Highway: Fairbanks to Manley Hot Springs (Alaska)

1. **CHATANIKA RIVER,** Mile 11. Campground and launching ramp. Good spring and fall fishing. (Grayling; whitefish; northern pike; sheefish; king and chum salmon.
2. **WASHINGTON CREEK,** Mile 18.3. Pulloff. Fair spring and fall fishing. Grayling.
3. **GLOBE CREEK,** Mile 38. Pulloffs. Fair spring and fall fishing. Grayling.
4. **TATALINA RIVER,** Mile 45.2. Pulloff and undeveloped use-site. Good fall fishing. Grayling; whitefish.
5. **TOLOVANA RIVER,** Mile 57. Campground. Good spring and fall fishing. Grayling; whitefish; salmon.
6. **WEST FORK OF TOLOVANA RIVER,** Mile 75.2. Pulloff and undeveloped use-sites. Good late summer and fall fishing. Grayling; whitefish.

7. **KUCK LAKE,** 8 miles southwest of Livengood; turn due south on bulldozer trail. Occasionally impassable due to mud. Undeveloped use-site. Northern pike.
8. **MINTO FLATS,** access 11 miles via new Minto Village road from Elliott Highway, Mile 109.7. Road passable to autos but may be bad during rainy periods. Boat launching and parking areas. Access to entire Minto Flats by boat. Good spring, summer and fall fishing. Road not maintained during winter. Northern pike; sheefish; whitefish; burbot.
9. **HUTLINANA CREEK,** Mile 129.3. Pulloffs and undeveloped use-sites. Good spring and fall fishing. Grayling; Dolly Varden.
10. **BAKER CREEK,** Mile 137.6. Pulloffs and undeveloped use-site. Good spring, summer and fall fishing. Grayling.
11. **HOT SPRINGS SLOUGH,** end of Elliott Highway at Manley, Mile 152. Pulloff, use-site and boat launch. Good spring, summer and fall fishing. Lodge, post office, store and charter aircraft available. Northern pike; whitefish; sheefish.

MAP NUMBER 17   Brooks Range: Bettles Area (Alaska)

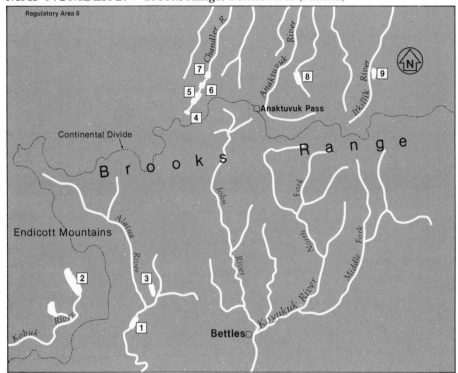

MAP NUMBER 17
Brooks Range: Bettles Area (Alaska)

All lakes accessible via floatplane from Bettles. Charter flights available. Appoximate flight time is given.

1. **HELPMEJACK LAKE** (35 minutes).Good lake trout; northern pike; whitefish.
2. **WALKER LAKE** (45 minutes). Excellent lake trout fishing; northern pike; whitefish; arctic char.
3. **INIAKUK LAKE** (35 minutes). Good lake trout fishing; northern pike; whitefish.
4. **FISH LAKE** (1 hour). Excellent lake trout; grayling; arctic char.
5. **CHANDLER LAKE** (1 hour by floatplane or small wheel plane). Short, rough airstrip. Excellent lake trout and grayling fishing; whitefish.
6. **LOWER CHANDLER LAKE** (1 hour). Good lake trout and grayling fishing; arctic char; whitefish.
7. **ROUND LAKE** (1 hour). Good lake trout and grayling fishing; arctic char; whitefish.
8. **SHAININ LAKE** (1 hour). Excellent lake trout and grayling fishing; whitefish.
9. **NANUSHUK LAKE** (1 hour). Lake trout; grayling; whitefish.

MAP NUMBER 18   Kotzebue Area (Alaska)

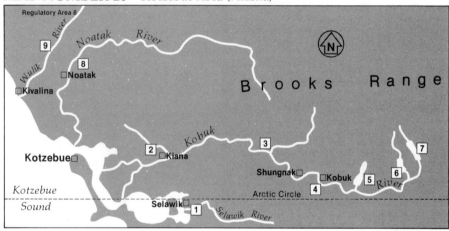

MAP NUMBER 18
Kotzebue Area (Alaska)

1. **SELAWIK RIVER** fly-in commercial or private charter from Kotzebue. Excellent fishing for small-medium sheefish; pike.
2. **KIANA VILLAGE,** fly-in from Kotzebue. Accommodations available. Excellent early summer fishing. Sheefish.
3. **KOBUK RIVER (LOWER),** fly-in via mail floatplane. Riverboats available for charter. Good sheefish fishing in June and July; northern pike; grayling.
4. **KOBUK RIVER (UPPER),** commercial flights from Kotzebue. Riverboats available for charter. Sheefish; northern pike; grayling; whitefish.
5. **SELBY LAKE,** charter floatplane from Kotzebue or Bettles. Summer fishing excellent. No accommodations or boats available. Lake trout; grayling; northern pike; burbot.
6. **NUTUVUKTI LAKE,** air charter from Kotzebue or Bettles. No accommodations or camps. Good summer fishing. Lake trout; grayling; northern pike; burbot.
7. **WALKER LAKE,** air charter from Kotzebue or Bettles. Good lake trout fishing; grayling; northern pike; burbot; arctic char.
8. **NOATAK RIVER,** commercial and air charters available from Kotzebue. Char fishing excellent in the fall; grayling; chum salmon.
9. **WULIK RIVER,** Kivalina. Fly-in commercial or private charters from Kotzebue. Accommodations available. Grayling.

MAP NUMBER 19 Nome Area (Alaska)

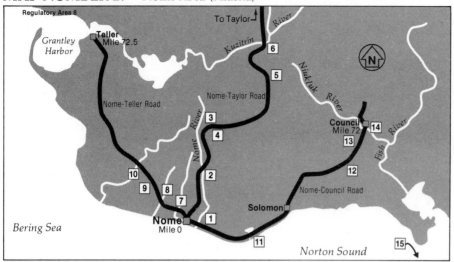

MAP NUMBER 21
Glenn Highway and Palmer-Matanuska Valley (Alaska)

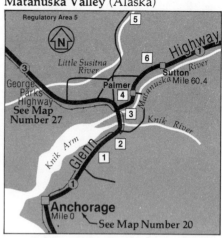

MAP NUMBER 20 Anchorage Area (Alaska)

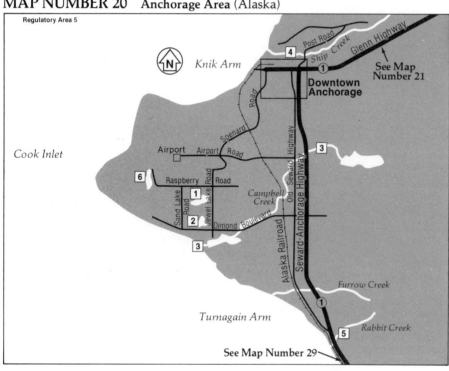

MAP NUMBER 19
Nome Area (Alaska)

1. **NOME RIVER,** 4 miles east of Nome via extension of Main Street. Junction of river and ocean. Arctic char; pink, silver, chum and king salmon.
2. **NOME RIVER,** Mile 10 Nome-Taylor Road. River closely parallels road, numerous pulloffs. Spring and fall fishing best. Pink, chum, king and silver salmon; grayling; arctic char.
3. **GRAND CENTRAL RIVER,** Mile 35 Nome-Taylor Road. Very small pulloff; excellent canoe/small boating river. Grayling; whitefish; arctic char; red salmon.
4. **SALMON LAKE,** Miles 36 to 44 Nome-Taylor Road. Lake is parallel to highway, numerous roads to lake shore. No accommodations. Airstrip. Red and chum salmon; whitefish; grayling; northern pike; arctic char.
5. **PILGRIM (KRUZGAMEPA) RIVER,** Mile 65 Nome-Teller Road. Pulloffs; undeveloped areas suitable for camping. Excellent fishing. Pink, chum and silver salmon; whitefish; arctic char; northern pike.

6. **KUZITRIN RIVER,** Mile 68 Nome-Taylor Road. Fine clear-water stream. King, chum and pink salmon; arctic char; grayling; northern pike.
7. **SNAKE RIVER,** Mile 6.7 Nome-Teller Road. Pulloff. Spring and fall fishing. Chum, pink and silver salmon; grayling; arctic char.
8. **PENNY RIVER,** Mile 12.3 Nome-Teller Road. Pulloff. Grayling; arctic char.
9. **CRIPPLE CREEK,** Mile 20 Nome-Teller Road. Grayling; arctic char.
10. **SINUK RIVER,** Mile 26.7 Nome-Teller Road. Best fishing stream on road. Chum and pink salmon; arctic char; grayling; northern pike.
11. **SAFETY LAGOON,** Mile 17.6 Nome-Council Road. Boat fishing recommended. Eskimo summer fishing camps throughout area. Pink and chum salmon; arctic char; flounder; occasional halibut.
12. **SOLOMON RIVER,** Miles 40 to 50 Nome-Council Road. River parallels road. Numerous old narrow-gauge engines alongside road; reindeer herds in summer. Fair grayling fishing; pink and chum salmon; arctic char.
13. **FOX RIVER,** Miles 60 to 67 Nome-Council Road. River parallels road several miles. Chum and pink salmon; grayling.
14. **NIUKLUK RIVER** at Council. Good silver, chum and pink salmon fishing in July and August. Good char fishing in August and September; grayling; whitefish.
15. **UNALAKLEET RIVER,** located on southeast side of Norton Sound. Good accommodations on lower Unalakleet River; boats available. Good fishing for king salmon, early July; silver, pink and chum salmon; grayling; arctic char.

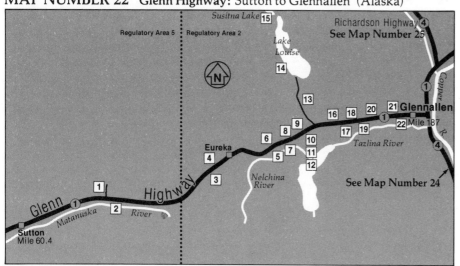

13. **Lake Louise Road**, Mile 159.8. **JUNCTION LAKE**, Mile 0.5, east side of road. Grayling; silver salmon. **CRATER LAKE**, Mile 1.5, west of road 200 yards. Rainbow. **PEANUT LAKE** and **40-FOOT LAKE**, Mile 6.5, east 2 miles on Oil Well Road, then 0.25 mile by trail. Grayling. **ELBOW LAKE** and **CARIBOU LAKE**, Mile 11.5. Grayling.
14. **LAKE LOUISE**, Mile 17. Accommodations available. Lake trout; whitefish; grayling; burbot.
15. **SUSITNA LAKE**, by boat across Lake Louise. Lake trout; whitefish; grayling; burbot.
16. **TEX SMITH**, Mile 162. Pulloff. Silver salmon; rainbow; fair fishing.
17. **LOST CABIN LAKE**, Mile 166. Trail across from Atlasta House, 0.75 mile to lake. Grayling.
18. **KAY LAKE**, Mile 168. Good trail north 0.75 mile to lake. Grayling.
19. **MAE WEST LAKE**, Mile 168. Pulloff a short distance from marked trail, 0.5 mile to lake. Try inlet stream. Grayling.
20. **TOLSONA-MOOSE LAKES**, Mile 170. turn north at sign. Parking space provided by lodge. Grayling; burbot.
21. **TOLSONA CREEK**, Mile 173. Adjacent to highway. Campground. Grayling.
22. **MOOSE CREEK**, Mile 186. Adjacent to highway. Grayling.

MAP NUMBER 20
Anchorage Area (Alaska)

1. **SAND LAKE**, access at Sand Lake School on Strawberry Road off Jewel Lake Road. Rainbow.
2. **JEWEL LAKE**, on Dimond Boulevard between Jewel Lake and Sand Lake roads. Rainbow.
3. **CAMPBELL CREEK**, numerous roads cross stream; located south of International Airport Road. Dolly Varden; silver and pink salmon.
4. **SHIP CREEK**, north of downtown and Glenn Highway. Dolly Varden; king, silver, pink and chum salmon. Fair to poor summer and fall fishing.
5. **RABBIT CREEK**, between DeArmoun and Rabbit Creek roads. Pink salmon; Dolly Varden; fair to poor summer-fall fishing.
6. **CAMPBELL POINT LAKE**, on Point Campbell Military Reservation, end of Raspberry Road at Sand Lake Road. Rainbow.

MAP NUMBER 21
Glenn Highway and Palmer-Matanuska Valley (Alaska)

1. **LOWER FIRE LAKE**, Mile 16.2. Rainbow; Dolly Varden; silver salmon.
2. **MIRROR (BEAR) LAKE**, Access from Mile 23.6 northbound or Mile 24.4 southbound. Boat launch. Rainbow; silver salmon.
3. **ECHO LAKE**, Mile 37. Boat launch. Silver salmon.
4. **KEPLER-BRADLEY LAKE COMPLEX**, Mile 37.3. **KEPLER LAKE**, roadside boat launch and public use-site. Rainbow. **BRADLEY LAKE**, roadside boat launch and public use-site. Rainbow. **VICTOR LAKE**, 0.5 mile by trail. Silver salmon. **IRENE LAKE**, 1 mile by trail. Rainbow. **CANOE LAKE**, 1 mile by trail. Rainbow; grayling. **LONG LAKE**, 1.1 mile by trail. Rainbow.

5. **UPPER LITTLE SUSITNA RIVER**, access from Mile 49 Glenn Highway on Fishhook-Willow Road; road closed in winter beyond Mile 7. Headwaters to Little Susitna Roadhouse, water cloudy but very good Dolly Varden fishing.
6. **SEVENTEEN MILE LAKE**, Mile 61. Turn north on Jonesville Road 1.8 mile, then left (about 3 miles). Public use-site. Excellent for grayling.

MAP NUMBER 22
Glenn Highway: Sutton to Glennallen (Alaska)

1. **RAVINE LAKE**, Mile 83.5. Turn north onto Bonnie Lake Road; 0.8 mile to lake. Rainbow. **LOWER BONNIE LAKE**, Mile 83.5. Turn north onto Bonnie Lake road 1 mile to campground; 2 miles to lake. Road not recommended beyond Ravine Lake for any vehicle during rainy season. Small rainbow; grayling.
2. **LONG LAKE**, Mile 86. Campground. Grayling.
3. **LEILA LAKE**, Mile 121. Gravel pit parking. Short hike through open country to outlet. Grayling; burbot.
4. **GUNSIGHT CREEK**, Mile 123.5. Good early fishing for grayling.
5. **ALABAMA LAKE**, Mile 147; 200 feet southeast of highway. Small pond, but good grayling fishing.
6. **CACHE CREEK**, Mile 147.3. Pulloff. Good grayling fishing early spring and fall.
7. **MIRROR LAKE**, Mile 149; 200 yards from road. Grayling, summer fishing.
8. **MENDELTNA CREEK**, Mile 152.8. Pulloff. Accommodations available. Grayling.
9. **GERGIE LAKE**, Mile 155.2. Trail 1.25 miles south to lake. Grayling.
10. **ARIZONA LAKE**, Mile 155.5. Grayling.
11. **BUFFALO LAKE**, Mile 156. Rainbow.
12. **SUCKER LAKE**, Mile 158. Grayling; burbot.

MAP NUMBER 23   Glenn Highway: Glennallen to Tok (Alaska)

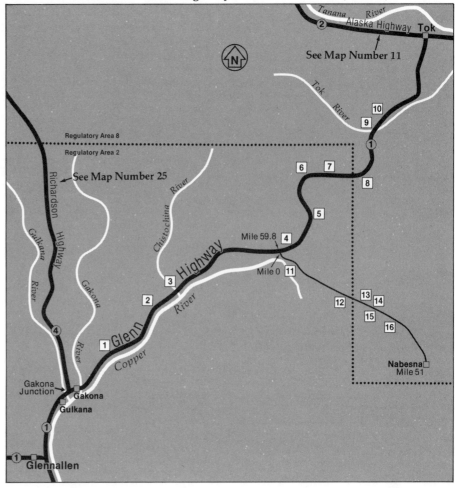

MAP NUMBER 23
Glenn Highway: Glennallen to Tok (Alaska)

Mileages given from Gakona Junction.
1. **TULSONA CREEK**, Miles 15 to 18. Creek parallels highway. Numerous pulloffs. Grayling.
2. **GRAVEL PIT LAKE**, Mile 30. North side of highway. Grayling.
3. **SINONA CREEK**, Mile 34. Grayling; Dolly Varden.
4. **AHTELL CREEK**, Mile 61. Use-site. Grayling.
5. **CARLSON LAKE**, Mile 64.9, 2.5 miles west up Carlson Creek. Grayling; Dolly Varden.
6. **MABLE CREEK**, Mile 76.5. Grayling.
7. **MENTASTA LAKE**, Mile 81.5. Turn north on old Slana-Tok bypass. Inlet and outlet best fishing. Grayling; whitefish.
8. **MINERAL LAKE**, Mile 89.2. Small pulloffs; 0.5-mile trail to lake outlet. Excellent spring grayling fishing; northern pike; whitefish.
9. **LITTLE TOK RIVER**, Mile 104.5. Pulloff. Grayling.
10. **CLEARWATER CREEK**, Mile 108. Use-site. Fair fall and early spring fishing. Grayling.

Nabesna Road, from Mile 59.8

11. **RUFUS CREEK**, Miles 4 to 7. Spring fishing. Dolly Varden.
12. **LONG LAKE**, Mile 23.2. Pulloff. Grayling; burbot.
13. **LITTLE TWIN LAKE**, Mile 28; 0.3 mile south. Grayling; lake trout; burbot.
14. **BIG TWIN LAKE**, Mile 29. Grayling; burbot.
15. **JACK LAKE**, Mile 31. Road deteriorates beyond Mile 29, check ahead. South of road 1 mile by old cat trail. Grayling; whitefish; lake trout; burbot.
16. **JACK CREEK**, Mile 38. Pulloff. Grayling.

MAP NUMBER 24
Richardson Highway: Valdez to Glennallen (Alaska)

1. **PORT VALDEZ**, Mile 0. Boat rentals at docks. Accommodations. Silver, pink and chum salmon; Dolly Varden; red snapper and other bottom fish.
2. **ROBE RIVER** and **LAKE**, Mile 2.7. Highway crosses river. Access road to lake at Mile 3.1. Dolly Varden.
3. **LOWE RIVER**, Mile 13. River emerges from canyon. Dolly Varden.

MAP NUMBER 24 Richardson Highway: Valdez to Glennallen (Alaska)

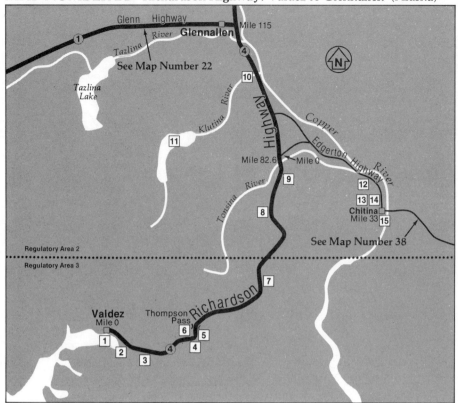

MAP NUMBER 25

Richardson Highway: Glennallen to Delta Junction (Alaska)

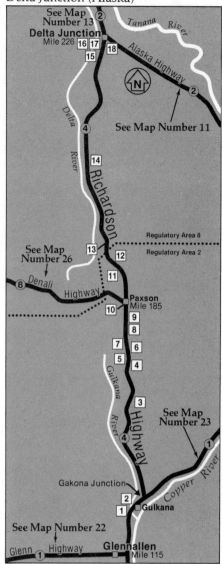

4. **BLUEBERRY LAKE**, Mile 23.6. Campground, access to lake. Rainbow.

5. **THOMPSON LAKE**, Mile 24. Lake is east and downhill from highway; can be seen from road. Rainbow.

6. **WORTHINGTON LAKE**, Mile 27. Parking area. Rainbow.

7. **TIEKEL RIVER**, Mile 47.9. Rest area alongside river. Fish run small in size. Dolly Varden.

8. **LITTLE TONSINA RIVER**, Mile 65. Campground. Dolly Varden; grayling; rainbow.

9. **SQUIRREL RIVER**, Mile 80. Campground. Grayling.

10. **KLUTINA RIVER**, Mile 100. Dolly Varden; grayling; king and red salmon.

11. **KLUTINA LAKE**, Mile 101; 25 miles by poor road. Burbot; Dolly Varden; grayling; lake trout; king and red salmon.

Edgerton Highway
Junction to Chitina (Alaska)

12. **LIBERTY FALLS CREEK**, Mile 23.6. Campground. Follow good trail to stream. Grayling.

13. **3-MILE LAKE**, Mile 29.7. Lake adjacent to road. Rainbow; grayling.

14. **2-MILE LAKE**, Mile 30.3. Lake adjacent to road. Rainbow; grayling.

15. **CHITINA LAKE**, lake bordered by town. Various pulloffs. Grayling.

See Map Number 36 for road from Chitina to McCarthy.

MAP NUMBER 25

Richardson Highway: Glennallen to Delta Junction (Alaska)

1. **BEAR CREEK**, Mile 127. Pulloff. Spring and fall fishing for grayling.

2. **GULKANA RIVER**, Miles 128 to 148. State campground at Mile 147.4. Marked fishing trails at Miles 129.1; 136.7; 139.6; 141.4; 146.5. (Recent highway construction may alter these mileages.) Rainbow; grayling; king and red salmon.

3. **SOURDOUGH CREEK**, Mile 148. Grayling.

4. **HAGGARD CREEK**, Mile 162. Grayling.

5. **JUNE** and **NITA LAKES**, Mile 166, west 0.25 mile. Whitefish; grayling.

6. **GILLESPIE LAKE** and **CREEK**, Mile 169.5. Walk up Gillespie Creek 0.25 mile. Grayling.

7. **MEIERS LAKE**, Mile 170. Campground. Best fishing at inlet. Grayling.

8. **DICK LAKE**, Mile 173, east of road. Grayling.

9. **PAXSON LAKE**, Mile 181. Wayside at Mile 179.6; boat launch. Good gravel road but a little steep for trailers. Lodge nearby. Lake trout; grayling; whitefish; burbot.

10. **MUD LAKE**, 1 mile southwest of Paxson Junction by rough road. Good early grayling fishing.

11. **FISH CREEK** and **LAKES**, Mile 192. Pulloff. Trail parallels creek 2 miles to lake. Grayling.

12. **SUMMIT LAKE**, Mile 195. Parking areas and accommodations available. Lake trout; grayling; whitefish; burbot.

13. **FIELDING LAKE**, Mile 200.5. Turn south on side road 1.5 miles to campground. Good fishing. Lake trout; grayling; whitefish; burbot.

14. **RAPID LAKE**, Mile 227. Lake 0.25 mile north of highway. Rainbow.

15. **NICKEL LAKE, CHET LAKE** and **"J" LAKE**, Mile 258.5. Southwest of highway 4.5 miles on military reservation. Grayling.

16. **BOLIO LAKE**, Mile 260. Turnoff marked. Lake 2.5 miles southwest of highway on military reservation. Excellent silver salmon fishing.

17. **MARK LAKE**, Mile 260. On Bolio Lake Road, 4.5 miles southwest of highway on military reservation. Rainbow.

18. **GOODPASTER RIVER**. Accessible by riverboat via Delta-Clearwater and Tanana rivers. Grayling; whitefish.

MAP NUMBER 26 Denali Highway: Paxson to Cantwell (Alaska)

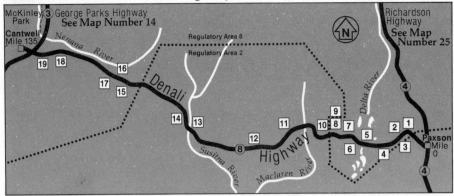

MAP NUMBER 27 George Parks Highway: Wasilla to Willow (Alaska)

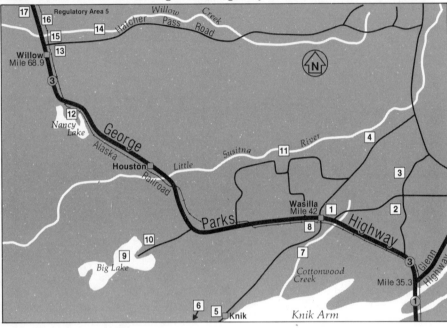

MAP NUMBER 28
George Parks Highway: Willow to Broad Pass (Alaska)

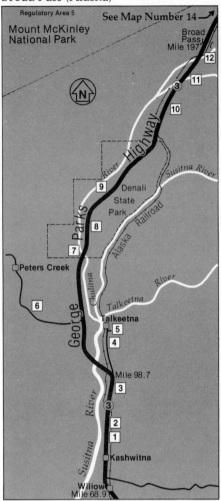

MAP NUMBER 26
Denali Highway: Paxson to Cantwell (Alaska)

1. **SEVEN-MILE LAKE**, Mile 7. Small pulloff. Follow bulldozer trail 0.75 mile across tundra to lake. Excellent summer fishing. Lake trout.

2. **TEN-MILE LAKE**, Mile 10. Small pulloff. Short hike downhill to outlet. Summer. Lake trout; grayling; burbot.

3. **TEARDROP LAKE**, Mile 10.8. Short hike down steep hill to the south. Good summer fishing. Lake trout; grayling; burbot. **OCTOPUS LAKE**, Mile 11. South of road 0.25 mile. Lake trout; grayling; whitefish.

4. **LITTLE SWEDE LAKE**, Mile 16.8. South of highway 2.5 miles by cat trail. Excellent fishing for lake trout. **BIG SWEDE LAKE**, Mile 16.8. South of Little Swede Lake 2 miles. Excellent fishing. Lake trout; grayling; whitefish; burbot. **16.8-MILE LAKE**, Mile 16.8. Walk north up creek 200 yards to lake. Lake trout; grayling. **RUSTY LAKE**, Mile 16.8. Behind 16.8-Mile Lake. Walk 0.5 mile northwest of 16.8-Mile

Lake. Lake trout; grayling. **17-MILE LAKE**, Mile 17. Small lake with fair to good summer fishing. Lake trout; grayling. **DENALI-CLEARWATER CREEK**, Mile 18.1. Road crosses creek. Parking area. Spring and summer. Grayling.

5. **TANGLE LAKES**, Mile 21.5. BLM campground and boat launch. Accommodations available. Excellent summer fishing. Lake trout; grayling; whitefish; burbot.

6. **ROCK CREEK**, Mile 25.3. Parking area. Fair summer fishing. Grayling.

7. **LANDMARK GAP LAKE**, Mile 26. Due north 3 miles from highway on cat trail. Good lake trout; grayling; whitefish.

8. **GLACIER LAKE**, Mile 30. Parking area on north side of highway. Follow cat trail 3 miles north to lake. Excellent summer fishing. Lake trout; grayling; whitefish.

9. **BOULDER (7-MILE) LAKE**, Mile 30. Due north of Glacier Lake 4 miles, or air charter from Summit Lake. Cabin and boats. Lake trout; grayling; whitefish.

10. **36-MILE LAKE**, Mile 36. Walk 0.5 mile north of road. Lake trout; grayling; whitefish.

11. **46.9-MILE LAKE**, Mile 46.9. North side of road. Lake and outlet excellent for large grayling. **CROOKED CREEK**, Miles 46.9 to 50. Creek parallels highway. Excellent fishing. Grayling. **50-MILE LAKE**, Mile 50. North side of road. Fair fishing. Grayling; whitefish.

12. **CLEARWATER CREEK**, Mile 55. Campground. Summer. Grayling.

13. **BUTTE CREEK**, Mile 79.7. Susitna River bridge crossing. Parking area south side of highway. Follow Susitna River downstream 5.5 miles to creek junction. Grayling; whitefish.

14. **STEVENSON'S LAKE**, Mile 84. South of road 0.5 mile. Grayling.

15. **BRUSHKANA CREEK**, Mile 104.5. BLM campground. Summer, small fish. Grayling; Dolly Varden.

16. **CANYON CREEK**, Mile 106.5. Parking site. Summer. Grayling.

17. **SEATTLE CREEK**, Mile 110.9. Use-site. Summer. Grayling; Dolly Varden.

18. **JERRY LAKE**, Mile 125.5. North of highway 0.13 mile. Grayling. **JOE LAKE**, Mile 125.5. South side of road. Parking area. Grayling.

19. **UNNAMED CREEK**, Mile 128.2. Grayling, good in summer.

MAP NUMBER 29
Seward-Anchorage Highway (Alaska)

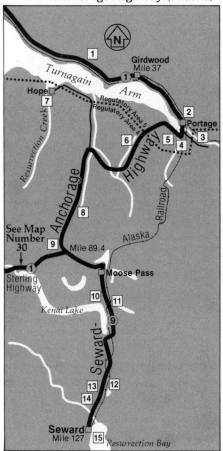

MAP NUMBER 27
George Parks Highway: Wasilla to Willow (Alaska)

1. **WASILLA LAKE**, Mile 41.7. Wayside. Boat launch facilities and accommodations. Rainbow; silver salmon.
2. **FINGER LAKE**, Mile 42.2. Turn right on Wasilla-Fishhook Road, then right just past town, on Bogard Road (about 8 miles to campground). Resorts in area. Also accessible from Palmer via Palmer-Wasilla Road. Rainbow; pan-sized silver salmon.
3. **CORNELIUS LAKE**, Mile 42.2. Take Bogard Road past Finger Lake to Engstrom Road, 1 mile to lake. Rainbow; silver and red salmon; Dolly Varden.
4. **REED LAKE**, Mile 42.2. Turn right on Wasilla-Fishhook Road 7 miles to lake. Public access. Rainbow.
5. **KNIK LAKE**, Mile 42.2. Turn left on Knik-Goose Bay Road 13.2 miles. Campground. Pan-sized rainbow.
6. **FISH CREEK**, Mile 42.2. Turn left on Knik-Goose Bay Road; 1 mile past Knik Lake. Rainbow; silver salmon; Dolly Varden.
7. **COTTONWOOD CREEK**, Mile 42.2. Turn left on Knik-Goose Bay Road. Access from several roads between Miles 2.5 and 4. July-August. Silver and red salmon; rainbow; Dolly Varden.

8. **LAKE LUCILE**, Mile 42.2. Located 0.5 mile from Wasilla. Public access area and resorts. Silver salmon.
9. **BIG LAKE**, Mile 52.3. Turn left 3.5 miles to fork. Both roads lead to numerous resorts and campgrounds on lake. Burbot; rainbow; Dolly Varden; silver and red salmon.
10. **ROCKY LAKE**, Mile 52.3. Turn left on Big Lake Road, 3.25 miles, turn right to lake. Use-site. Silver salmon.
11. **LITTLE SUSITNA RIVER.** Accessible from Miles 42.2, 43.5, 48.8 and 56.5. Fair fishing. Early August best for silver salmon; Dolly Varden; rainbow; silver, pink and chum salmon.
12. **NANCY LAKE**, Miles 64 to 67. Several access points. Wayside and marinas. Rainbow; Dolly Varden; burbot; whitefish; silver and red salmon.
13. **DECEPTION CREEK**, Mile 71.2. Turn right on Hatcher Pass Road 1 mile to creek. Wayside. July-August. Rainbow; Dolly Varden; silver, pink and chum salmon.
14. **UPPER WILLOW CREEK** (above rapids), Mile 71.2. Turn right on Hatcher Pass Road. Abundant small Dolly Varden.
15. **LOWER WILLOW CREEK** (below rapids), Mile 71.4. Rainbow; Dolly Varden; grayling; silver, chum and pink salmon.
16. **LITTLE WILLOW CREEK**, Mile 74.7. Rainbow; grayling; silver and pink salmon.
17. **KASHWITNA LAKE**, Mile 76.4. Poor fishing for small silver salmon.

MAP NUMBER 28
George Parks Highway: Willow to Broad Pass (Alaska)

1. **CASWELL CREEK**, Mile 85.6. Summer-fall. Rainbow; grayling; silver, pink and chum salmon.
2. **SHEEP CREEK**, Mile 88.6. Access at bridge. Rainbow; grayling; Dolly Varden; whitefish; silver, pink and chum salmon.
3. **MONTANA CREEK**, Mile 96.6. Good access site at bridge. Rainbow; grayling; Dolly Varden; whitefish; silver, pink and chum salmon.
4. **BIRCH CREEK**, Mile 98.7. Turn right 9.5 miles on road to Talkeetna. Access limited. Rainbow; whitefish; silver and red salmon.
5. **CHRISTIANSEN LAKE**, Mile 98.7. Talkeetna Spur Road 12 miles; turn east 0.7 mile then north (left) 0.8 mile, turn right 0.2 mile to lake. Silver salmon.
6. **MOOSE CREEK, KROTO CREEK** and **MARTIN CREEK**, Mile 114.9. Turn left on Petersville Road. Rainbow; grayling; silver and king salmon.
7. **CHULITNA RIVER**, Mile 132.8. Rainbow; grayling; whitefish.
8. **TROUBLESOME CREEK**, Mile 137.3. Clear runoff stream. Trail extends 15 miles coming out at Mile 147. Grayling.

9. **BYERS LAKE**, Mile 147.5. Wayside. Access to lake. Lake trout; burbot; whitefish.
10. **HONOLULU CREEK**, Mile 178.1. Camping and parking area below bridge on the creek. Grayling.
11. **EAST FORK CHULITNA RIVER**, Mile 185.1. Wayside at Mile 185.7 with RV sanitary stations. Rainbow; grayling; whitefish.
12. **MIDDLE FORK CHULITNA RIVER**, Mile 194.5. Rainbow; grayling; whitefish.

See Map Number 14 for northern portion of George Parks Highway.

MAP NUMBER 29
Seward-Anchorage Highway (Alaska)

1. **BIRD CREEK**, Mile 25.5. Campground at Mile 25.8. Summer. Dolly Varden; pink salmon.
2. **TWENTY-MILE RIVER**, Mile 46.1. Dip-net fishing for smelt (also called hooligan, eulachon or candlefish) in May; silver salmon.
3. **PORTAGE CREEK**, Mile 47.6. Dolly Varden; red and silver salmon.
4. **PLACER RIVER**, Mile 49.2 to 49.6. Good dip-net fishing for smelt in May.
5. **INGRAM CREEK**, Mile 51.8. Summer. Dolly Varden; pink salmon.
6. **GRANITE CREEK**, Mile 63.7. Campground at Mile 64.2. Creek parallels highway; numerous pulloffs. Summer. Dolly Varden.
7. **RESURRECTION CREEK**, Mile 56.4. Turn off onto Hope Access Road, drive 16.5 miles to Hope. Campground. Summer. Dolly Varden; pink salmon.
8. **SUMMIT LAKES**, Miles 80 to 82. Campground at Upper Summit Lake. Year-round fishing for Dolly Varden.
9. **JEROME LAKE**, Mile 88.5. Year-round fishing for rainbow and Dolly Varden.
10. **TRAIL RIVER**, Mile 101.7. Campground at Mile 102.9. Summer and fall. Dolly Varden; rainbow; lake trout.
11. **PTARMIGAN CREEK**, Mile 103.9. USFS campground. Rainbow; Dolly Varden.
12. **GOLDEN FIN LAKE**, Mile 116. Trail 0.5 mile through Divide Ski Area. Year-round fishing for Dolly Varden.
13. **GROUSE LAKE**, Mile 119. Spring and fall. Dolly Varden.
14. **SALMON CREEK**, Mile 121.1. Late summer and fall. Dolly Varden.
15. **RESURRECTION BAY**, Mile 127 at Seward. Campground, commercial facilities. Boat rentals and charters. Spring, summer and fall. Silver and pink salmon; Dolly Varden; bottom fish.

MAP NUMBER 30
Sterling Highway: Junction with Seward-Anchorage Highway to Soldotna (Alaska)

1. **QUARTZ CREEK,** Mile 45.1. Campground 0.5 mile from Mile 45.1. Summer and fall. Silver salmon; rainbow; Dolly Varden.
2. **CRESCENT CREEK,** Mile 45.1. Campground. Summer and fall. Grayling.
3. **CRESCENT LAKE,** Mile 45.1. Trail leads 6.5 miles to lake. Spring, summer and fall. Grayling.
4. **COOPER LAKE,** Mile 49. Lake is 12 miles from turnoff. Summer and fall. Small Dolly Varden.
5. **JUNEAU LAKE,** Mile 49. Trail leads 6 miles to lake. Campground. Summer. Rainbow; lake trout; whitefish.
6. **SWAN LAKE,** Mile 49. Trail leads 9 miles to lake. Campground area. Summer. Rainbow; lake trout; Dolly Varden; red salmon.
7. **RUSSIAN LAKES,** Mile 52.8. Trail leads 2.6 and 12 miles to lakes. Camping area. Summer and fall. Rainbow; Dolly Varden.
8. **RUSSIAN RIVER,** Mile 55. Campground. Summer and fall. Dolly Varden; silver salmon; sockeye salmon, mid-August to September; good fishing for rainbow following salmon run.
9. **SOUTH FULLER LAKE,** Mile 57.2. Trail leads 2 miles to lake. Grayling.
10. **Skilak Loop Road,** Miles 57.7 and 75.1. See Map Number 31.
11. **JEAN LAKE,** Mile 61. Rainbow; Dolly Varden.
12. **UPPER JEAN LAKE,** Mile 63. Campground. Year-round fishing for rainbow.
13. **KELLY** and **PETERSON LAKES,** Mile 68.5. Drive 1 mile from turnoff. Camping area. Summer and fall. Rainbow.
14. **WATSON LAKE,** Mile 71. Drive 1 mile to camping area. Rainbow.
15. **EAST FORK MOOSE RIVER,** Mile 70.3. Summer and fall. Rainbow.
16. **MOOSE RIVER,** Mile 82. State campground. Commercial accommodations nearby. Boat rentals. Summer and fall. Dolly Varden and red salmon.

Swanson River Road from Mile 83.5

17. **SUNKEN ISLAND LAKE,** Mile 4. Camping area. Year-round. Silver salmon.
18. **FOREST LAKES,** Mile 9.5. Summer and fall. Rainbow.
19. **DOLLY VARDEN LAKE,** Mile 14. Campground. Year-round. Rainbow; arctic char.
20. **RAINBOW TROUT LAKE,** Mile 16. Campground. Year-round. Rainbow; arctic char.
21. **SWANSON RIVER,** Mile 18. Campground. Summer and fall. Rainbow; Dolly Varden; silver salmon.
22. **SWAN LAKE CANOE PORTAGE SYSTEM,** Mile 22. Parking area. Maps available at Department of Fish & Game and U.S. Fish & Wildlife offices. Summer and fall. Rainbow; arctic char.
23. **SWANSON RIVER CANOE PORTAGE SYSTEM,** Mile 29. Parking area. Maps available at U.S. Fish & Wildlife offices. Summer and fall. Rainbow; arctic char.

MAP NUMBER 30
Sterling Highway: Junction with Seward-Anchorage Highway to Soldotna (Alaska)

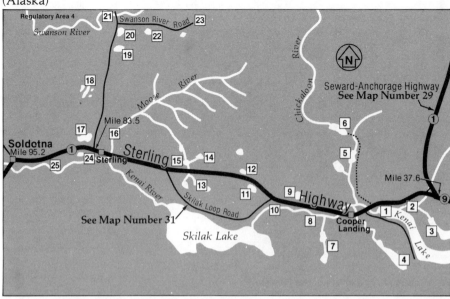

MAP NUMBER 31   Skilak Loop Road from Mile 57.7 (Alaska)

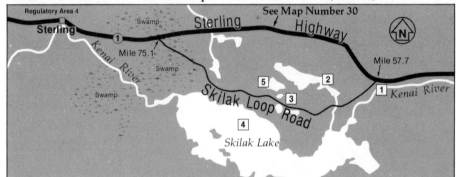

Sterling Highway (continued) (Alaska)

24. **SCOUT LAKE,** Mile 87 Sterling Highway. Year-round. Silver salmon.
25. **LONGMARE LAKE,** Mile 90. Year-round. Rainbow.

MAP NUMBER 31
Skilak Loop Road from Mile 57.7 (Alaska)

1. **East Entrance of Skilak Loop Road,** Mile 57.7 Sterling Highway.
2. **HIDDEN LAKE,** Mile 57.7 Campground. Year-round. Rainbow; lake trout; Dolly Varden; kokanee.
3. **OHMER LAKES,** Mile 7. Campground. Summer and fall. Rainbow; Dolly Varden.
4. **SKILAK LAKE,** access roads at Miles 7 and 12. Campground and boat launching facilities. Summer and fall. Rainbow; lake trout; Dolly Varden; silver salmon; whitefish.
5. **ENGINEER LAKE,** Mile 8. Campground. Summer and fall. Silver salmon.

MAP NUMBER 32
Sterling Highway: Kenai-Soldotna to Homer (Alaska)

1. **STORMY LAKE,** Mile 36.5 North Kenai Road. Year-round. Arctic char; rainbow.
2. **BISHOP CREEK,** Mile 35.1 North Kenai Road. Parking area. Summer and fall. Rainbow.
3. **CABIN LAKE,** Mile 21.5 North Kenai Road turnoff; 3 miles on Miller's Loop Road. **BERNICE LAKE,** campground at Mile 21.4. Rainbow.
4. **BEAVER CREEK,** Mile 6 Kenai Spur Road. Limited parking area. Summer and fall. Rainbow; Dolly Varden.
5. **SPORT LAKE,** junction 2 miles north of Soldotna leads 1 mile to lake. Parking area. Rainbow.
6. **KENAI RIVER,** Soldotna area. Summer and fall. Rainbow; Dolly Varden; silver, pink, red and king salmon.
7. **ARC LAKE,** Mile 98.2 Sterling Highway. Parking area. Year-round. Rainbow.
8. **JOHNSON LAKE,** Mile 110.4 Sterling Highway. Campground. Year-round. Rainbow.
9. **CENTENNIAL LAKE,** Mile 110.6 Sterling Highway turnoff; 3 miles on Tustumena Lake Road. Parking area. Year-round. Silver salmon.

MAP NUMBER 32
Sterling Highway: Kenai-Soldotna to Homer (Alaska)

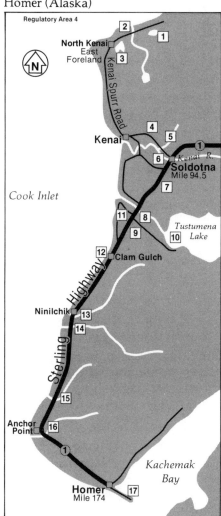

MAP NUMBER 33 Bristol Bay-Alaska Peninsula (Alaska)

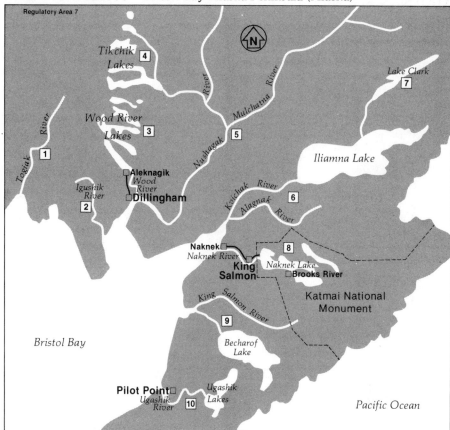

10. **TUSTUMENA LAKE,** Mile 110.6; 5 miles on Tustumena Lake Road. Caution advised in boating. Spring fishery at outlet. Lake trout; Dolly Varden; whitefish; silver salmon.
11. **CROOKED CREEK,** Mile 114. Summer and fall. Rainbow; Dolly Varden.
12. **CLAM GULCH,** Mile 118.5. Access road leads 2 miles to clam beaches. Parking area. Spring, summer and fall. Minus tides recommended. Razor clams.
13. **NINILCHIK RIVER,** Mile 135. Parking and campground areas. Commercial facilities. Spring through fall. Dolly Varden; steelhead; king and silver salmon.
14. **DEEP CREEK,** Mile 136.7. Parking and campground areas. Spring through fall. Dolly Varden; steelhead; king and silver salmon.
15. **STARISKI CREEK,** Mile 151. Campground 1 mile south. Summer and fall. Dolly Varden; steelhead; silver salmon.
16. **ANCHOR RIVER,** Mile 157. Campground and commercial facilities. Spring through fall. Dolly Varden; steelhead; king and silver salmon.
17. **HOMER SPIT,** campground and commercial facilities. Spring through fall. Dolly Varden; silver and pink salmon; halibut; bottom fish.

MAP NUMBER 33
Bristol Bay-Alaska Peninsula (Alaska)

Access via scheduled flights to King Salmon, Dillingham, Pilot Point with floatplanes available from these points. Distances given are approximate. No accommodations unless listed.

1. **TOGIAK SYSTEM: TOGIAK RIVER** and **LAKE, ONGIVINUK, GECHIAK** and **PUNGOKEPUK LAKES,** 60 miles west of Dillingham. Togiak River is a popular river to float. All salmon; grayling; arctic char; rainbow; northern pike.
2. **IGUSHIK SYSTEM:** 20 miles west of Dillingham. Red salmon; grayling; arctic char; rainbow; northern pike.
3. **WOOD RIVER SYSTEM:** 20 to 60 miles north of Dillingham. Access to **LAKE ALEKNAGIK** via road from Dillingham in summer. Entire system navigable with a river boat and jet unit or can be floated. Fantastic scenery. Private lodges. All salmon; grayling; arctic char; rainbow; northern pike.
4. **TIKCHIK SYSTEM:** 80 miles north of Dillingham. One private lodge. Grayling; arctic char; rainbow; northern pike; lake trout; red and pink salmon.
5. **NUSHAGAK-MULCHATNA SYSTEM: MULCHATNA, KOKTULI** and **KING SALMON RIVERS** are popular for float trips. Hundreds of miles of river fishing from **TWIN** and **TURQUOISE LAKES** north of **LAKE CLARK** downstream to Dillingham. Grayling; arctic char; rainbow; northern pike; lake trout.

6. **BRISTOL BAY WILD TROUT AREA:** Kvichak watershed (except Lake Clark and its tributaries above Six-Mile Lake). Special regulations; check regulation book. All salmon; grayling; arctic char; rainbow; northern pike; lake trout.
7. **LAKE CLARK AREA,** 30 miles north of Iliamna. Several private lodges. Lake trout; northern pike; red salmon; arctic char; burbot; whitefish; grayling.
8. **NAKNEK RIVER SYSTEM** extends 75 miles east of Naknek and much of the system is included in Katmai National Monument (subject to additional federal regulations). Access by plane, foot or boat from King Salmon. Campground in monument, lodge at Brooks River and hotel in King Salmon. All salmon; grayling; arctic char; rainbow; northern pike; lake trout; whitefish; smelt in winter.
9. **EGEGIK RIVER SYSTEM,** 40 miles south of King Salmon. Access by boat from Egegik, plane from King Salmon. All salmon; grayling; arctic char; rainbow; northern pike; lake trout.
10. **UGASHIK SYSTEM,** 80 miles south of King Salmon. Private lodges at Ugashik Lake. All salmon; grayling; arctic char; northern pike; lake trout.

MAP NUMBER 34
Kodiak Area (Alaska)

1. **MONASHKA BAY**, 4.5 to 11 miles northeast of Kodiak via Rezanof-Monashka Road. Dolly Varden; rockfish; silver and pink salmon; greenling; halibut.
2. **ABERCROMBIE LAKE**, 4.25 miles northeast of Kodiak. Picnic, camping and swimming area. Rainbow; grayling.
3. **ISLAND** and **DARK LAKES**, 3 miles north of Kodiak on Rezanof-Monashka Road. Picnic and swimming area. Rainbow; Dolly Varden.
4. **GENEVIEVE** and **MARGARET LAKES**, picnic and swimming area. Rainbow.
5. **CASCADE LAKE**, access to trail at Mile 8.7 Anton Larsen Bay Road; 1.5-mile hike over steep trail. Rainbow; grayling.
6. **ANTON LARSEN BAY**, 10.1 miles northwest of Kodiak. Boat launch. Pink, chum and silver salmon; Dolly Varden; halibut; crab.
7. **BUSKIN RIVER**, Mile 5 Chiniak Road. Dolly Varden; pink, silver and red salmon.
8. **WOMENS BAY**, Miles 7 to 9 Chiniak Road. Fishing off side of road. Dolly Varden; pink, silver and chum salmon; halibut, crab.
9. **BELL'S FLATS LAKES**, 10 miles south of Kodiak; 7 small lakes accessible by short trails. Rainbow; grayling; Dolly Varden.
10. **RUSSIAN RIVER**, 10 miles south of Kodiak. Dolly Varden; pink and chum salmon.
11. **CLIFF POINT LAKES**, 14 miles south of Kodiak via Chiniak Road. Rainbow.
12. **MIDDLE BAY**, 18 miles south of Kodiak. Small picnic area. Halibut; pink, silver and chum salmon; Dolly Varden; crab; clams.
13. **AMERICAN RIVER**, Mile 20.8 Chiniak Road. Silver, pink, and chum salmon; Dolly Varden.
14. **OLDS RIVER** and **KALSIN RIVER**, Mile 28 Chiniak Road. Dolly Varden; pink and silver salmon.
15. **KALSIN BAY**, Mile 30 Chiniak Road. Pink and silver salmon; Dolly Varden.
16. **ROSLYN RIVER** and **BEACH**, Mile 37 Chiniak Road. Good beach and small camping area. Pink and silver salmon; Dolly Varden.
17. **TWIN FORKS** and **CHINIAK CREEKS**, Mile 40 to 40.5 Chiniak Road. Silver salmon are scarce. Dolly Varden; pink and silver salmon.
18. **PONY LAKE**, Mile 40 Chiniak Road. Silver salmon; Dolly Varden.
19. **PASAGSHAK POINT LAKES**, Mile 7.6 Pasagshak Road. Rainbow.
20. **LAKE ROSE TEAD** and **PASAGSHAK RIVER**, Mile 6.6 Pasagshak Road. Good beach. Dolly Varden; silver, pink and red salmon.
21. **MIAM LAKE**, 15 to 20 minute air charter from Kodiak. Rainbow; steelhead; pink and silver salmon; Dolly Varden.
22. **SALTERY LAKE** and **RIVER**, 36 miles southwest of Kodiak via a 4-wheel-drive road to Saltery Cove, or a 15 to 20 minute air charter from Kodiak. Rainbow; steelhead; red, pink and silver salmon; Dolly Varden.
23. **WOODY** and **LONG ISLAND LAKES**, 2 to 4 miles east of Kodiak; also accessible by boat. Good camping, hiking, picnicking and beachcombing. Rainbow; silver salmon; Dolly Varden; grayling.

MAP NUMBER 34   Kodiak Area (Alaska)

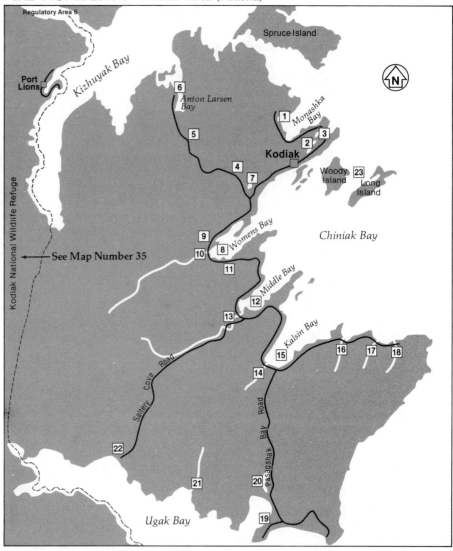

MAP NUMBER 35   Kodiak National Wildlife Refuge (Alaska)

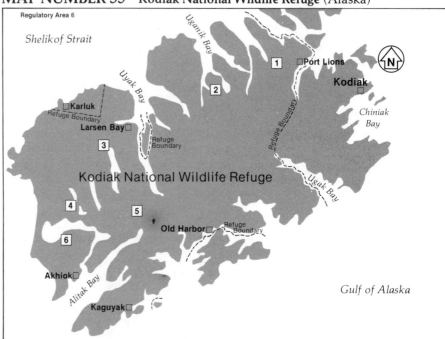

MAP NUMBER 36
Afognak Island (Alaska)

MAP NUMBER 37   Copper River Highway (Alaska)

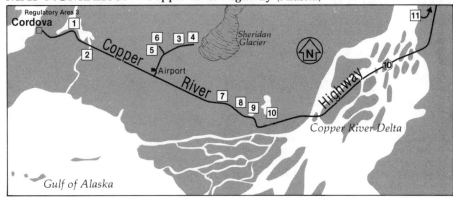

MAP NUMBER 35
Kodiak National Wildlife Refuge
(Alaska)

1. **BARBARA LAKE**, 21 air miles west of Kodiak. Rainbow; Dolly Varden; red and silver salmon.
2. **UGANIK LAKE** and **RIVER**, 36 air miles southwest of Kodiak. Rainbow; steelhead; Dolly Varden; red, pink and silver salmon.
3. **KARLUK LAKE, RIVER** and **LAGOON**, approximately 75 air miles southwest of Kodiak. Public-use cabins at lake and mid-river. Rainbow; steelhead; Dolly Varden; red, pink, silver and king salmon.
4. **RED LAKE** and **RIVER**, approximately 85 air miles from Kodiak. Rainbow; steelhead; Dolly Varden; red, pink, silver and king salmon.
5. **UPPER STATION LAKES**, approximately 90 air miles southwest of Kodiak. Rainbow; steelhead; Dolly Varden; pink, red and silver salmon.
6. **AKALURA LAKE**, approximately 80 air miles southwest of Kodiak. Rainbow; steelhead; Dolly Varden; silver, red and pink salmon.

MAP NUMBER 36
Afognak Island (Alaska)

1. **AFOGNAK LAKE** and **RIVER**, 28 air miles northwest of Kodiak. Rainbow; steelhead; Dolly Varden; red, pink and silver salmon.
2. **MALINA LAKES**, 36 air miles northwest of Kodiak. USFS cabin. Rainbow; steelhead; Dolly Varden; red, pink and silver salmon.
3. **LITTLE AFOGNAK LAKE**, 26 air miles northeast of Kodiak. Rainbow; steelhead; Dolly Varden; red and silver salmon.

MAP NUMBER 38   Chitina-McCarthy Road (Alaska)

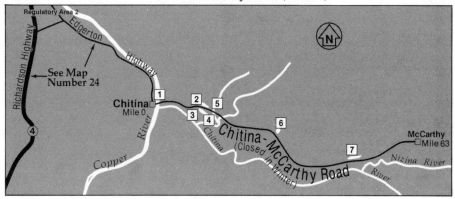

4. **KITOI LAKES**, 30 air miles northeast of Kodiak. Rainbow; Dolly Varden; silver and red salmon.
5. **PORTAGE LAKE**, 35 air miles north of Kodiak. USFS cabin. Rainbow; steelhead; Dolly Varden; red, pink and silver salmon.
6. **WATERFALL LAKE**, 40 air miles northwest of Kodiak. USFS cabin. Dolly Varden.
7. **PAULS-LAURA LAKE**, 40 air miles northeast of Kodiak. Best rainbow trout fishing on Afognak Island. Rainbow; steelhead; Dolly Varden; red, pink and silver salmon.

MAP NUMBER 37
Copper River Highway (Alaska)

1. **EYAK LAKE**, Miles 0 to 4. Silver and red salmon; cutthroat.
2. **EYAK RIVER**, Mile 5.7. Silver and red salmon; cutthroat.
3. **BEAVER LAKE**, Mile 12.1. Drive 3 miles north on good dirt road; 1 mile by trail. Dolly Varden; cutthroat.
4. **UPPER BEAVER LAKE**, Mile 12.1. Just above Beaver Lake. Fish are small. Dolly Varden; cutthroat.
5. **CABIN LAKE**, Mile 12.1. Access road 2.7 miles to lake and USFS campsite. Fish are small. Cutthroat.

6. **ISLAND LAKE**, 1 mile by good trail from Cabin Lake. Cutthroat.
7. **19-MILE LAKE**, Mile 19. Adjacent to road. Fish are small. Dolly Varden; cutthroat.
8. **PIPELINE LAKE**, Mile 21.5. North by trail 0.75 mile. Grayling; Dolly Varden; cutthroat.
9. **22-MILE LAKE**, Mile 21.5. North by trail 0.5 mile. Dolly Varden; cutthroat.
10. **McKINLEY LAKE**, Mile 22.1, North by trail 3 miles. Dolly Varden; cutthroat.
11. **CLEAR CREEK**, Mile 42. Dolly Varden.

MAP NUMBER 38
Chitina-McCarthy Road (Alaska)

1. **COPPER RIVER**, Mile 1.1. Campground. Red and king salmon.
2. **STRELNA LAKE**, Mile 10.6. Trail, 0.3 mile north. Rainbow; silver salmon.
3. **VAN LAKE**, Mile 11.1. Trail, 0.25 mile south. Rainbow; silver salmon.
4. **SCULPIN LAKE**, Mile 12.6. South 0.25 mile. Rainbow.
5. **STRELNA CREEK**, Mile 15.4. Fair fishing. Dolly Varden.
6. **LOU'S LAKE**, Mile 25.7. North 0.75 mile. Silver salmon; grayling.
7. **LONG LAKE**, Mile 45. Grayling; burbot; lake trout; silver salmon; Dolly Varden.

MAP NUMBER 39
Yakutat Area (Alaska)

1. **YAKUTAT BAY.** King and silver salmon; halibut.
2. **LOST RIVER,** by trail or air from Yakutat. Silver salmon; Dolly Varden.
3. **SITUK RIVER,** by air or road from Yakutat. USFS cabin. Guides and accommodations available in Yakutat. One of the top fishing spots in Alaska, spring and fall. Steelhead; Dolly Varden; king, silver, red and pink salmon; smelt.
4. **AHRNKLIN RIVER,** 25 miles by road from Yakutat. Fall. Dolly Varden; red and silver salmon.
5. **ITALIO RIVER,** 21 air miles southeast of Yakutat. Silver salmon; cutthroat; Dolly Varden; smelt.
6. **AKWE RIVER,** 32 air miles southeast of Yakutat. Private airstrip. Excellent fall fishing at fork with **USTAY RIVER.** Dolly Varden; cutthroat; red, king and silver salmon.

MAP NUMBER 40
Haines and Skagway Area (Alaska)

1. **BIG BOULDER CREEK,** Mile 34 Haines Highway. Pulloff. Dolly Varden.
2. **31-MILE SLOUGH,** Mile 31 Haines Highway. Road shoulder parking along meandering slough. Late summer and fall. Dolly Varden; chum and silver salmon.
3. **MOSQUITO LAKE,** Mile 28.5 Haines Highway; turn north at sign and drive 2.5 miles to lake. Use-site. Shore fishing available. Dolly Varden; cutthroat; whitefish.
4. **CHILKAT RIVER,** Miles 16 to 19 Haines Highway. River adjacent to road at intervals. Fall and winter. Cutthroat; Dolly Varden; chum, silver and pink salmon.
5. **CHILKAT LAKE,** Mile 19 Haines Highway; turn west 5 miles. Access by boat or air. Red salmon; whitefish; Dolly Varden; kokanee; cutthroat.
6. **14-MILE SLOUGH,** Mile 14 Haines Highway. Off-highway parking. Late summer and fall. Dolly Varden; chum, silver and pink salmon.
7. **CHILKOOT RIVER,** 10 miles northeast of Haines on Chilkoot Lake Road. Fall and winter. Red and pink salmon; Dolly Varden.
8. **LOWER DEWEY LAKE,** trail starts east of Skagway near water tanks. Hike 0.3 mile to lower lake. Rainbow.
9. **BLACK LAKE,** 3 miles north of Skagway on Skagway River Road. Information may be obtained locally. Large Dolly Varden.
10. **DYEA SLOUGH,** 10 miles north of Skagway by road at head of Taiya Inlet. Fall best. Dolly Varden; pink, chum and silver salmon.
11. **LOST LAKE,** 10 miles from Skagway by road to head of Taiya Inlet; then a stiff 2-mile hike westerly to lake. Use of guide recommended. Information may be obtained locally. Large rainbow.

See Map Number 4 for northern portion of Haines Highway.

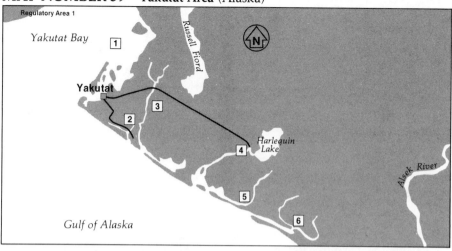

MAP NUMBER 39 Yakutat Area (Alaska)

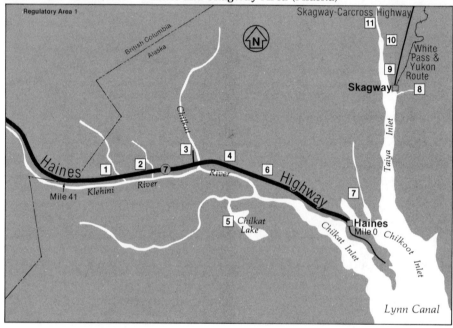

MAP NUMBER 40 Haines and Skagway Area (Alaska)

MAP NUMBER 41
Juneau Area (Alaska)

1. **ANTLER LAKE,** 39 air miles northwest of Juneau. Grayling.
2. **ECHO COVE,** Mile 40.6 Glacier Highway. Dolly Varden; cutthroat; king, silver, chum, and pink salmon; halibut.
3. **COWEE CREEK,** Mile 39.7 Glacier Highway. Dolly Varden; cutthroat; silver, chum and pink salmon.
4. **EAGLE RIVER,** Mile 25 Glacier Highway. Dolly Varden; silver salmon.
5. **NORTH PASS,** by boat from Juneau, Auke Bay or Tee Harbor. King, silver, pink and chum salmon; Dolly Varden; halibut; rockfish.
6. **WINDFALL LAKE,** Mile 27.4 Glacier Highway; 3-mile trail to lake. Dolly Varden; cutthroat; silver and red salmon.
7. **PETERSON CREEK,** Mile 24.4 Glacier Highway. Dolly Varden; cutthroat; steelhead; silver, chum and pink salmon.
8. **PETERSON LAKE,** Mile 24 Glacier Highway. Trail 4 miles to lake. Dolly Varden; rainbow.
9. **MONTANA CREEK,** Mile 4.6 Mendenhall Loop Road. Dolly Varden; cutthroat; silver, chum and pink salmon.
10. **AUKE LAKE** and **CREEK,** Mile 11 Glacier Highway. Campground. Check regulations for salmon season. Dolly Varden; cutthroat; red, silver, chum and pink salmon.
11. **AUKE BAY,** Mile 12.1 Glacier Highway. King, silver, pink, chum and red salmon; Dolly Varden; halibut; rockfish.
12. **FISH CREEK,** 7.6 miles north of the Gastineau Channel Bridge on North Douglas Road. Check regulations for salmon season. Dolly Varden; cutthroat; chum and pink salmon.
13. **SALMON CREEK RESERVOIR,** take the 3-mile trail that begins at Mile 2.3 Glacier Highway. No facilities. Good ice fishing. Brook trout.
14. **TURNER LAKE,** by boat and trail or air 25 miles east of Juneau. 2 USFS cabins, 3 boats. Excellent kokanee and cutthroat.

MAP NUMBER 41 Juneau Area (Alaska)

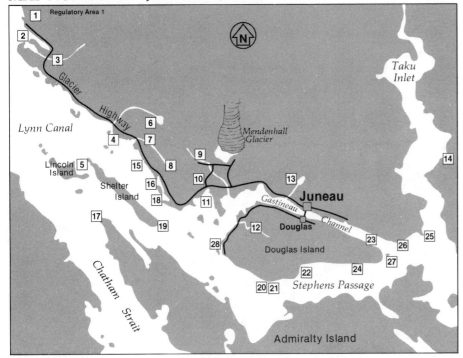

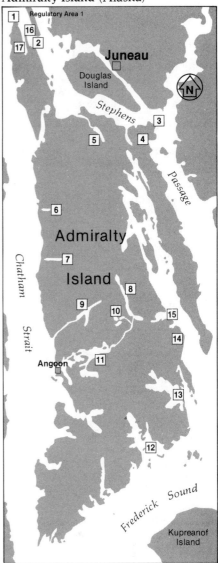

The following fishing spots are accessible by boat from Juneau, Auke Bay or Tee Harbor.

15. **THE BREADLINE.** King, silver, pink and chum salmon; Dolly Varden; halibut; rockfish.
16. **AARON ISLAND.** King, silver, pink and chum salmon; Dolly Varden; halibut; rockfish.
17. **POINT RETREAT.** King, silver, pink and chum salmon; Dolly Varden; halibut; rockfish.
18. **LENA POINT.** King, silver, pink and chum salmon; Dolly Varden; halibut; rockfish.
19. **SOUTH SHELTER ISLAND.** King, silver, pink and chum salmon; Dolly Varden; halibut; rockfish.
20. **MIDDLE POINT.** King, silver, pink and chum salmon; Dolly Varden; halibut; rockfish.
21. **WHITE MARKER.** King, silver, pink and chum salmon; Dolly Varden; halibut; rockfish.
22. **POINT HILDA.** King, silver, pink and chum salmon; Dolly Varden; halibut; rockfish.
23. **DUPONT,** 2-mile trail at end of Thane Road for offshore fishing. King, silver, pink and chum salmon; Dolly Varden; halibut; rockfish.
24. **ICY POINT.** King, silver, pink and chum salmon; Dolly Varden; halibut; rockfish.
25. **POINT BISHOP.** King, silver, pink and chum salmon; Dolly Varden; halibut; rockfish.
26. **POINT SALISBURY.** King, silver, pink and chum salmon; Dolly Varden; halibut; rockfish.
27. **MARMION ISLAND.** King, silver, pink and chum salmon; Dolly Varden; halibut; rockfish.
28. **OUTER POINT.** King, silver, pink and chum salmon; Dolly Varden; halibut; rockfish.

MAP NUMBER 42
Admiralty Island (Alaska)

1. **POINT RETREAT,** by boat from Juneau, Auke Bay or Tee Harbor. King, silver, pink, chum and red salmon; Dolly Varden; halibut; rockfish.
2. **PILING POINT,** by boat from Juneau, Auke Bay or Tee Harbor. King, silver, pink, chum and red salmon; Dolly Varden; halibut; rockfish.
3. **POINT ARDEN,** by boat from Juneau, Auke Bay or Tee Harbor. King, silver, pink, chum and red salmon; Dolly Varden; halibut; rockfish.
4. **DOTY'S COVE,** by boat from Juneau, Auke Bay or Tee Harbor. King, silver, pink, chum and red salmon; Dolly Varden; halibut; rockfish.
5. **YOUNGS LAKE,** 15 miles south of Juneau by boat or plane. USFS cabin and boat. Rainbow; steelhead; cutthroat; Dolly Varden; silver salmon.
6. **LAKE KATHLEEN,** 28 air miles southwest of Juneau. USFS cabin and boat. Cutthroat; Dolly Varden.
7. **LAKE FLORENCE,** 33 air miles southwest of Juneau. USFS cabin and shelter with boats. Cutthroat; Dolly Varden.
8. **HASSELBORG LAKE,** 37 air miles south of Juneau. Several USFS cabins and boats. Cutthroat; Dolly Varden; kokanee.
9. **THAYER LAKE,** 42 air miles south of Juneau. Modern lodge with all facilities. Cutthroat; Dolly Varden.
10. **DAVIDSON, DISTIN** and **GUERIN LAKES,** 45 air miles south of Juneau. USFS cabins and boats. Cutthroat; Dolly Varden; kokanee.

11. **MITCHELL BAY,** 49 air miles south of Juneau, or by boat from Angoon. Shelter. Excellent cutthroat trout, spring; Dolly Varden.
12. **PYBUS BAY,** 80 miles south of Juneau. Good summer fishing for large king salmon. King, pink and silver salmon; halibut; Dolly Varden.
13. **GAMBIER BAY,** 70 boat miles south of Juneau. USFS cabin. King, silver and pink salmon; halibut; Dolly Varden.
14. **PLEASANT BAY CREEK,** 50 air miles, 65 boat miles south of Juneau. Popular for steelhead; Dolly Varden; pink and silver salmon; cutthroat.
15. **MOLE HARBOR,** 45 air miles, 70 boat miles south of Juneau. Dolly Varden; pink, chum and silver salmon; cutthroat; steelhead.
16. **BARLOW COVE.** King, silver, pink and chum salmon; Dolly Varden; halibut; rockfish.
17. **FAVORITE REEF.** King, silver, pink and chum salmon; Dolly Varden; rockfish.

MAP NUMBER 43
Sitka Area (Alaska)

1. **SITKOH LAKE**, 30 air miles northeast of Sitka on Chichagof Island. Excellent fishing. Cabin and boat. Cutthroat.
2. **SITKOH CREEK**, good steelhead fishing in April and May. Dolly Varden; silver and red salmon; cutthroat.
3. **LAKE EVA**, 20 air miles northeast of Sitka. Excellent fishing. Cabin and skiff. Cutthroat; Dolly Varden.
4. **LITTLE LAKE EVA**, 20 air miles northeast of Sitka. Excellent fishing. Cutthroat.
5. **NAKWASINA RIVER**, 15 miles north of Sitka by boat. Excellent Dolly Varden fishing in July and August; Silver salmon; sea-run Dolly Varden.
6. **KATLIAN RIVER**, 11 miles northeast of Sitka by boat. Dolly Varden; cutthroat; silver, pink and chum salmon.
7. **STARRIGAVIN BAY**, Mile 7.8 Halibut Point Road. Campground. Excellent fishing from shore. Dolly Varden; pink and silver salmon.
8. **KAMENOI BEACH**, 10 miles northwest of Sitka by boat or plane. Minus-3-foot tide recommended. Razor clams.
9. **SITKA SOUND**, boats, tackle and guides available in Sitka. Excellent fishing. Dolly Varden; king and silver salmon; rockfish; halibut.
10. **SWAN LAKE**, within Sitka city limits. Small skiff or rubber boat recommended. Rainbow.
11. **THIMBLEBERRY LAKE**, Mile 3.7. Sawmill Creek Road. Trail 2.8 miles to lake. Brook trout.
12. **HEART LAKE**, 0.2 mile beyond Thimbleberry Lake. Brook trout.
13. **BLUE LAKE**, Mile 5.5 Sawmill Creek Road. Take Blue Lake Road 2.2 miles to parking area and short trail to lake. Excellent fishing. Lightweight skiff or rubber boat recommended. Rainbow.
14. **BEAVER LAKE**, 0.5-mile hike from Sawmill Creek campground, Mile 1.4 Blue Lake Road. Excellent fishing. Grayling.
15. **BARANOF LAKE**, 18 air miles east of Sitka. Cabin and skiff. Cutthroat.
16. **MEDVEJIA LAKE**, 8 miles up Silver Bay southeast of Sitka by boat. Dolly Varden.
17. **GREEN LAKE**, at southeast end of Silver Bay by boat with short hike to lake; or by plane. Skiffs. Brook trout.
18. **SALMON LAKE**, at southeast end of Silver Bay by boat, 11 miles, with 1-mile hike. Skiff. Cutthroat; steelhead; Dolly Varden; silver, red, pink and chum salmon.
19. **REDOUBT LAKE**. Trail 5.5 miles to lake from head of Silver Bay; 12 miles south of Sitka by boat. USFS cabin. Cutthroat; Dolly Varden; pink, chum, silver and red salmon.

20. **AVOSS LAKE**, 29 air miles southeast of Sitka. Excellent fishing. Cabin and skiff. Rainbow.
21. **PASS LAKE**, 33 air miles southeast of Sitka. Rainbow.
22. **DAVIDOF LAKE**, 35 air miles southeast of Sitka. Excellent fishing. Cabin and skiff. Rainbow.
23. **PORT BANKS**, 35 air miles southeast of Sitka. Excellent fishing in late July and August. Silvers.
24. **LAKE PLOTNIKOF**, 38 air miles southeast of Sitka. Cabin and skiff. Rainbow.
25. **KHVOSTOF LAKE**, 39 air miles southeast of Sitka. Rainbow.
26. **REZANOF LAKE**, 40 air miles southeast of Sitka; 2 cabins and skiff. Rainbow.
27. **GAR LAKE**, 39 air miles southeast of Sitka. Good fishing. Cabin and skiff. Rainbow.

MAP NUMBER 43   Sitka Area (Alaska)

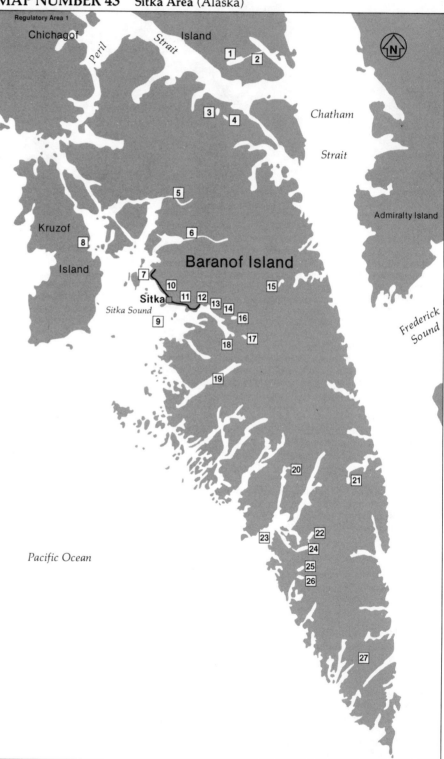

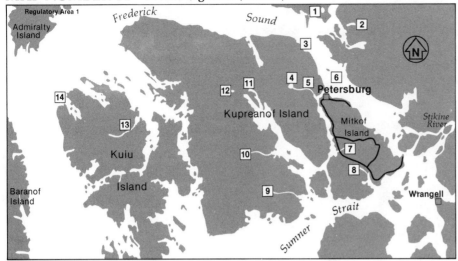

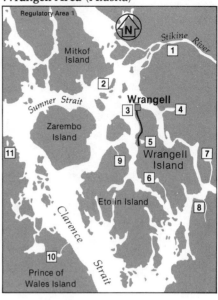

MAP NUMBER 44
Petersburg Area (Alaska)

1. DeBOER LAKE, 20 air miles north of Petersburg. Rainbow.
2. SWAN LAKE, 18 air miles north of Petersburg. Excellent fall fishing. Boat and cabin. Rainbow.
3. CAPE STRAIT, 12 miles north of Petersburg off the Kupreanof Island shoreline. King and silver salmon; halibut; rockfish; ling cod.
4. PETERSBURG LAKE, 4.5 miles by trail up Petersburg Creek. Boat and cabin. Dolly Varden; cutthroat; silver salmon.
5. PETERSBURG CREEK, across Wrangell Narrows from Petersburg by boat. Boats available in Petersburg. Cutthroat; Dolly Varden; steelhead; rainbow; silver, chum, red and pink salmon.
6. FREDERICK SOUND, northeast of Petersburg by boat. King and silver salmon.
7. FALLS CREEK, 11 miles south of Petersburg by road. Use-site. Fall best. Silver, pink and chum salmon; cutthroat; Dolly Varden; steelhead.
8. BLIND RIVER, Mile 12.3 Mitkof Highway. Excellent fall silver salmon fishing; cutthroat; Dolly Varden; king salmon.
9. KAH SHEETS CREEK, 21 miles southwest of Petersburg by boat. Shelter present at head of tide flats. Excellent fall silver salmon fishing; steelhead; cutthroat; Dolly Varden; pink, chum and red salmon.

10. CASTLE RIVER, 22 miles southwest of Petersburg on west shore of Duncan Canal. Rainbow; steelhead; cutthroat; Dolly Varden; silver, pink and chum salmon.
11. SALT CHUCK, 28 miles by boat west of Petersburg at the head of Duncan Canal. Cutthroat; Dolly Varden; silver salmon; steelhead.
12. TOWERS LAKE, 20 air miles west of Petersburg. Cutthroat; Dolly Varden.
13. KADAKE CREEK, 60 miles by boat or 20 minutes by plane west of Petersburg on Kuiu Island. Cabin and boat. Excellent in spring for cutthroat; steelhead; Dolly Varden; silver, chum and pink salmon.
14. SECURITY BAY, 60 miles by boat west of Petersburg on Kuiu Island. King and silver salmon; halibut; rockfish; ling cod.

MAP NUMBER 45
Wrangell Area (Alaska)

1. STIKINE RIVER, by boat or plane from Petersburg or Wrangell. USFS cabins. Use of guide recommended. Excellent fishing. Steelhead; cutthroat; Dolly Varden; silver, pink and chum salmon; whitefish; sturgeon.
2. GREYS PASS, 8 miles northwest of Wrangell by boat. Excellent spring fishing. King salmon; halibut.
3. WRANGELL HARBOR, skiff fishing, mainly for king and silver salmon; halibut; rockfish.
4. VIRGINIA LAKE, 8 miles east of Wrangell by boat and short hike. Cabin and boat. Cutthroat; Dolly Varden; red salmon.
5. PATS CREEK and LAKE, Mile 11 Zimovia Highway. Campground. Cutthroat; Dolly Varden; silver salmon.

6. THOMS LAKE, 18 miles south of Wrangell by boat with a 2-mile hike, or by plane. Cabin. Cutthroat; silver and red salmon; steelhead.
7. MARTEN LAKE, 30 air miles southeast of Wrangell. Boat and cabin. Dolly Varden; rainbow; kokanee; chum salmon.
8. ANAN CREEK, 40 miles south of Wrangell by boat or plane. Cabin. Rainbow; steelhead; cutthroat; Dolly Varden; pink, chum, red and silver salmon.
9. KUNK LAKE, 14 miles south of Wrangell on Etolin Island, by boat and short hike or by plane. Cabin and boat. Cutthroat; Dolly Varden; silver salmon; steelhead.
10. LUCK LAKE, 35 miles southwest of Wrangell on Prince of Wales Island, inland from Luck Point. USFS cabin. Rainbow; steelhead; cutthroat; Dolly Varden; silver, pink, red and chum salmon.
11. SALMON BAY LAKE, 40 miles west of Wrangell on Prince of Wales Island. Boat and cabin at outlet of lake. Rainbow; steelhead; cutthroat; Dolly Varden; pink, chum, red and silver salmon.

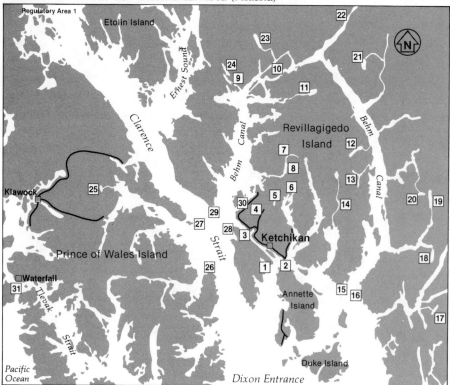

MAP NUMBER 46
Ketchikan Area (Alaska)

1. **BLANK INLET,** 7 miles south of Ketchikan by boat. King, silver, pink and chum salmon; rockfish; ling cod; halibut.
2. **MOUNTAIN POINT,** Mile 5.5 South Tongass Highway. Boat launching ramp. King, silver, pink and chum salmon; rockfish; ling cod; halibut.
3. **WARD COVE CREEK** and **LAKES,** Mile 1.1 Ward Lake Road. System consists of 4 lakes. Pulloffs. Rainbow; steelhead; Dolly Varden; brook trout; chum, silver and red salmon.
4. **SILVIS LAKE,** 1.5 miles from end of South Tongass Highway. Rainbow.
5. **HARRIET HUNT LAKE,** Mile 7.1 Ward Lake Road, then left 2.4 miles to lake. Rainbow.
6. **SALT LAGOON CREEK,** 22 miles north of Ketchikan at head of George Inlet, by boat. Rainbow; steelhead; cutthroat; Dolly Varden; silver, pink and chum salmon.
7. **NAHA RIVER,** 21 miles north of Ketchikan by boat; 6-mile trail follows river. USFS cabin. Grayling; rainbow; steelhead; cutthroat; Dolly Varden; silver, pink, red and chum salmon.
8. **PATCHING LAKE,** 19 air miles from Ketchikan near the Naha River on Revillagigedo Island. USFS cabin. Grayling; cutthroat; Dolly Varden.

9. **YES BAY,** 44 miles north of Ketchikan, by boat, in North Behm Canal. Resort. King, pink, chum and silver salmon; steelhead; cutthroat; Dolly Varden; halibut; rockfish.
10. **BELL ISLAND,** 45 miles north of Ketchikan, by boat, in North Behm Canal. Resort. King, pink, chum and silver salmon; steelhead; cutthroat; Dolly Varden; halibut; rockfish.
11. **ORCHARD LAKE,** 32 air miles north of Ketchikan above Shrimp Bay, Revillagigedo Island. USFS cabin. Cutthroat; Dolly Varden.
12. **GRACE LAKE,** 30 air miles from Ketchikan, inland from east coast of Revillagigedo Island. Brook trout.
13. **MANZANITA LAKE,** 28 air miles northeast of Ketchikan above Manzanita Bay. USFS cabin. Cutthroat; Dolly Varden; kokanee.
14. **FISH CREEK,** 21 miles east of Ketchikan by boat at head of Thorne Arm. USFS cabin. Rainbow; steelhead; cutthroat; Dolly Varden; silver, pink and red salmon.
15. **POINT ALAVA,** 20 miles southeast of Ketchikan by boat. King, silver, pink and chum salmon; rockfish; ling cod; halibut.
16. **POINT SYKES,** 25 miles southeast of Ketchikan by boat. Use of guide recommended. King, silver, pink, chum and red salmon; ling cod; halibut.
17. **HUMPBACK LAKE,** 48 miles southeast of Ketchikan above Mink Bay, Boca de Quadra. Lodge and USFS cabin. Grayling; cutthroat; Dolly Varden.
18. **BAKEWELL LAKE,** 39 air miles northeast of Ketchikan or by boat with a 0.8-mile hike from beach in Smeaton Bay. Cutthroat; Dolly Varden.
19. **WILSON LAKE,** 43 air miles northeast of Ketchikan. USFS cabin. Cutthroat; Dolly Varden; kokanee.
20. **BIG GOAT LAKE,** 38 air miles northeast of Ketchikan. USFS cabin. Grayling.

21. **LeDUC LAKE,** 49 air miles northeast of Ketchikan above Chickamin River. Rainbow.
22. **UNUK RIVER,** 50 miles north of Ketchikan at the head of Burroughs Bay. Rainbow; silver, pink and chum salmon; steelhead; cutthroat; Dolly Varden.
23. **REFLECTION LAKE,** 46 air miles north of Ketchikan above Short Bay, Cleveland Peninsula. USFS cabin. Rainbow; steelhead; cutthroat; silver salmon.
24. **McDONALD LAKE,** 45 air miles north of Ketchikan above Yes Bay. USFS cabin. Rainbow; steelhead; cutthroat; Dolly Varden; silver and red salmon; grayling.
25. **KARTA RIVER,** 42 air miles northwest of Ketchikan above Karta Bay, Prince of Wales Island. USFS cabin. Rainbow; steelhead; cutthroat; Dolly Varden; silver, pink, red and chum salmon.
26. **CHASINA POINT,** 22 miles southwest of Ketchikan by boat. Use of guide recommended. King, silver, pink and chum salmon; rockfish; ling cod; halibut.
27. **GRINDALL ISLAND,** 20 miles northwest of Ketchikan by boat. Use of guide recommended. King, silver, pink and chum salmon; rockfish; ling cod; halibut.
28. **VALLENAR POINT,** 11 miles northwest of Ketchikan by boat. King, silver, pink and chum salmon; rockfish; ling cod; halibut.
29. **CAAMANO POINT,** 18 miles northwest of Ketchikan by boat. Use of guide recommended. King, silver, pink and chum salmon; rockfish; ling cod; halibut.
30. **CLOVER PASS,** 11 miles northwest of Ketchikan by road or boat. Resort. King, silver, pink and chum salmon; rockfish; ling cod; halibut.
31. **WATERFALL,** on Tlevak Strait, west side of Prince of Wales Island, 40 minutes from Ketchikan by air. Resort. Steelhead; king, pink and silver salmon; halibut; rockfish; ling cod; crab; clams.

INDEX

There's a whole lot more to ALASKA than meets the eye

If you're like most outdoor people, you think of a hunting or fishing trip as one of the best possible ways to see the countryside. But one trip or even a hundred won't show one pair of eyes all the Alaska there is to see.

That's where we come in . . . with a variety of publications that give you the use of hundreds of pairs of eyes, countless trips into the countryside, unbeatable perspective on the Great Land. Help yourself to these long looks at Alaska:

ALASKA® magazine, every month, captures Life on the Last Frontier® in top quality color photography and vivid, true stories that have a strong emphasis on the great outdoors. 12 monthly issues, just $15 — a $3 saving over the newsstand price.

ALASKA GEOGRAPHIC® is uniquely designed to show you an Alaska few people are privileged to see for themselves. Each issue concentrates on just one subject and explores it thoroughly with maps, spectacular photography and the latest information about Alaska's vast resources. Membership in The Alaska Geographic Society — $20 per year — brings you 4 quarterly editions, at a vast saving over single copy price.

The ALASKA JOURNAL® gives you a window on Alaska's colorful past, its arts, artists and photographers, and the people who shape its future. Quarterly subscription, $8 a year.

The MILEPOST® All-the-North Travel Guide® is annually updated to bring you the last word about traveling anywhere in Alaska, Yukon Territory, British Columbia, Northwest Territories and Alberta. Nearly 500 pages of how-to, where-to data, maps and photos galore, plus a color fold-out map of the whole area. Just $5.95 plus $.75 fourth-class postage and handling per copy ($2.50 first class).

TO ORDER ANY OF THESE LONG LOOKS AT ALASKA, just fill out one of the handy coupons below and send it to us today with your check or money order. And don't forget to check the other side of the coupon for some fine selections from our list of Northland books.

ALASKA NORTHWEST PUBLISHING COMPANY

BOOKS from ALASKA NORTHWEST

IF IT'S NORTH . . . WE'VE GOT IT COVERED

ALASKA® magazine's ALASKA FISHING GUIDE and ALASKA HUNTING GUIDE are just two samples from a long list of books you'll want if you enjoy Alaska's wide wonderful outdoors. Please use one of the coupons below to ask for a FREE COPY of our latest BOOK CATALOG. In it

you'll find many more books for the sports-minded, travel guides, guides to Northland flora and fauna, cookbooks and how-to books, history, geography, adventure. . . . If it's North, we've got it covered.

While you're at it, why not select a sample or two from these sportsmen's favorites:

SELECTED ALASKA HUNTING & FISHING TALES, Volumes 2, 3 and 4, edited by Jim Rearden, Outdoors Editor of *ALASKA*® magazine — Here's Sportsman's Paradise all wrapped up in three adventure-packed volumes of stories that are told by the folks who lived them. Sharp, first-person accounts for

many hours of good fireside reading. Vols. 2 and 3 are each $3.95; Vol. 4, $4.95; plus $.50 postage and handling per book.

LOWBUSH MOOSE (And Other Alaskan Recipes) by Gordon R. Nelson — *Not* a "trail" cookbook, but a complete soup-to-nuts chef's delight that emphasizes foods a hunter or fisherman brings home. Moose, yes, and *lowbush* moose (otherwise known as rabbit) and crab souffle with an Alaskan flair. Vying with the recipes are Nelson's wonderful stories about growing up in Alaska. Softbound, $5.95 plus $.50 postage and handling per book.

THE ALASKAN CAMP COOK *is* a "trail" cookbook filled with mouthwatering recipes that have been campfire tested — recipes for large and small game, game birds, fish and shellfish, wild fruits and vegetables and sourdough. Handy comb-binding, $3.95 plus $.50 postage and handling per copy.

ALASKA GAME TRAILS WITH A MASTER GUIDE, compiled by Charles J. Keim; foreword by Lowell Thomas Sr. — Dozens of first-person stories that pay tribute to the fun and excitement of hunting with Alaska's first master guide. Softbound, $6.95 plus $.50 postage and handling per book.

FAIR CHASE WITH ALASKAN GUIDES — Master guide Hal Waugh and journalist/guide Charles J. Keim join up to swap 20 "can you top this" stories of the hunt. Softbound, $3.95 plus $.50 postage and handling per book.

 ALASKA NORTHWEST PUBLISHING COMPANY

☐ **YES,** please send me a copy of your **FREE BOOK CATALOG.** I have filled out my name and address on the other side of this coupon.

I'd also like to receive the following books:

SELECTED ALASKA HUNTING & FISHING TALES

☐ Vol. 2, $4.45 ppd. ☐ Vol. 3, $4.45 ppd. ☐ Vol. 4, $5.45 ppd.

☐ LOWBUSH MOOSE (And Other Alaskan Recipes), **$6.45 postpaid**

☐ THE ALASKAN CAMP COOK, **$4.45 postpaid**

☐ ALASKA GAME TRAILS WITH A MASTER GUIDE, **$7.45 postpaid**

☐ FAIR CHASE WITH ALASKAN GUIDES, **$4.45 postpaid**

PLEASE FILL OUT NAME AND ADDRESS ON THE OTHER SIDE OF THIS COUPON AND INDICATE THE AMOUNT OF THE CHECK OR MONEY ORDER YOU HAVE ENCLOSED FOR BOOKS AND MAGAZINE SUBSCRIPTIONS.

Send order to:
ALASKA NORTHWEST PUBLISHING COMPANY
Box 4-EEE, Dept. AFHG, Anchorage, Alaska 99509

☐ **YES,** please send me a copy of your **FREE BOOK CATALOG.** I have filled out my name and address on the other side of this coupon.

I'd also like to receive the following books:

SELECTED ALASKA HUNTING & FISHING TALES

☐ Vol. 2, $4.45 ppd. ☐ Vol. 3, $4.45 ppd. ☐ Vol. 4, $5.45 ppd.

☐ LOWBUSH MOOSE (And Other Alaskan Recipes), **$6.45 postpaid**

☐ THE ALASKAN CAMP COOK, **$4.45 postpaid**

☐ ALASKA GAME TRAILS WITH A MASTER GUIDE, **$7.45 postpaid**

☐ FAIR CHASE WITH ALASKAN GUIDES, **$4.45 postpaid**

PLEASE FILL OUT NAME AND ADDRESS ON THE OTHER SIDE OF THIS COUPON AND INDICATE THE AMOUNT OF THE CHECK OR MONEY ORDER YOU HAVE ENCLOSED FOR BOOKS AND MAGAZINE SUBSCRIPTIONS.

Send order to:
ALASKA NORTHWEST PUBLISHING COMPANY
Box 4-EEE, Dept. AFHG, Anchorage, Alaska 99509

3516